Criminality and
the Modern

Criminality and the Modern

Contingency and Agency in Twentieth-Century America

Stephen Brauer

LEXINGTON BOOKS

Lanham • Boulder • New York • London

Published by Lexington Books
An imprint of The Rowman & Littlefield Publishing Group, Inc.
4501 Forbes Boulevard, Suite 200, Lanham, Maryland 20706
www.rowman.com

86-90 Paul Street, London EC2A 4NE, United Kingdom

British Library Cataloguing in Publication Information Available

Library of Congress Cataloging-in-Publication Data

Names: Brauer, Stephen, 1967– author.
Title: Criminality and the modern : contingency and agency in twentieth-century America / Stephen Brauer.
Description: Lanham : Lexington Books, [2022] | Includes bibliographical references. | Summary: "Using modernism as a lens, Stephen Brauer examines Americans' understanding of criminality in the twentieth-century and how the powerful figure of the criminal is key to exploring cultures, social norms, and, ultimately, laws"— Provided by publisher.
Identifiers: LCCN 2021049064 (print) | LCCN 2021049065 (ebook) | ISBN 9781793608444 (cloth) | ISBN 9781793608468 (paperback) | ISBN 9781793608451 (epub)
Subjects: LCSH: Criminals—United States—History—20th century. | Criminology—United States—History—20th century. | Crime—United States—History—20th century.
Classification: LCC HV6789 .B73 2022 (print) | LCC HV6789 (ebook) | DDC 364.973—dc23/eng/20211130
LC record available at https://lccn.loc.gov/2021049064
LC ebook record available at https://lccn.loc.gov/2021049065

To Joan, Finn, and Wilson, with the deepest gratitude
for your encouragement and patience

Contents

List of Illustrations   ix

Acknowledgments   xi

Introduction: The Cultural Work of American Crime Narratives   1

1   The Face of Crime, a Killer Body: Imagining the
    Criminal Type   21

2   "I Had to Have Her, If I Hung for It": Impulse, Repression,
    and Repetition Compulsion   59

3   Reforming the "Bad" Boy: Juvenile Delinquency,
    Intervention, and Choice   97

4   The Criminal as Self-Made Man   133

Conclusion: The Crime Narrative in Late Capitalism   169

Bibliography   181

Index   191

About the Author   199

List of Illustrations

Figure 1.1   Flattop Jones from Chester Gould's *Dick Tracy*   22
Figure 1.2   The Bertillon System with Alphonse Bertillon
              as Subject   28
Figure 1.3   An Example of Galton's Composite Photography.
              Frontispiece of Inquiries into Human Faculty and Its
              Development.   30
Figure 1.4   Paul Muni as Tony Camonte in *Scarface* (1932)   35
Figure 2.1   Ruth Snyder and Judd Gray   60
Figure 2.2   Ngram of Uses of "Sex Drive"   68
Figure 2.3   Nathan Leopold (Left) and Richard Loeb   81
Figure 3.1   Spencer Tracy as Father Flanagan in *Boys Town*   98
Figure 3.2   An Illustration from Harvey Warren Zorbaugh,
              The Gold Coast and the Slum   103
Figure 3.3   Jimmy Cagney as Rocky Sullivan, along with the
              Dead End Kids, in *Angels with Dirty Faces*   118
Figure 4.1   James J. Hill   140
Figure 4.2   Arnold Rothstein   148
Figure 4.3   Al Capone's Mugshot Photo, Miami, FL, 1930   151
Figure 4.4   Al Pacino (Left) and Marlon Brando as Michael
              and Vito Corleone in *The Godfather*   156

Acknowledgments

A gardener once told me that planting shrubs and waiting for them to take hold requires patience. First they sleep, she said, then creep, and then finally leap. But the process can take years. You must wait for them, but then you will be so pleased with the result.

She might have been speaking about this book.

I have been working on and with the ideas of this book for many years, playing with them in classrooms and testing them out at conferences, in workshops, and in writing groups. I have many people to thank for their help and support along the way. The earliest support came at New York University, especially from Cyrus Patell and Philip Brian Harper. Over time I have received valuable feedback from colleagues in seminars and on panels on which I presented at conferences for the Modern Language Association, the American Studies Association, the Modernist Studies Association, and the American Comparative Literature Association. Leonard Cassuto pointed me in an especially valuable scholarly direction and Jackson Bryer was very helpful with my writing on Fitzgerald and James J. Hill. Closer to home, I would like to thank the members of the Rochester US History Group, especially Alison Parker and Rachel Remmel, for their suggestions and contributions to this project. I also would like to thank colleagues at the Rochester Institute of Technology and at St. John Fisher College for their contributions to the development of this work: Richard Santana and Babak Elahi at RIT and Melissa Bissonette and Deborah Uman at St. John Fisher College were helpful members of my writing group in the early stages. Mark Rice at St. John Fisher College has also been a valued colleague and support during the length of this project. John Michael at the University of Rochester has always provided an ear for concerns, anxieties, and questions and Stephen Belber has provided steady friendship and encouragement during the entirety of this work.

I have had strong institutional support from administrators at St. John Fisher College as I have worked on this book. I would like to single out David Pate, Deborah VanderBilt Ann Marie Fallon, and Bill Waddell for helping me secure funds to research and write. I also am indebted to the library staff at Lavery Library at St. John Fisher for their help in locating many of the primary documents that I use in this project, along with the staffs at Rush Rhees Library at the University of Library, the Monroe County Library in downtown Rochester, and the New York Public Library.

For many years, the ideas in this book crept forward. Then, in Fall 2018 Gabriella Fernandes and Daniel Gutierrez reached out to me about presenting some of my research at a conference on criminology in Washington, DC. My paper at that conference eventually found its way to Becca Rohde Beurer at Lexington Books, who reached out to me in 2019 about submitting a book proposal to her. I believed at that moment that the project was then ready to blossom. But at that point, in March 2020, the COVID-19 pandemic hit. During what has been a challenging time, Becca has been an incredibly patient and professional editor, allowing me time to think, to write, and to revise. Almost all of this book has been written during the pandemic and I am deeply appreciative of her help during this time as the book has finally taken its leap into bloom. Part of that process was responding to the helpful comments from the anonymous reviewer and I appreciate that reader's valuable insights.

I would like to thank the Brauer and Saab families for their long-standing support of my research and my work. Many of them have even ventured to attend sessions at academic conferences where I was presenting, an act that speaks volumes about their tolerance and love.

Finn Brauer and Wilson Brauer inspire me on a daily basis. They have consistently supported me and encouraged me in my work. More tellingly, though, their persistence, work ethic, and positivity during the last two years have been indelible reminders to me of the values of commitment and endurance. I could not be prouder of them.

Finally, I owe my deepest debt of gratitude to Joan Saab. I could not have written this book without her. She has encouraged me, challenged me intellectually, has made me laugh every day, has propped me up when I was feeling overwhelmed, and has made literal and figurative space for me to write. For over two decades, she has helped me grow as a thinker and a writer. As a scholar and educator, she is inquisitive, rigorous, and expansive. But more importantly for me personally, as a partner, she is loving, generous, compassionate, and fiercely loyal. I could not be luckier. To her, and to Finn and Wilson, I dedicate this book.

Introduction

The Cultural Work of American Crime Narratives

On the night of November 15, 1959, Perry Smith and Dick Hickock entered the Clutter family home in Holcomb, Kansas. Smith, thirty-one, had met Hickock, twenty-eight, while in prison. One of Hickock's cellmates, Floyd Wells, had worked as a farmhand at the Clutters, and he told Hickock that Herb Clutter had a safe in his house that regularly contained a great deal of cash, upwards of $10,000. Hickock convinced Smith to join him and they drove 400 miles, from Olathe, Kansas, to rob the family. They brought a shotgun and a large knife to use as intimidation, should they need it. Hickock feared going back to prison and wanted to avoid that at all costs. One of the main reasons he had brought Smith along was that he believed him to be a "natural killer."[1] It wasn't that he expected problems, but he wanted to be prepared should they arise, and he imagined Smith as the one who could ensure there were no witnesses should there be any issues.

There were four family members at home—Herb Clutter, the patriarch of the family; his wife Bonnie; seventeen-year-old daughter Nancy; and fifteen-year-old son Kenyon. Hickok and Smith separated them and tied them up individually in different rooms. They then asked Herb where the money was and his answer presented their problem. Unfortunately for their plans, Herb told them that there was no safe in the house and that he did not keep cash at home. Smith and Hickock did not believe him and they became flustered the longer that Herb insisted that this was true. They were tired and uncertain of how to proceed. They had already committed a crime by entering the house and tying up the family. They had traveled a long distance for what they had imagined to be an easy, straightforward job, and now they faced an obstacle they weren't sure how to overcome. How could they get the money they had come for if there was no money to take? What should they do now? They had thought this would be an easy robbery, but it had turned into something different.

Smith and Hickock had thought that they would be safe from capture because they had traveled so far from their own homes and because no one had seen them or would recognize them if they had. But after things went sideways when they got to the Clutter home, they acted decisively. Hickock had repeatedly told Smith that he didn't want any witnesses to the robbery, so after listening to Herb repeatedly claim that there was no safe in the house, nor any cash of substance, Smith cut his throat wide open in frustration and shot him in the head with the shotgun. He and Hickock then proceeded to shoot each of the three others with shotgun blasts to the head. They left the home with about $50, a transistor radio, and a pair of binoculars and immediately drove the 400 miles back home to Olathe.

The impact of the murders was immediate. Four members of the family were killed. Two other daughters had married and had moved out of the Clutter home, and they lost the bulk of their family that night, a devastating blow. Farmhands who worked for Herb Clutter lost their employer. Friends and neighbors lost people who were close to them.

In his highly successful nonfiction novel entitled *In Cold Blood*, Truman Capote made famous these murders and the investigation into what happened. Capote details what happened that night and during the weeks and months that followed. He also tells the backstories of Perry Smith and Dick Hickock, with their histories of abuse and trauma that scarred them and perhaps changed them, in order to provide a type of logic to what they did. Their abuse and traumas, he rather blatantly implies, created the men who would respond in just that violent a way to the situation in the Clutter home. The decision to kill them all, Capote suggests, was born from their own individual pasts. In his framing of the killings, he gives narrative shape to the murders and their impact. He writes,

> At the time not a soul in sleeping Holcomb heard them—four shotgun blasts that, all told, ended six human lives. But afterward the townspeople, theretofore sufficiently unfearful of each other to seldom trouble to lock their doors, found fantasy re-creating them over and over again—those somber explosions that stimulated fires of mistrust in the glare of which many old neighbors viewed each other strangely, and as strangers.[2]

The shotgun blasts ended six lives, not four, because Capote factors in the death sentence executions of Smith and Hickock as part of the inherent results of the murders. Indeed, their lives become an intricate part of the story Capote tells. Likewise, the lives of the people of Holcomb change as a result of the murders. Although the murders did not have the same type of material impact on their lives, they had a powerful effect nonetheless. As the investigation of the murders dragged on for weeks and then months, with little motive apparent, neighbors who had once trusted one another implicitly, who had once left all their doors unlocked whether they were home or not, came to no longer have that same faith in one another. Residents became suspicious of others' intentions and actions and the town lost one of its vital and distinctive qualities of good fellowship. They no longer felt safe in a place that they had always assumed was safe. A threshold had been breached.

Capote builds the structure of *In Cold Blood* on two central elements: the personal and communal destabilization that often results from violent crime. The horribly violent murders were senseless, illogical, and seemingly inexplicable. Smith and Hickock had other options. They could have just left the family tied up and walked away. However, they had come for a big score and didn't seem able to recognize that there wasn't going to be one; or, at the least, didn't seem able to reconcile themselves with the reality of what they found at the Clutter home. Moreover, Dick Hickock had come to Holcomb with the intent of leaving no witnesses, even if that intent made little logical sense for a robbery where it would have been near impossible to identify them as the culprits. And so they killed all four members of the family who were there, a violence that is hard to fathom in its brutality.

I begin this book with this story in order to illustrate how violent crimes can have a frighteningly destabilizing effect on families, towns, and cultures, but also to demonstrate how such narratives can provide frames for crimes that might seem impossible to comprehend. Crime, on its most basic level, represents a breaking of a law. In theory, laws act as articulations and codifications of a community's beliefs, values, and principles. They are less a set of prescribed behaviors than they are reflections of accepted customs and social norms, which is why laws are often expressed in the negative, so that the violation of the norm is what is actually articulated. Laws define the boundaries, within the particular society that enacts them, between what is considered right and wrong, what is acceptable behavior and what is not. They mark a threshold. According to anthropologist E. Adamson Hoebel, "A social norm is legal if its neglect or infraction is regularly met, in threat or in fact, by the application of physical force by an individual or group possessing the legally recognized privilege of so acting."[3] It is worth noting that Hoebel defines law through the negative—the notion that we know if an action is legal not by if it is done but by whether that action is regularly met with a response that indicates that the action has been a violation of accepted practice. The "individual or group possessing the legally recognized privilege of acting"— a tribal chief, a criminal prosecutor, a king—operates as an embodiment of a government (a democracy, a monarchy, an oligarchy, a theocracy, etc.) that institutes a set of laws that provide oversight for behavior and that also manages the enforcement of those laws.

Hoebel's definition, in part, derived from the work of Bronislaw Malinowski, who wrote of law as an "effective social restraint," in one of the foundational texts in the field of anthropology in 1926, entitled *Crime and Custom in Savage Society*. Malinowski recognized that the institution of laws and the oversight of the enforcement of those laws were rarely if ever simple or straightforward: "the element or aspect of law, that is of effective social restraint, consists in the complex arrangements which make people keep to their obligations."[4] The workings of the law, in Malinowski's experience, was rarely if ever rigid. Those "complex arrangements" both have to do with what moves ordinary citizens to operate within the social restraint of the law but also with when, where, and in what form the enforcement of the law would take place. Malinowski allows us to recognize the complex ways that the social function of the law takes shape. A violation of the social restraint, an infraction of the accepted norm, is not necessarily treated universally throughout a culture. Context matters. Different crimes come with different punishments. Indeed, some crimes are prosecuted, some are not. And some convictions come with a harsh punishment, while others do not. Nonetheless, all crimes can have an impact, culturally speaking, in that they are violations. That impact need not be earth-shattering or culture-changing, but certainly, as in the Clutter murders, it can lead to substantial changes in individual lives and in the community.

The figure of the criminal is a powerful one. In *Purity and Danger*, her canonical study of pollution and taboo, the anthropologist Mary Douglas suggests, "Danger lies in transitional states, simply because transition is neither one state nor the next, it is undefinable."[5] The act of transgression, the criminal act, I would propose, creates a transition such as the one Douglas postulates—from one state to another, something new, but something "undefinable." That lack of stability is what makes crime so very dangerous and threatening. It obviously can have immediate results, such as death, but it also can lead to a loss of material goods, or devastating injury, or other physical or material consequences. And it can have secondary impacts: a community riddled with suspicion and distrust. Douglas argues that individuals who transgress established social boundaries are understood as "polluting" the culture: "A polluting person is always in the wrong. He has developed some wrong condition or simply crossed some line which should not have been crossed and this displacement unleashes danger for someone."[6] Whether the criminal consciously seeks to pollute the culture through his actions or not, those actions instigate the transition, in Douglas's formulation. The actions that both demarcate and also create the pollution establish that liminal space as dangerous, because that transgressor is operating outside of accepted norms and values, or in relation to criminality, outside of the law. For this project, I am identifying that liminal space as criminality.

Criminality, I am arguing, provides us with a way to think about what a culture values and how it operates. Indeed, notions of criminality—even more than laws—offer us a specific understanding of the boundaries of the acceptable and the not within and across cultures. Laws rarely cover or govern the whole panoply of human behavior. By breaking laws, criminals help us reinforce social norms by giving us the opportunity to affirm what we believe to be right and acceptable. By operating outside the bounds of acceptable behavior, in other words, the criminal serves as a useful figure to understand what is at stake in the culture, what the central issues of that culture might be, and what our fears and anxieties are. This, then, is what this project will explore: how criminality serves as a lens through which we can read ourselves and how the criminal operates as a cultural figure to reveal something about ourselves to ourselves, how he signifies the things we are negotiating in our lives and in our communities.

I am aware that this type of project is not without precedence.[7] No scholar has had as powerful an influence on my thinking as Karen Halttunen, the cultural historian whose 1998 award-winning *Murder Most Foul: The Killer and the American Gothic Imagination* lays the groundwork for this book. Through her examination of how American crime narratives in early America served as a reflection of American culture, Halttunen demonstrates how those narratives operated as a space for the articulation of a tug-of-war about ideas and values that were taking place at the time. Halttunen unpacks how shifts in representing and thinking about murder reflected evolving cultural ideals about human nature, faith, and religion, and ultimately mark the emergence of the social sciences, with their privileging of empiricism when it comes to the analysis of human behavior.

As a central element of her book, Halttunen examines how crime narratives provide a means for working through the "pollution" of murder. She writes that murder

> demands that a community comes to terms with the crime—confront what has happened and endeavor to explain it, in an effort to restore order to the world. In literate societies, the cultural work of coming to terms with this violent transgression takes crucial form in the crafting and rendering of written narratives of the murder, the chief purpose of which is to assign meaning to the incident.[8]

For Halttunen, the "cultural work" of the narrative is to assign meaning and reestablish order and is fundamental to how we deal with the rupture of murder. Similarly, in his seminal *Reading for the Plot*, Peter Brooks writes,

We live immersed in narrative, recounting and reassessing the meaning of our past actions, anticipating the outcome of our future projects, situating ourselves at the intersection of several stories not yet completed. The narrative impulse is as old as our oldest literature: myth and folktale appear to be stories we recount in order to explain and understand where no other forms of explanation will work.[9]

Narratives are one of the central forms that give shape to our world, "one of the large categories in which we think," as Brooks puts it.[10] A narrative can provide cohesion to events that are not inherently structured. In so doing, it constructs an apparatus, of sorts, that helps us understand what things signify, in that the narrative imposes a semblance of cause and effect. Finally, in its construction, it generates certain types of structures that serve to articulate the meaning of what happened and language that gives shape to the experience that otherwise might exist beyond meaning, motive, and reason.

In her book, Halttunen lays out these how these models, tropes, and rhetorics operated in early American crime narratives.[11] She is particularly effective in delineating the rise of these particular storytelling elements within cultural and sociological shifts in late eighteenth- and early nineteenth-century America and in articulating the cultural work that the construction, distribution, and consumption of these narratives performed during this time period.[12] The narrative frames, models, and tropes provide a structure for the story of crime and assign meaning to it, in Brooks's terms. Starting around the mid-1800s—the time period where Halttunen ends her survey of murder narratives—the conception of criminality has significantly evolved. Few scholars, however, have looked closely at that change within these terms. While writers continue to rely on horror and mystery and other genres as a means of structuring crime stories, I would argue that the concerns and questions derived from the social sciences have taken on a greater prominence and the cultural work of American crime narratives has shifted concurrently. Indeed, it is within this context of the cultural work of American crime narratives that I write this project.

Because of their fundamental interest in classifying and then predicting human behavior through an examination of empirical evidence, the social sciences offer a seductive means through which we as a society can perhaps achieve answers to the questions we have regarding the "logic" of crime. The social sciences were founded upon the principle of analyzing human behavior and choices through the scientific method—as disciplines, they organize and classify data and evidence and suggest theories that make sense of that data to better understand human behavior. When it comes to the study of criminality, those theories often lead to proposals as to how best to recognize causes or issues related to criminal behavior and to intervene in a positive manner to steer individuals and groups away from that behavior. When I look at the majority of criminal narratives in American culture over the last 125 years, I see stories that, at their heart, negotiate issues of autonomy and control, fault and responsibility. I see narratives that strive to offer some sense of cause and effect and order. The writers of the stories—journalists, novelists, filmmakers—have looked to the social sciences for the language and the rhetoric that structure and encompass what they tell of crime and the men and women who commit it as a way to explain human behavior and to make logical sense of it. The social sciences of sociology, psychology, anthropology, and economics have come to shape what we make of criminals, how we construct criminality, and how we respond to the destabilizing effects of what criminals do.[13] In this book, through a consideration of all sorts of crime narratives—novels and autobiographies, comic strips and films, scholarly treatises and actual trials—I will delineate how these analyses have taken shape through these disciplines and demonstrate that the shift in how we think about criminality has to do with the foundational questions of Modernism about individual agency and contingency.

This book is not a work *of* criminology; instead, it is a work *about* criminology and its indebtedness to the social sciences and how those disciplines informed the construction and articulation of criminality and crime narratives over the last 125 years. The rise of the social sciences in the nineteenth century and early twentieth century came at the same time as increasing modernization in Europe and America, leading to "the highly developed, differentiated and dynamic new landscape in which modern experiences takes place," Marshall Berman argues in *All That Is Solid Melts into Air*.[14] He continues,

> This is a landscape of steam engines, automatic factories, vast new industrial zones; of teeming cities that have grown overnight, often with dreadful human consequences; of daily newspapers, telegraphs, telephones and other mass media, communicating on an ever wider scale; of increasingly strong national states and multinational aggregations of capital; of mass social movements fighting these modernizations from above with their own modes of modernization from below; of an ever-expanding world market embracing all, capable of the most spectacular growth, capable of appalling waste and devastation, capable of everything except solidity and stability.[15]

What Berman describes here is a world of radical technological, social, political, and economic change in a highly compressed time period. The individual's attempts to navigate his way successfully through this landscape—with its ever-increasing speed, production, and consumption, and also with its ever-increasing divisions of wealth and access to social and economic opportunities—are how Berman defines Modernism: "any attempt by modern men and women to become subjects as well as objects of modernization, to get a grip on the modern world and make themselves at home in it."[16] That attempt to locate oneself as a subject within the modern maelstrom, as well as an object of it, entailed a complicated dynamic that had at its foundation debates over issues of agency and contingency, free will and determinism. Do we have agency as individuals? Is that agency differentiated based on elements (class, race, gender, and so much more) outside of the individual's control? Indeed, even with great social and economic privilege, how much can an individual actually control? What constitutes individual autonomy or agency, or even the potential of these conceits, when so many things are beyond our capabilities and we operate less as subjects and more as mere objects of forces greater than us?

The social sciences emerged as intellectual and professional endeavors at the same time as the rise of modernization in the nineteenth century and they tend to focus on the dynamic that Berman articulated as Modernism. They provided a language and a logic for how to imagine, understand, and represent that dynamic of an individual seeking to be a subject. They provided a way to answer the question, "Why?" As a way to illustrate how the emergence of the social sciences over the last 125 years in academic and popular cultures has influenced how we see, imagine, and represent criminality, I would like to consider the story of Andy Williams.

On Monday, March 5, 2001, at 9:20 in the morning, Charles Williams—known as Andy—walked into a boy's room in Santana High School in Santee, CA. Andy was a freshman at Santana High who had moved to Twentynine Palms, CA, with his father in August 1999 from Maryland and then relocated to Santee in the summer of 2000 so that his father could more readily commute to his job at the Naval Medical Center in San Diego. His parents were divorced and he rarely saw his mother or older brother Michael, who lived back in Maryland. Things were difficult with his father, who worked long hours at his job and was also emotionally distant when at home with Andy. They didn't seem to interact much or with any real connection. While Andy had had only some trouble adjusting to his new life in Twentynine Palms, he found things in Santee much more difficult. Although a well-behaved child while living in Maryland and then in Twentynine Palms, in Santee he befriended a group of skateboarding students who liked to hang out at the park, skateboard, smoke marijuana, and drink tequila. He adopted their habits. Nonetheless, even with a peer group of friends, Andy was the victim of bullying from a number of classmates at Santana High and even from some of the new friends he had made in Santee. Moreover, about a month previously, in February, just a few days before his fifteenth birthday, Andy had learned that one of his good friends from his year in Twentynine Palms had died tragically in a bus accident.

As he walked into the restroom the morning of the fifth, Andy had the worst of intentions. Over the weekend of March 2–4, he had told some of his friends that he was going to "pull a Columbine" on Santana High, threatening to go on a rampage that would be the equivalent of what Eric Harris and Dylan Klebold did on April 20, 1999, when they killed thirteen people and wounded twenty-one others at Columbine High School. Some of Andy's friends egged him on, calling him a pussy and daring him to do it. Other friends took his threat more seriously and sought to talk him out of it and a few of them even patted him down as he prepared to enter Santana High that Monday morning. They didn't find any weapon on him and they apparently felt no need to alert any authorities.

That morning, before school, Andy had smoked a joint with some friends outside an apartment complex and then went to hang out at a local Jack in the Box with other friends. He told them that he needed to leave at 9:06, which a few friends noted as rather specific and a bit earlier than they usually went to school. Andy left then, however, and headed into Santana High. As he got to the restroom, he pulled out a .22-caliber Arminius revolver, which he had stolen from his father's locked gun cabinet and which he had successfully hidden from his friends. He went into the restroom and immediately shot Bryan Zuckor, a fellow freshman. He then stepped out of the restroom and began to shoot his gun at random students in the hallway and into an adjacent courtyard before heading back into the room. He repeated this process a number of times. He reloaded his gun at least once. How much he targeted specific students is not clear, although the specificity of his arrival time at the restroom and his immediate attack on Zuckor suggest that Williams believed that Zuckor would be there at that point in time.

The scene, as one can imagine, was chaotic. Some students believed the shots to be fireworks and headed toward the noise, only to discover Williams shooting. Other students were at first instructed to head to exits by way of the hallways and then told to return to classrooms. Some witnesses claimed they saw Williams smiling as he fired his gun, while others described him as extremely calm. A student teacher and campus security supervisor Peter Ruiz went to the restroom to try to stop Williams but he wounded them both, shooting Ruiz five times. Eventually, after what seemed like ages for those there but was actually less than 6 minutes after the original 911 call, a group of police officers and sheriff's deputies were able to enter the restroom and take Williams into custody.

In his shooting spree that morning, Andy Williams killed two students—Zuckor and seventeen-year-old Randy Gordon, a senior at the school—and wounded thirteen others, including the student teacher and Ruiz. The school and the community were immediately overwhelmed by feelings of panic, confusion, and fear. Parents wanted to know if their children were safe.

Santee residents wanted to know if their town was safe. On March 8, the *San Diego Union-Tribune* published an article by Kelly Thornton entitled, "Why Gunman Did It Is Big Unanswered Question." One longtime resident of Santee described the town as "a middle-class, white, Christian, typical neighborhood."[17] The mayor called it a place "of Little League and doctors—it is America."[18] The underlying question in these comments was, "How could it happen here?" At the heart of their fears was the desire to know what had driven a fifteen-year-old child to take up a gun and shoot so many people? Why did Andy Williams do it? He wasn't a likely candidate. He did not have a history of violent or disruptive behavior. San Diego County District Attorney Paul Pfingst described him, after the shooting, as "articulate" and "unexceptional."[19] In fact, Pfingst called his ordinariness a "frustration. We cannot tie all this up neatly for you."[20] That longing for a reason, something that would "tie this up neatly," was widespread. In an article the next day in the *New York Daily News*, writer Dave Goldliner quoted cheerleader Courtney Guthaus as saying, "I don't hate him for what he did. I just want to know why."[21] District Attorney Pfingst himself said, after Williams had made a statement to authorities in which he did not provide any answers regarding a motive, "I am not sure in any real way we will ever know why."[22]

The desire to know why is one we can certainly recognize, for it is the question we so often ask following the horror of murder, as we look for an explanation for what seems to us to be inexplicable. How do we understand why Williams proceeded with this plan? This is, of course, parallel to how we understand why Smith and Hickock decided to kill all four members of the Clutter family when they could have just driven away. How do we explain murder and other violent crime? Murder is our culture's most transgressive act and it is often beyond our sense of understanding, seemingly operating outside the realm of reason. The desire to know why is a desire for motive and meaning, for logic and reason, for things making sense. To explain such crimes is to conceive of a cause and effect, a recognizable motivation. Recalling what Brooks and Halttunen have to say about narratives and their function, we can recognize that narratives often provide cohesion to events that are not inherently structured. They can impose a semblance of causality that enables us to try to understand why something has happened. This, I would argue, is what Capote does in detailing the abuse and trauma that Perry Smith and Dick Hickock faced in their pasts and that he suggests led them to killing the Clutters. Writers who construct these narratives and who perform this type of cultural work tend to generate certain types of tropes that serve to articulate the meaning of what happened, tropes that give shape to the experience that otherwise might exist beyond meaning, motive, and reason.

In the days following the Santee shooting spree, the media coverage illustrated an overwhelming desire for a narrative that could articulate a motivation or underlying cause for the horrific events of March 5. The varying crime narratives that reporters and columnists constructed "explained" the mystery of why Williams fired those shots while employing particular frames and rhetorics that demonstrated a specific logic at the heart of each writer's thinking. Most of the journalists writing about the killings sought to lay out some psychological reasoning behind Williams's actions. For instance, Kristen Green and Bruce Lieberman, writing in the *San Diego Union-Tribune*, located the origins of the murders in the abuse that Williams faced from bullies in California.

> They flicked a lighter in front of his face.
> They called him "faggot" and "geek."
> They stole his cigarettes, his wallet and his skateboard.
> The taunting began soon after Charles "Andy" Williams moved to Santee last summer. His new classmates tested him to see how he would react.
> He never fought back.[23]

The implication of the narrative that Green and Lieberman trace here is that Williams finally decided that he was not going to take the abuse anymore and that he had decided that it was time to do something about it. In essence, this perspective suggests, Williams was a ticking time bomb, prompted by a group of bullies who didn't recognize that their victim was about to strike back. This was the dominant logic articulated in the days after the shootings. Williams made a conscious choice to say "enough" and to say it with force, to put a stop to the abuse and the bullying. In this narrative, the responsibility clearly lies with Williams, who is acting of his own volition to end a pattern of mistreatment.

Some journalists, however, did not see Williams himself so much at fault but instead understood him to be a victim of sociological effects that were beyond his control, an object of those effects rather than the subject of his own story. Timothy Egan, in the *New York Times*, notes the "explanations child psychiatrists, educators and other researchers were looking to understand why teenagers had been shooting other teens at suburban high schools." Egan writes,

> Their explanations point to the easy availability of guns, but they also wonder whether the violent student outbursts are a byproduct of communities like this one, where children come and go as they please, and where the ups and downs of student life and cliques are magnified by a school's position as the center of the local universe.[24]

Egan's notion of Williams's violence as a "by-product" of the community's structure locates the origin of blame not with the individual but with some external sociological force beyond Williams's control. In essence, he is contending that Williams had little agency over what he did or that the individual has little autonomy in the choices he makes. His analysis is the flipside of the thinking of Green and Lieberman in relation to this question of choice; at the same time, the issue of choice is central to how each conceive of the story of the shooting.

A look at two other writers demonstrates a variance. Gary Behrman, writing in the *St. Louis Post-Dispatch*, argued,

> When a young person is isolated, using mood-altering substances, struggling with untreated depression and abused by peers, we have the ingredients for a bomb that is lit and ready to explode. . . . We have to remember we are dealing with children who have severe mental illness. . . . These young people will focus only on the one thing they believe will release the pressure, not the consequences of their action.[25]

In some ways, Behrman's take sounds similar to that of Green and Lieberman, in that he seems to be saying that Williams was a time bomb ready to explode. But whereas Green and Lieberman see volition in Williams's actions, Behrman does not. Indeed, Behrman not only does not believe there is volition, he goes further as to say that Williams is "struggling with untreated depression" and that he has a "severe mental illness," unable to see or understand "the consequences" of his actions. Ignore for a moment that Behrman makes these claims without ever speaking to or even seeing Williams and that therefore he is fully unqualified to even make such judgments about him. Instead, note how Behrman employs psychological rhetoric to explain what has happened and why it has occurred. That rhetoric shapes his narrative of the shooting. Daniel Weinberger takes this approach even further in his interpretation of the events:

> Everyone gets angry; everybody has felt a desire for vengeance. The capacity to control impulses that arise from these feelings is a function of the prefrontal cortex. . . . But the evidence is unequivocal that the prefrontal cortex of a 15-year-old is biologically immature. . . . The young school shooter probably does not think about the specifics of shooting at all. The often-reported lack of remorse illustrates how unreal the reality is to these teenagers.[26]

Like Behrman, Weinberger looks to psychiatry to explain the shootings— they are the result of "impulses that arise from these feelings" of anger and vengeance. Weinberger, though, asserts "unequivocally" that the prefrontal cortex of fifteen-year-olds is not mature enough to control those impulses. Rooting his explanation in this scientific "fact," he feels comfortable asserting that Williams had no ability to respond appropriately to his anger and desire for revenge. Note, though, his use of "probably" and "often" in the last two sentences of the passage. Although Weinberger believes that he has situated his logic in hard science, his language at the end of the passage demonstrates a lack of certainty. He has no idea whether Williams thinks about the specifics of the crime, and apparently some shooters do feel remorse. The contradiction is a result of Weinberger's attempt to affix meaning to something that cannot be certain. Some fifteen-year-olds might respond inappropriately and are unable to control their impulses for vengeance. But others can. And do. And one cannot simply assert this biological "fact" as the cause of the crime—not convincingly anyway.[27]

My interest in the conception of criminality and in the representation of criminals has much to do with the rhetorical moves that these journalists made in the days after Andy Williams entered that bathroom and began to shoot. As is clear, violent crime can have an amazingly destabilizing effect on how people feel about themselves, their families, and their communities. As an act, it frightens us, understandably. We want to know why it happened not out of curiosity but out of a desire to assuage our fears and insecurities. It's human nature. To live in insecurity and fear is to struggle. And the construction of a narrative, as Brooks reminds us, is to give shape to our world and to assign meaning. In telling stories we construct ways of understanding what happened, ways of understanding why it happened, and therefore we seek to come to an emotional, intellectual, and perhaps even spiritual stability that helps us move forward. In how I think about the construction of criminality and the representation of the criminal, I will return often to the function of story as an assertion of logic and order.

For instance, in Williams's case, the multiple stories of criminality that the media generated were ones that had to do with responsibility, autonomy, and control. How much was Williams at fault? How much were other factors—bullying, drugs, video games, divorce, suburban sprawl, psychological illness? The journalists writing the varying narratives of the Santee spree shooting were very good at making assertions about the causes of the crime—even without knowing Williams or knowing that much of the background of the events. What led to their confidence, their certainty that what they were arguing was somehow "true"? I would assert that the answer for this lies in the very stories that they told. Most of them looked to sociological and psychological causes for why it happened. Others considered economic reasons. Pretty much all of them looked to the language and the logic of social science as a way to understand Andy Williams and to understand why he turned so very violent that morning. That gesture is worth noting, it seems to me, as the language and the logic of social science is the very language of the narrative of crime over the last 125 years.

As I have tried to demonstrate in my review of the media's attempt to make sense of the Santee spree murders, crime narratives tell us as much as, if not more, about the person writing the narrative than they do about the crime or criminal. Our desire for a logic for a crime that help us make sense of it is often at the heart of *how* we tell the story of that crime. We construct a cause and effect, a reason for the actions that give it an order: he had been bullied or abused and was psychologically damaged, he had become inured to violence because of his exposure to certain types of music/films/video games, the sociological conditions of his living environs made connection to others difficult and he felt isolated and alone. These "answers" offer a type of solace to the community because they provide a motive that perhaps we can do something about, a reason that we can address through public policy or individual or community actions. The narratives that we construct about a crime—using particular rhetorics, tropes, and models—ultimately demonstrate our fundamental thinking about criminality itself and how it operates, where it originates, and sometimes even what to do about it. Those narratives, in other words, do deeply important cultural work.

Even though the journalists constructing these narratives had neither met nor spoken to Williams himself, the fact that they believed that their stories were "true" tells us something about how much they valued a logic of criminality that could make sense of what was so frightening. In *Murder Most Foul*, Halttunen argues that the nineteenth-century Gothic narrative of murder led to the "ultimate incomprehensibility of any given crime of murder." She writes that the "Gothic narrative of criminal transgression proved central to the modern liberal construction of the concept of criminal deviance . . . [which] was eventually to shape modern social-scientific views of the criminal in such fields as psychology, sociology, criminology, and criminal law."[28] This book continues Halttunen's project of examining the cultural work of criminal narratives in American culture that she and others have sought to articulate.

Of course, other scholars have similarly engaged in the consideration of the cultural work, as Halttunen described it, of criminals and crime narratives in American culture. In *Natural Born Celebrities*, for instance, David Schmid unpacks the figure of the serial killer in modern culture and situates that figure historically and socially within the contexts of celebrity culture and consumerism in the late nineteenth and twentieth centuries.[29] David Ruth, in *Inventing the Public Enemy*, and Jonathan Munby, in *Public Enemies, Public Heroes*, have done an especially nice job in thinking about a particular type of criminal—the gangster of the 1920s and 1930s, particularly as configured in the gangster films of the time. Both writers recognize the ways in which these characters acted first to demonstrate the allure of the narrative of ethnic socioeconomic mobility but also to point to the dangers of consumption and commercialism as a marker of individual or ethnic advancement. Munby has also written a close consideration of criminal representation within specifically African American popular culture in *Under a Bad Sign*, which argues that the self-representation of criminality within African American operates as a response to being marginalized by the broader American culture.[30] In *At Stake: Monsters and the Rhetoric of Fear in Public Culture*, Edward Ingebretsen looks to late twentieth-century versions of "moral monsters," such as Andrew Cunanan and Susan Smith, to consider the function of the monster, as a representation in popular culture, to instill fear and to reflect central questions of faith and religion in contemporary culture.[31]

On a broader scale than these studies, some critics have sought to look less at a particular figure and more at a way of thinking about crime and the criminal in general. In *War on Crime*, Claire Bond Potter delves into the New Deal years and the way in which the "war on crime" took place in newspapers and films and the radio, with real guns and fake guns, and actual government hearings and criminal trials. In this book Potter lays out the ways in which the highly public actions of criminals and lawmen—both actual and fictional—refracted broader cultural issues within a nation undergoing seismic social and economic changes.[32] Jonathan Finn's *Capturing the Criminal Image*, on the other hand, examines the way that images of criminals have shifted and also remained the same over the last 100–125 years. In interrogating the visual representations of criminals and the technologies of representation itself, Finn asks questions especially about issues of identity and identity formation, demonstrating once again the resonance and the reach of the figure of the criminal in American culture.[33]

I believe that representations of criminality in the late nineteenth and twentieth centuries are central to our understanding of American culture more broadly. Ultimately, I argue, the criminal is an emblematic figure of American modernity.[34] In this book, I articulate two main concepts of criminality: one focused on the idea that the individual might not be in control of his own deviance, and the other on the notion that the criminal makes a conscious choice to use crime as a means of economic and social success. The criminal, in this schema, operates as a key figure in American culture to explore how the idea of the Modern is exemplified in the ongoing debate over how much control the individual has over his own behavior.

The first three chapters of this book explore how social scientists categorized criminal behavior and how they sought to change that behavior, each chapter examining a discipline in relation to cultural representations of criminality that is tied to conceits within that discipline. In the first chapter, I explore the idea of the criminal type, an idea that grew out of criminological advances in the late nineteenth century—such as fingerprinting and the taking of mugshots—that criminologists used to create an archive of criminals.

Many of these criminologists posited that the physical traits that these archives earmarked were associated with specific types of crimes. Embedded as it is in a system of classification, the notion of the criminal type as a model for criminality has appeal in that it suggests that if we can know the criminal type in advance of the crime, we can identify the threat he poses and act to defuse that danger before he acts upon it—and potentially us. By looking at criminal trials, at the *Dick Tracy* comic strips, and at how anthropologists promulgated this theory not only in the late nineteenth century but even in the 1940s, I demonstrate how this idea was used to shape and construct criminal narratives for public consumption and ultimately the alleviation of public anxiety about crime.

In the second chapter, I turn from anthropology to a different discipline by considering the ways that psychologists in the early part of the twentieth century explained how the body and the mind "compelled" individuals toward certain actions. Sigmund Freud's theories of the sex and death drives, for instance, were one way to propose why people might do things that were clearly not in their best interests. Another approach was more rooted in quantifiable data that suggested that, at the cellular level, some individuals did not have the response to stimuli as other people did and therefore did not feel remorse or regret or fear or a host of other emotions that might stop them from doing certain things. At the heart of the rhetoric of compulsion that these psychologists proposed was a suggestion that many individuals could not control their impulses. As a way to explore this rhetoric and how it manifested itself in the culture I examine the defense of Leopold and Loeb, the teenage thrill killers in Chicago in 1925, as well as the separate autobiographies of Ruth Snyder and Judd Gray, who together killed Snyder's husband. The Snyder and Gray story was the impetus behind James Cain's *The Postman Always Rings Twice*, and I situate that novel—as well as his follow-up, *Double Indemnity*—within this same rhetoric of compulsion, one that criminal defendants continue to use to this day.

The third chapter examines a similar rhetoric of criminality that imagines criminals as individuals who are not always able to control their actions. The Chicago School of Sociology was a group of scholars, specializing in urban sociology, who articulated a theory of social ecology that behavior was determined by social structures and the influence of the surrounding physical environment. Through their application of quantitative methods to track and map an array of problems across the city of Chicago, they not only recognized a correlation between one's socioeconomic upbringing and crime, but also actually demonstrated such a correlation, thereby providing evidence for how one's environment could influence how individuals imagined only limited behavioral choices. They also demonstrated how intervention—especially in relation to juvenile delinquency—could play a powerful role in swaying those individuals to broaden what they saw as available choices and to make better decisions. Two films of the late 1930s—*Angels with Dirty Faces* and *Boys Town*—dramatized this concept of a successful intervention to steer young men away from crime through positive intervention.

All three of these chapters examine ways in which criminality was imagined as either explicitly or implicitly out of the control of individual will. In contrast, the fourth chapter considers ways in which criminality was also understood as a choice—as an act of agency—and that certain criminals approached their work as a businesslike endeavor that sought to maximize profit, influence, and cultural authority. In 1899, Thorstein Veblen argued in *The Theory of the Leisure Class* that a focus on accumulating wealth, no matter the costs, was inevitable for capitalism. Although crime is a morally and ethically dubious avenue to pursue, for those individuals who are seeking socioeconomic mobility, according to Veblen's theory, it makes sense for them to choose criminality as a "legitimate" means to reach the socially approved goal of financial success. Gatsby, Fred Pasley's Al Capone, and Coppola's Corleone family all operate as portrayals of criminality under the cloak of "business." Their stories are self-making narratives and illustrate how the idea of self-making had shifted from its traditional emphasis on making a better "self" by focusing on virtue to making a "better" self by focusing on individual wealth. In that shift lies an indictment of the American Dream and its corruption over time. The notion that killing someone is justified because it's "not personal, it's strictly business"—and that this phrase is widely cited in other films and among the greater public—is perhaps an indication that American culture has come to privilege the pursuit of financial accumulation over responsible moral behavior.

The conflicts between choices and control that the narratives in these four chapters dramatize get at a central component of the crime narrative, especially in light of issues of agency and contingency. The modern crime narrative is a key site for dramatizing these issues, I am arguing, for we map these issues on to the figure of the criminal, the figure that most threatens us and leaves us feeling out of control of our lives and makes us feel the most vulnerable. My conclusion, an analysis of Mario Van Peebles's 1991 film, *New Jack City*, argues that these ways of imagining criminality continue to inform our thinking in the public sphere today. Although social scientists regularly moved away from some of the theories of the late nineteenth and early twentieth centuries—such as the notion of a criminal type or the death drive articulated by Freud—these ideas often held on longer in the academy and beyond much longer than perhaps we might have expected, even to the present day. Indeed, many of these ideas continue to have broad cultural currency in the current moment and have been defined by a rhetoric and logic that are derived from the establishment of the social sciences over 100 years ago.

That rhetoric and logic has to do with how we can understand criminality in relation to what we can control as individuals and as a culture. Moreover, I would suggest that the currency of these ideas—even the ones that the academy itself has moved away from—is due to the type of anxiety that we can identify in Holcomb, Kansas, in 1959 and in Santee, California, in 2001. Crime scares us, it makes us question our sense of security, and it leads to uncertainties and concerns about what we know and what we don't, about what we can and can't do, and about what we can predict and whom we can protect. That is the cultural power of a murder, and even a home invasion. It's destabilizing for individuals and for our culture and we—perhaps not surprisingly—imagine ideas of criminality itself in the very terms of agency and contingency that mimic what we ourselves feel in the aftermath of crime. We tell stories of crime that reveal not only what we think about criminality, but also what we think about ourselves.

NOTES

1. Capote, Truman. *In Cold Blood* (New York: New American Library, 1965), 55.
2. Capote, *In Cold Blood*, 5.
3. Hoebel, E. Adamson. *The Law of Primitive Man* (Cambridge, MA: Athenaeum, 1954), 28.
4. Malinowski, Bronislaw. *Crime and Custom in Savage Society.* 1926 (Totowa, NJ: Littlefield, Adams & Co., 1982), 31–32.
5. Douglas, Mary. *Purity and Danger.* 1966 (London: Ark Paperbacks, 1984), 92.
6. Douglas. *Purity and Danger*, 113.
7. Michel Foucault's *Discipline and Punish* and Peter Stallybrass and Allon White's *The Politics and Poetics of Transgression* both served as inspirations when many years ago I first began thinking about criminality and its cultural function. Malinowski, Douglas, and other early anthropologists likewise provide means of thinking about how crime can operate within cultures and also how it can help define cultural values.
8. Halttunen, Karen. *Murder Most Foul: The Killer and the American Gothic Imagination* (Cambridge, MA: Harvard University Press, 1998), 2.
9. Brooks, Peter. *Reading for the Plot* (Cambridge, MA: Harvard University Press, 1992), 2.
10. Brooks, *Reading for the Plot*, 323.
11. She explicitly identifies the models of the execution sermon and the Gothic narratives of the horror and mystery. Similarly, she provides key tropes—including, among others, the pornography of violence—as she argues that these emerged in the nineteenth century alongside changes in literacy rates and shifts in technological advances (such as the rise of the penny press), which made murder narratives so captivating and also available for the general public.

12. She is, for instance, quite persuasive in linking murder narratives of this time period to key shifts within family and gender dynamics in the evolving nation. She also skillfully indicates how these models and tropes are often still foundational to crime narrative to this day—slasher films, detective fiction, and television franchises such as *Law & Order* and *C.S.I.* all come to mind as indebted to the models that Halttunen identifies.

13. Exemplary scholarly treatises on the history of criminology over the last thirty years include Piers Beirne's *Inventing Criminology: Essays on the Rise of* Homo Criminalis (Albany, NY: State University of New York Press, 1993) and Michael Dow Burkhead's *The Search for the Causes of Crime: A History of Theory in Criminology* (Jefferson, NC: McFarland & Company, 2006).

14. Berman, Marshall. *All That Is Solid Melts into Air* (New York: Penguin, 1988, with new preface, reprint of original 1982 edition): 18.

15. Berman, *All That Is Solid Melts Into Air*, 18–19.

16. Berman, *All That Is Solid Melts Into Air*, 5.

17. Thornton, Kelly. "Why Gunman Did It Is Big Unanswered Question," *San Diego Union- Tribune*, 3/8/2001: A-14.

18. Thornton, "Why Gunman Did It Is Big Unanswered Question," A-14.

19. Thornton, "Why Gunman Did It Is Big Unanswered Question," A-14.

20. Thornton, "Why Gunman Did It Is Big Unanswered Question," A-14.

21. Goldliner, Dave. "Teen Suspect Silent in Court," *New York Daily News*, 3/8/2001: 5.

22. Purdum, Todd. "Shooting at School Leaves 2 Dead and 13 Hurt," *The New York Times*, 3/6/2001: A1.

23. Green, Kristen and Bruce Lieberman. "Bullying, Ridicule of Williams Were Routine, Friends Say," *San Diego Union-Tribune*, 3/10/2001: A1.

24. Egan, Timothy. "Santee is Latest Blow to Myth of Suburbia's Safer Schools," *The New York Times*, 3/09/2001: A1, continued on A16.

25. Behrman, Gary. "We Must Learn to Understand Mental Illness," *St. Louis Post-Dispatch*, 3/8/2001: 21.

26. Weinberger, Daniel. "A Brain Too Young for Good Judgment," *New York Times*, 3/10/2001: A13.

27. Another frequent "site" of blame was "youth culture" itself: Scott Bowles and Martin Kasindorf of *USA Today* suggested that "Williams and his friends were wild about the bands Linkin Park and Limp Bizkit. It is angry-sounding music that's popular with many young people" ("Friends Tell of Picked-On but 'Normal' Kid," 3/6/2001: 4A). Diana Steele and Dave Goldliner, writing in the *New York Daily News*, claimed that following his move to California, Williams "took refuge in video games and rock music with anguished lyrics about death and violence" ("All Were Targets at HS," 3/7/2001: 23). These writers suggest that the sociological effects of angry or anguished music lead teens to take out their frustration or anger or anguish and to kill others, an argument clearly lacking in evidence or common sense. For instance, certainly not all those teens who listen to these bands or play video games kill other teens. The desire for an answer, for a logic to contain the uncertainty of not

knowing why, seemed to inspire many to affix responsibility in ways that just didn't hold up to basic reason.

28. Halttunen, *Murder Most Foul: The Killer and the American Gothic Imagination*, 5.

29. Schmid, David. *Natural Born Celebrities: Serial Killers in American Culture* (Chicago: University of Chicago Press, 2005).

30. Ruth, David. *Inventing the Public Enemy: The Gangster in American Culture, 1918–1934* (Chicago: University of Chicago Press, 1996); Munby, Jonathan. *Public Enemies, Public Heroes: Screening the Gangster from* Little Caesar *to* Touch of Evil (Chicago: University of Chicago Press, 1999); and, Munby, Jonathan. *Under a Bad Sign: Criminal Self-Representation in African American Popular Culture* (Chicago: University of Chicago Press, 2011).

31. Ingebretsen, Edward. *At Stake: Monsters and the Rhetoric of Fear in Public Culture* (Chicago: University of Chicago Press, 2001).

32. Potter, Claire. *War on Crime: Bandits, G-Men, and the Politics of Mass Culture* (New Brunswick, NJ: Rutgers University Press, 1998).

33. Finn, Jonathan. *Capturing the Criminal Image: From Mug Shot to Surveillance Society* (Minneapolis, MN: University of Minnesota Press, 2009).

34. Other recent scholars have seen the criminal as an emblematic figure of modernity. These include Lisa Downing, *The Subject of Murder: Gender, Exceptionality, and the Modern Killer* (Chicago: University of Chicago Press, 2013); Paul Sheehan, *Modernism and the Aesthetics of Violence* (Cambridge: Cambridge University Press, 2013); Jonathan Eburne, *Surrealism and the Art of Crime* (Ithaca, NY: Cornell University Press, 2014); and Matthew Levay, *Violent Minds: Modernism and the Criminal* (Cambridge: Cambridge University Press, 2019). These are all admirable works of scholarship that I would recommend to readers who work within this field, especially in relation to their interrogation of the figure of the criminal within modernity. While I would identify a variety of commonalities between my research and that of these critics, where my work differs from these studies is first in their linking of British and American modernity and second in my specific interest in the language and logic of the social sciences as central to the imagining of the criminal and to the construction of the crime narrative of the last 125 years.

Chapter 1

The Face of Crime, a Killer Body

Imagining the Criminal Type

In Chester Gould's comic strip *Dick Tracy*, on December 26, 1943, a group of hoodlums kidnap Tracy with the intent to kill him for a $5,000 payoff. Gould had begun the storyline a few days earlier, following one of the characters as he got off a train, took a taxi to a hotel, and arranged the details of the job and the payoff. On December 27, readers see the plot come to fruition as the villains trick Tracy into a car and hold him hostage with a pair of guns. The last panel in the strip that day introduces two of the gang. The first is named Ed. The second is the man readers have been following for days, who goes by the moniker Flattop. This character is appropriately named. In many ways he was average—regular height and weight with a full head of dark hair, parted in the middle. But he had an unusually large head, which was—of course—flat on top.

Flattop Jones was the most popular villain that Chester Gould created for *Dick Tracy*, the serial comic strip that followed the title character's work as a police detective who relied on high-tech gadgets and scientific detective methods to fight crime.[1] *Dick Tracy* was first published during Prohibition, in 1931, originally in the *Detroit Daily Mirror*, and then a week later in the *New York Daily News*, which had a readership of over 2 million people. By the end of the 1930s *Dick Tracy* was a phenomenal success, distributed through the Chicago Tribune Company Syndicate and appearing in 160 newspapers around the country. By the middle of the 1940s its estimated readership was 27 million.[2] The square-jawed Tracy was the hero, but the bad guys gave the strip its sense of character and originality. Flattop, appearing first in December 1943, was the most original of the gangsters.

Hired by a group of black marketeers who wanted him to kill Tracy, Flattop was more clever, more conniving, and more imaginative than Gould's previous villains and proved appealing enough to readers that his narrative

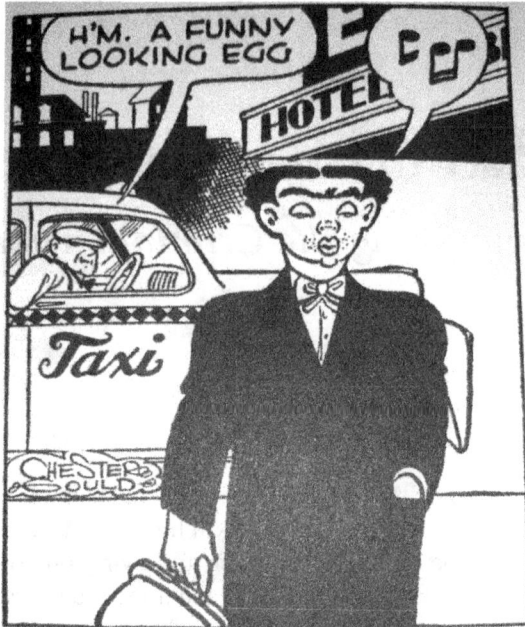

Figure 1.1 Flattop Jones from Chester Gould's *Dick Tracy*. *Source:* Dick Tracy/*Chicago Tribune*/TCA.

arc lasted six months, much longer than most of the strip's other bad guys. Gould extended that arc first by changing Flattop's plan to kill Tracy to a plan to blackmail his employers for extra money, then by concocting a series of escapes that Flattop was able to pull off, followed by a chase that lasted a period of weeks. Eventually, in May 1944, Flattop drowned while trying to escape Tracy one last time. The character was popular enough to generate a legacy, however, as Gould was moved to create a whole family of characters related to Flattop, including Mrs. Flattop, Flattop, Jr., Angeltop, Blowtop, Sharptop, Hi-Top, Poptop, and Frizzletop Jones-O'Copper.[3] When it came to the phenomenally popular *Dick Tracy*, Flattop was the face of crime. And what a face it was.

Key to understanding Flattop is recognizing the function of his appearance (See Figure 1.1.). He looked different from the other characters in the strip with whom he interacted. Indeed, on December 22, in the first full strip in which he is featured, Gould draws Flattop walking away from a cab and whis-tling while the cabdriver says, "H'm. A funny looking egg." [4] He is drawn similarly enough to other characters that he comes across as one of them, but at the same time looks odd enough that he is noticeably unique. Gould's rendering of Flattop as physically distinct from those others put him in the tradition of a number of villains that he drew in the late 1930s and 1940s. They were what came to be known as the Grotesques, men and occasionally women who were markedly different from other characters in how Gould rendered them visually. Each of the Grotesques had a physical distinction that was immediately apparent. Sometimes this meant an unusual body shape or size, as with Jerome Trohs, a midget, at times pictured making an escape riding on the back of a dog or sliding down a laundry chute. However, usually the differences had to do with facial features, as with The Mole, Little Face, Scardol, and Professor M. Emric. The most famous of the Grotesques were the Brow, Pruneface, and Flattop. The Brow was drawn as something of a common street thug, with a bald head, a strong nose that was perhaps once broken, and a sharp and pointy jaw, but what set this character apart were the deep and heavy furrows of skin making up his forehead that essentially elided the space between the top of his head and his eyes. Pruneface had distinguishing long and deep wrinkles running vertically down his face, mainly from his cheekbones on down. His eyes and nose were likewise quite lined, and his puckered mouth was virtually swallowed by the mapline of wrinkles.

Drawn with bulging, scarred foreheads or the eyes, nose, and teeth of a mole, or with tiny facial features or deep wrinkles covering their entire faces, the Grotesques interacted each day with other characters who were drawn with more commonly rendered bodies and features. The stylized differences between these types of characters were not articulated by anyone in the strip itself. Instead, they treated each other on equal terms without comment. Gould's emphasis on the variances in his drawing of them, though, made it quite clear that these characters were different than the other characters and that they played a particular function in the strip. "I never looked at them as ugly," Gould said of the Grotesques, therein implying that his drawing of these characters of a world has as much a moral as an aesthetic purpose.[5] Simply put, his use of the Grotesques was a direct ploy to visually differentiate the morally deviant from the morally good.

By emphasizing the physical uniqueness of these characters, by drawing them as "funny looking egg[s]," Gould alerted readers that they should be recognized immediately as the bad guys. In speaking of the Grotesques, Gould said, "I wanted my villains to stand out definitely so that there would be no mistake who the villain was."[6] This is a rather startling statement. If we go back to the scene where Flattop kidnaps Tracy, there really isn't much doubt as to who the villains are: the bad guys are the ones pointing the guns at our hero. They are the ones who have just kidnapped him. Moreover, we know Flattop is the leader of this gang because he is the one who both gives the orders to the others and the one who instructs Tracy how to cooperate so that he won't get hurt. Gould's statement implies that the reader needed physical markings to tell bad from good, as opposed to following the plotline to determine who the bad guy was. In other words, in Gould's imagination, the reader knows the bad guy in the strip not because of the action, but because he has a distinguishing face or body that functions as an emblem of danger. The drawings are meant to connote criminality: even though neither the action nor the dialogue in the strip ever explicitly allude to the physical reality of the Grotesques, their distinctive physical attributes isolate them from the other characters and we therefore can readily identify them as the ones who will commit the kidnapping/robbery/murder.

Gould wanted there to be "no mistake who the villain was." It was a highly effective strategy, evident in the strip's broad commercial success that especially took off during the years of the Grotesques. While implications that physical difference is tantamount to moral deviance were a frequent mode of representation through which cartoonists might caricature public figures or exaggerate issues for a particular editorial message, Gould's method of drawing the Grotesques relied upon a logic that there was a quantifiable criminal type that one could recognize.[7] Through his drafting style, Gould essentialized the criminal body as a physiological other and asserted that this other was, in essence, a killer body. Because recognizing the Grotesques was so straightforward, it was not difficult for readers to decode the figurative meaning of the characters who were drawn as literally unique in their body or facial type. With the stroke of the pen, Gould quantified the criminal threat for his readers and identified those individuals who appeared different as "the face of crime," the members of society to fear as threats to public safety and security. These threats, in this logic, were those individuals whose appearance was—in whole or even in part—biologically determined. [8]

The Grotesques serve as a prime example of the representation of the criminal type in popular culture. Although the theory of the criminal type had been articulated four decades prior to Gould's introduction of Flattop, and although it had been subsequently rejected by scholars as deeply problematic, the concept of the criminal type wielded a powerful influence on the public imagination when it came to its anxiety about crime. Crime makes people nervous, understandably. They want safety for themselves and their loved ones. The dynamic that plays out within the theory of the criminal type offers a type of anxiety release: it proposes that criminals are identifiable by how they look and once we learn what "danger" looks like, we can be prepared. For Gould, as draftsman for *Dick Tracy*, the logic was straightforward: readers could take a look at the comic and immediately identify the Grotesques as different than the other characters. They could tell immediately who was the criminal in the scene, even before the criminal had committed a crime. This dynamic, after all, is the endpoint of the thinking behind the theory of the criminal type. If criminality is something that is physically identifiable, then working to classify those physical traits associated with distinct criminal tendencies allows us to not only create a catalog of those traits, but also allows us to potentially predict criminality. Finally, identifying the criminal in advance of the crime helps us recognize a threat and act on it before it becomes manifest. There would be "no mistake who the villain was" because the appearance of difference served as a physical embodiment of criminality itself.[9] That endpoint, however, is central to why scholars and so many others ultimately rejected the concept of the criminal type. Interiority is not inherently mapped onto exterior appearance and difference, of course, does not inherently equal deviance and danger.

The concept of the criminal type itself arose in the late nineteenth and early twentieth centuries. At first, it was mainly limited to anthropological studies of criminality: there were a group of social scientists within the field of anthropology who sought to use emerging technologies to better understand criminality and criminals. These technologies helped these researchers classify criminals by the crime they had committed, creating an archive for police to use in their attempts to solve crime. That archive, though, allowed for other possibilities, in that some of these early classifiers grouped the criminals not only by crime but also by physical appearance. What began as a potential correlative relationship between criminality and appearance shifted rather quickly: perhaps not surprisingly, researchers began to assert a causal relationship between physical appearance and crime, and even between physical appearance and certain crimes. Over time this logic morphed into a theory of the criminal type and it began to filter into the broader culture, culminating in representations of criminals in the 1920s–1930s that often imagined them as distinctly "different" physically. That physical difference was often figured as ethnic and racial difference, leading to an assumption that one's ethnicity and race was a marker of deviance and a predisposition for crime.

The association of external appearance and inner character had its origin in what Shawn Michelle Smith has called the nineteenth-century interest in "interiority" and the way in which one's interiority either was externally mapped onto the face and body or was hidden from view. "Studies of the criminal body, in particular," she writes, "answered to middle-class concerns about the essences some bodies might mask and hide, and attempted to make those bodies transparent to the technologically aided, professional middle-class eye."[10] The categorizing of criminals into types began in the nineteenth century when Allan Sekula writes,

The law-abiding body recognized its threatening other in the criminal body, recognized its own acquisitive and aggressive impulses unchecked, and sought to reassure itself [in part through] the invention of a criminal who was organically distinct from the bourgeois: a *biotype*. The science of criminology emerged from this latter operation.[11]

Central to the development of criminology was Cesare Lombroso, the Italian criminal anthropologist, whose work was widely influential in Europe and America in the late nineteenth and early twentieth centuries. Lombroso's influence was most readily seen in Europe (since his work was not translated into English and published in America until 1911).[12] That year brought the publication of both *Criminal Man* and *Crime: Its Causes and Remedies*. However, a number of followers in America had been tracking and translating his work for many years before the publication in English of these two volumes. These men included Arthur McDonald, Henry Boies, C. R. Henderson, August Drahms, among others.[13]

Nicole Hahn Rafter, a leading chronicler of the history of criminology, has suggested that, in their files and documents, the criminal anthropologists sought to produce "a means of signifying science and objectivity. . . . They would measure criminals' bodies with scientific equipment such as calipers, the dynamometer, and the aesthesiometer, objectively recording facts. And they would use induction and quantitative methods to formulate causal laws."[14] The methodology of the early criminal anthropologists—recording and documenting the measurements of their subjects—was crucial in their efforts to garner respect from their peers in other sciences and to establish followers. In *An Organ of Murder: Crime, Murder, and Phrenology in Nineteenth-Century America*, Courtney E. Thompson denotes the long Continental and American history of phrenology, including a consideration of its connections to Lombroso and the rise of criminology at the end of the century. She writes, "While phrenologists did not apply a systematic or classificatory system to criminals, as did Lombroso, these two areas of scientific inquiry shared a set of methods, assumptions, sites, and thematic interests. . . . Lombroso's contemporaries often made comparisons between phrenology and criminal anthropology as a means to critique Lombroso."[15] Criminal anthropologists' emphasis on scientific objectivity, however, led them to too readily assume that criminals embodied their own criminality. Rafter says, "Their material premises led criminal anthropologists to their central assumption that the body must mirror moral capacity. Lombrosians took for granted a one-to-one correspondence between the criminal's physical being and unethical behavior."[16] In the presumption of the reflection of the individual's interiority on the body, the "correspondence" between the body and morality was certainly helpful in appeasing those who feared the presence of the criminal, for it offered the possibility that the criminal could be demarcated as somehow separate from the rest of society, and therefore isolated and marginalized and ultimately contained. The documenting of distinctive physical features and the categorizing of these features in relation to the crimes that the individuals had committed rather readily led to the conclusion that there were distinctive criminal types who were liable to commit particular crimes. Anthropologists "used their texts to demonstrate that there exists a criminal class, physically and psychologically different from normal citizens."[17]

This is the basis of the logic, I would suggest, that underlies Gould's statements that he didn't see his Grotesques as "ugly," but that he was merely trying to demarcate criminality in his draftsmanship so that the reader could more readily tell who the criminal was in the story. Of course, in that draftsmanship Gould was also—consciously or unconsciously—subscribing to a causal relationship between one's appearance and one's behavior, that criminality can be linked causally to a particular appearance. And that notion of causality makes a leap of logic that leads to an essentialist understanding of criminality and biology that suggests an inherent relationship between one's biological traits and one's future behavior. That essentialism is a biological determinism that presupposes, a priori later individual behavioral choices, that particular individuals will commit crimes.

Shawn Michelle Smith has argued that "criminologists following Lombroso sought to map the social body, to make the innate character of any given individual readable according to his or her physical 'type.'"[18] This mapping coincided with the establishment of criminal archives that were pioneered in the nineteenth century. As a means of creating "a bureaucratic-clerical-statistical system of 'intelligence,'" a number of criminologists created archives in which they stored measurements, photographs, and eventually fingerprints of the bodies and faces of known criminals.[19] These archives, along with the publication of photographs of criminals in such pamphlets as the "Rogues Gallery," offered a means of identifying criminals more readily. In doing so, criminologists used fundamental social science methods to codify and categorize crimes and to address concerns about the place of the criminal in society, especially in regards to the inability to know who posed a threat.

The two men at the forefront of the establishment of the criminal archive were Alphonse Bertillon and Francis Galton, who employed significantly different methodologies but whose work had rather similar applications and implications.[20] Using what became known eponymously as the Bertillon system, Bertillon indexed individual criminal bodies with an emphasis on quantitative methods, closely measuring faces, heads, and hands, for instance, and noting scars and other distinguishing marks, and completing the process with a photograph of a sort that ultimately became known as the mugshot.[21] Bertillon's intent was to cut down on recidivism but also to aid police in their attempts to solve a criminal act. These indices emphasized, in Sekula's words, the "body's physical history. . . . For Bertillon, the criminal body expressed nothing. No characterological secrets were hidden beneath the surface of this body."[22] The archive created, therefore, was comprised of a series of individual criminals; however, that archive could be used to place those

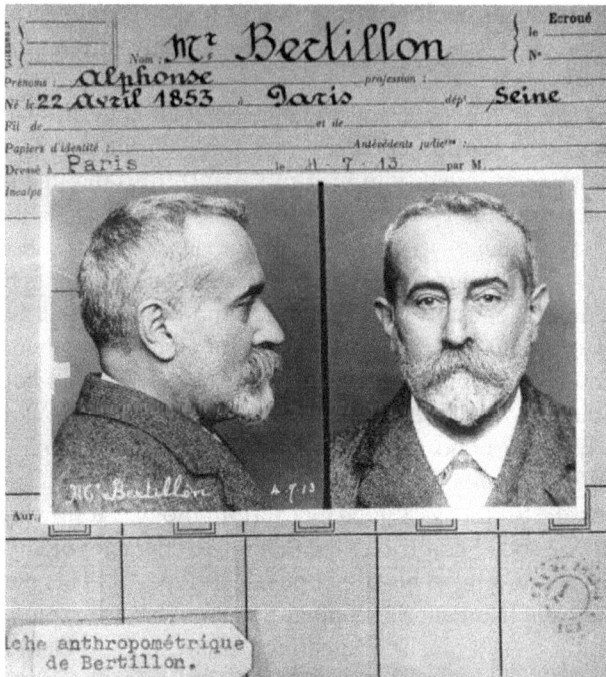

Figure 1.2 The Bertillon System with Alphonse Bertillon as Subject. *Source:* Apic/ Hulton Archive/Getty Images.

individuals into different groups—categorized and classified, in other words, as much by physical characteristic as by crime committed. It is worth pausing to note, however, that the system's varying ways of indexing individual criminals was used to locate a culprit following the commission of the crime.[23]

Thompson writes of the success of Bertillon's system of criminal classification in the public imagination, "Bertillonage made its practices and instrumentation visible, legible, and simple to understand—a transparent system with clear methods and goals. The prominent use of technology inspired faith in Bertillonage: the objectification of the criminal, explicitly and specifically, did not cause great concern for the public (See Figure 1.2.)."[24]

Galton's methodology and purpose were markedly different from Bertillon's. Galton was a pioneer in statistical theory, articulating such crucial concepts as standard deviation, correlation, and regression. He also was a leading researcher in fingerprinting, which he recognized had real value in criminology and for which he devised a system of classification that is still in use. However, he also was a pioneer in the field of eugenics, coining the term in fact. Related to this, his interests in heredity and population stability—which began with the study of animals but ultimately shifted to the study of humans—led him to consider such fields as psychiatry and criminology as he sought out ways to understand how individuals vary (and especially regress) across time and generations. The concept of variance itself often led him to look for "types" that he could examine for similarities and differences, directed toward his desire to understand regressions and deviations to better promote population and cultural stability.

Galton's focus on deviations and types was the basis of his promotion of composite photography for criminologists, which he hoped would help them identify "average" criminal faces. Using the latest photographic technologies, Galton compiled what he called composite photographic portraits, in which he combined multiple exposures of different images of criminals onto a single photographic plate. In this way, he would take the images of a large number of individuals and through a composite process produce a single image of one representative or "average" man. In this way, for instance, the portraits of individual rapists were compiled into a single composite portrait of a rapist. The portraits, therefore, represent the erasure of the individual criminals and leave in their place a visual representation of a criminal type.[25]

Bertillon's system was not wholly distinct from Galton's. Like the latter, Bertillon's emphasis on the visual aspect of the archive—through the documentation of the body in charts, diagrams, and photographs—privileged the physical appearance of the criminal body above that of the other evidence of the particular crime that he committed.[26] However, the differences in Galton's composites from Bertillon's mugshots—and the other measurable data that was included with the photograph—are significant and have to do with the representation (or lack thereof) of the individual criminal, as well as the purpose of the image itself. The mugshots specifically referenced individual criminals and individual crimes as a means to help victims and witnesses identify the perpetrator(s). While they could be used for correlative purposes—in that the files could reference types of crimes as well as particular physical features—Bertillon did not imagine his system as in any way predictive. Galton did. In not focusing on individual criminals but on criminal "types," Galton's composites did not enable investigators to identify specific individuals responsible for specific crimes. However, the composites did enable investigators to single out all sorts of individuals who "fit" the type, in essence implicating if not criminalizing a wide swath of individuals who may not actually have committed a crime but who seemed to fit the type of person who would have committed it. That type of classification, clearly, is different than the system that Bertillon instituted. It seeks to predict, through the assumption of the direct mapping on the body of interior character that Shawn Michelle Smith identified and that I referenced earlier. In other words, Galton's composites operate as visualizations of the belief that the appearance of the body predicts one's behavior—in this case, specific criminal

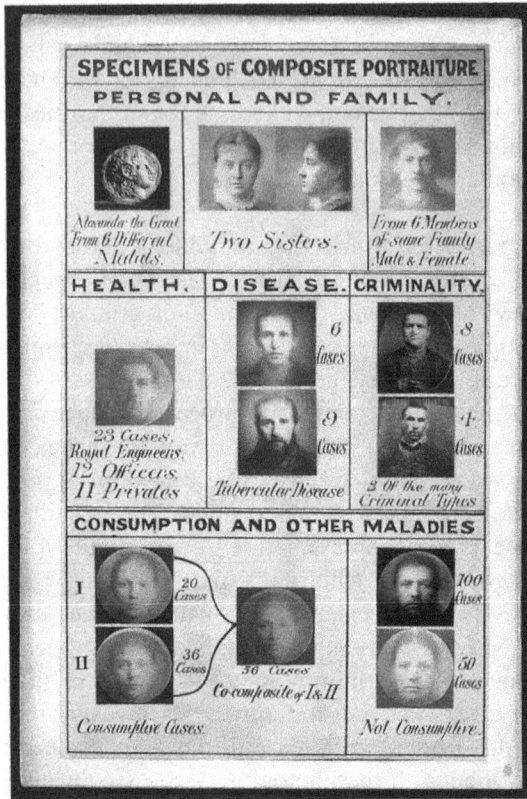

Figure 1.3 **An Example of Galton's Composite Photography. Frontispiece of Inquiries into Human Faculty and Its Development.** *Source:* Metropolitan Museum of Art.

behavior that can be "classified" by physical type. This is, then, a variation of the logic on which Chester Gould based his drafting of the Grotesques—they were drawn that way to offer a visual representation of their criminality, so that there "would be no mistake who the villain was."

Indeed, Galton's composite photographs function as portraits of criminality itself (See Figure 1.3.). They are visual representations of particular physical features in connection with specific crimes, implying a relationship between those features and criminal actions. Moreover, that relationship is less correlative than causal. By treating the composites as "types," Galton did more than suggest a correlation between people with particular features and particular crimes. His composites, in his own language, represented the "average" culprit for that crime, which would in essence not only eliminate people with other features as suspects but would also implicate individuals who had those particular features. This is important in that it presupposes that individuals with particular physical characteristics are—at the least—likely to commit particular crimes. This is how the composites are predictive. They presuppose the criminal behavior a priori any actual criminal behavior. Again, consider Gould and his introduction of Flattop Jones. Jones is a "funny-looking egg," and Gould's draftsmanship of the character signals to the reader that he is a criminal—even before the reader has seen Flattop commit a crime. In fact, the crime act is not the signifier of his criminality; instead, it is his physical appearance that signals it to the reader. Gould offers a fictional, comic strip example of the logic of the criminal type. Both he and Galton embrace a concept that links particular physical characteristics and criminal behavior, and ultimately that points to a version of biological determinism.

Considering Galton's deep intellectual and ideological investment in eugenics, his embrace of biological determinism should not come as much of a surprise, nor should it be surprising that much of his work had problematic racial and ethnic implications. Through the composite photographs, Galton implicated a "type" of person as criminal and sought to create a "scientific" justification for identifying those types as criminals.[27] That work was essential in order to allay public anxieties about crime and the criminal, which were most strikingly connected to anxieties about racial and ethnic "others"—those who could be identified legibly as physically "different."[28] And although Bertillon focused on individual criminals, his classification system—with its codification of distinct physical features— likewise implied that physical and biological characteristics were the means to locate foundational signs of criminality. But Bertillon and Galton were not alone in this work. The anxiety of and emphasis on these "others" as criminals was the result of study in the field of criminal anthropology that coexisted with that of Bertillon and Galton.[29] We can locate evidence of this study in the work of Lombroso himself.

Even in his own time, Lombroso had been widely criticized for his perceived attacks on what he called "atavistic races" and "savages." He often readily conflated race with criminality, as when he wrote that "many of the characteristics presented by savage races are very often found among born criminals."[30] In *Crime: Its Causes and Remedies*, he sought to answer those critics "who . . . object that there are savage peoples who are honorable and chaste." "The proof," he writes, "that [criminal] tendencies exist in the germ in the savage, is that when they begin to pass from their stage of savagery and take on a little civilization they always develop the characteristics of criminality in an exaggerated form."[31] The tension between civilization and savagery, and the powerfully negative influence of the former on the latter, is quite distinct in his reasoning. He continues in this vein, "Repressed in civilized man by education, environment, and the fear of punishment, [animal instincts] break out in the born criminal without apparent causes, or under the influence of certain circumstances, such as sickness, atmospheric influences, sexual excitement, or mob influence."[32]

Lombroso's readiness to assert equivalency between race and crime, based on a spurious notion of "proof," was one of the reasons that his ideas found such fertile soil in America.[33] As Rafter has suggested, in the late nineteenth and early twentieth centuries in America there existed the perception of "a deterioration in the nation's health. One source of weakness seemed to be the hordes of 'new immigrants' from southern and eastern Europe."[34] The work of the criminal anthropologists demonized these immigrants as inherently inferior and indeed even dangerous. Rafter writes, "According to these criminal anthropologists, members of the criminal class are bestial, childish, drunken and drawn to urban squalor. Including disproportionate numbers of foreigners, Catholics and Negroes, the criminal class breeds more rapidly than upright citizens, producing ever more paupers, imbeciles, and criminals."[35]

Criminal anthropologists of the late nineteenth and early twentieth centuries relied on a logic of biological determinism that readily led them to isolate distinct races and ethnicities as savage, uncivilized, and criminalistic. They treated the physical body as the most material means to define and establish a criminal type, and in so doing tended to suggest that there was a direct relationship between physical appearance and moral action. Lombroso insisted that criminal tendencies "exist in the germ in the savage" and that these tendencies "always develop" when the savages "take on a little civilization"[36] (366–367). That "always" is rather important in that it implies that these individuals have no choice but to become criminals. They are, as Sekula put it, criminals who are "organically distinct from the bourgeois: a *biotype*."[37] The demonization of difference in the logic of these criminologists worked doubly—to define "traditional," Anglo-Saxon looks as normal and to identify the overtly ethnicized bodies as dangerous. Along with criminal archivists such as Galton and Bertillon, the criminal anthropologists "put a face" on crime. It was a face that the public could recognize as a threat, a face that rarely conjured the term "middle class" and a face that most would associate with the terms "foreign" or "immigrant."

In the United States, the discipline of anthropology itself continued to gain widespread respect as a social science during the early decades of the twentieth century and the field of criminal anthropology did not disappear. Still, scholars working in the field of criminal anthropology itself were quite active in the fin de siècle years. There were at least eight American books published in the late nineteenth and early twentieth centuries as emerging from Lombroso's lead: McDonald's *Criminology* (1893), Boies's *Prisoners and Paupers* (1893), Henderson's *An Introduction to the Study of the Dependent, Defective, and Delinquent Classes* (1893), Eugene Talbot's *Degeneracy* (1898), August Drahms's *The Criminal* (1900), W. D. McKim's *Heredity and Human Progress* (1900), G. F. Lydston's *The Diseases of Society* (1904), and Philip Parsons's *Responsibility for Crime* (1909). Havelock Ellis's *The Criminal*, a treatise written in England and about English criminals but published in 1900 in America, further helped to popularize criminal anthropology in America. Early photographic processes were widespread in their use by the turn of the century: daguerreotypes of criminals had been used for decades in major American cities, for instance, rogues' galleries widely served as criminal archives, and after the Paris police accepted Bertillon's system in 1883, it was quickly adopted across Europe and North America. Identifying the criminal through physical characteristics was widespread investigative practice.

The conceit of the criminal type along racial and ethnic lines, along with a growing support of eugenics, seeped into the American popular consciousness through the early decades of the twentieth century. Inspired in part by the Red Scare of 1919–1920 but also in part by simple xenophobia, the Immigration Act that Congress enacted in 1924, which effectively banned all immigration from Asia and set very strict limitations on any immigrants from non-Western countries, had an explicitly racialist and eugenicist rationale that focused on alien radicals jeopardizing American institutions and immigrants threatening to change the fundamental nature of American identity. In 1920, for example, Lothrop Stoddard published *The Rising Tide of Color Against White World-Supremacy*, a book decrying the collapse of white supremacy, advocating for severe immigration restrictions from nonwhite countries, and embracing a separation of the races. Stoddard's book was commercially successful, received a number of positive reviews from major news outlets, and was singled out by then-president Warren Harding in a 1922 rally in Alabama, in which Harding pushed his pro-segregation agenda. Stoddard's book was well known enough that Tom Buchanan's mere mention of it in Fitzgerald's *The Great Gatsby*—with a slight fictionalizing of the author as Goddard and the title as *The Rise of the Colored Empires*—served to sum up Buchanan as a eugenicist and white supremacist.

In *The Gangs of New York*, his 1927 "informal history" of New York's criminal underworld, Herbert Asbury told the story of the rise of gangs from the 1800s to the early 1900s, especially as situated in the locales of Five Points, Hell's Kitchen, and Chinatown—all New York neighborhoods heavily populated with immigrants from Ireland, Italy, and China, respectively. His history focused on gangsters' ethnic backgrounds and he explicitly located criminality in New York with these specific neighborhoods. In constructing his portrait of crime as an ethnography of these areas, Asbury reified nativist beliefs about immigrants and their inherent criminality that they brought with them to America.

Asbury's attempt to compile a popular history of violence and crime in New York, coming as it did during the years of Prohibition and its attendant

rise in crime, displays an adherence to notions of the criminal type as articulated by the criminal anthropologists of the beginning of the century. Like
Lombroso and many of the others, Asbury includes a series of illustrations
of crimes and criminals, along with a rogues' gallery of conmen, prostitutes,
thieves, and murderers. These gangsters embodied a vision of criminality
that was especially evocative. Indeed, the rogues' gallery, taken as a whole,
serves as a group portrait of criminals that actually operates as a portrait of
criminality. The individuals who are photographed in the book—although
almost always arrayed in a tie and jacket in the photo—are often bruised,
scarred, and swollen. Although they look directly into the lens of the camera, they do not smile nor invite an emotional connection to the observer.
These are photos of identification used to enter these gangsters into the
judicial system, and readers would recognize the staging, lighting, and
cropping of the photograph as that of mugshots. Readers therefore would
recognize, through popular visual literacy, that these men are dangerous, on
some level, which is why they are photographed in this manner. Moreover,
their names underneath the photos serve to further identify them as both
threatening and specifically ethnic. With names like Sheeny Mike Kurtz,
Googy Corcoran, Baboon Connolly, Louie the Lump, Kid Twist, Humpty
Jackson, Dago Frank, and Gyp the Blood, the gangsters connote animality,
deviance, and distinct danger. These are men to be scared of and men to
avoid.

Asbury complemented these images with descriptions of the gangsters that
emphasized their physical deficiencies. Take, for instance, this description of
Monk Eastman:

> So far as looks were concerned, and actions, too, for that matter, Eastman was a
> true moving picture gangster. He began life with a bullet-shaped head, and dur-
> ing his turbulent career acquired a broken nose and a pair of cauliflower ears,
> which were not calculated to increase his beauty. He had heavily veined, sag-
> ging jowls, and a short, bull neck, plentifully scarred with battle marks, as were
> his cheeks. He seemed always to need a haircut, and he accentuated his fero-
> cious and unusual appearance by affecting a derby hat several sizes too small,
> which perched precariously atop his shock of bristly, unruly hair.[38]

Asbury presents Eastman as something of a freak, with features such as the
broken nose and cauliflower ears that immediately identified him as someone
who engaged in violence. The scars on his neck came from somewhere, after
all. But Asbury also implies that Eastman's other features, such as the "heavily veined, sagging jowls" and the "shock of bristly, unruly hair" also serve
as emblems of his criminality and this implication bears further scrutiny.
Certainly these features do not signal violence, in either the past or the future.

Figure 1.4   Paul Muni as Tony Camonte in *Scarface* (1932). *Source:* Hawks, Howard. 1932. *Scarface*. United States. The Caddo Company.

But Asbury conflates the way in which a photograph serves as a document of an individual arrested for a crime with a portrait that foretells further criminal behavior. Not everyone with bristly, unruly hair will commit a crime, and heavily veined, sagging jowls do not necessarily signal anything other than an unhealthy diet. Asbury's implication is nonetheless clear. Eastman's is the face of crime—violent and scarred, ethnic and different, a threat to good citizens everywhere.

Asbury's description of Eastman as having the looks of a "moving picture gangster" points to other examples of the criminal type in popular culture in the Prohibition years and beyond. In Howard Hawks's *Scarface*, which premiered in 1932, Paul Muni plays Tony Camonte with a raw physicality that represented Tony's savage and brutal nature (See Figure 1.4.).

Scarface, a story of crime in 1920s Chicago, found a wide commercial audience and exerted a profound influence on representations of criminals over the next decade, as the genre of the gangster film became a mainstay in the United States. At the beginning of the film, Muni has long and somewhat unruly hair, hunches his shoulders, and allows his arms to hang loose and long at his sides. His physical presence is distinctively simian.[39] Muni acts the part with a manner that corresponds with how he holds his body, leering and rolling his eyes and gesticulating broadly with his arms, for instance, while emphasizing Tony's lack of sophistication in terms of his cultural knowledge of clothes, furnishings, and proper demeanor in social settings. In the film, the way he carries himself physically, as well as his lack of culture, is equated with his Italian heritage and its limitations. As Muni plays him, Tony is all id, a creature who wants; and our understanding of Tony is that he is indeed a

creature. He seems less a man than something savage, not only a metaphori-
cal but also a somewhat literal ape.[40]

In the early decades of the twentieth century, the criminalized body operated as an a priori device within crime narratives (the novel, the film, the
sociological history)—a means to identify and signal a threat, and therein a
means to alleviate the anxiety that first generated the desire to demarcate the
threat. Within popular culture, this function of the criminalized body reached
its apogee in the representation of the cinematic character of *Scarface* or even
more so in the Grotesques in *Dick Tracy*. In fact, the theory of the criminal
type remained prevalent in popular consciousness long after most criminal
anthropologists and social scientists rejected it or at the least recognized its
logical faults. Many would argue it continues to have relevance today, in the
logic of racial profiling and the manner in which immigrants continue to be
portrayed as inherently criminal.

Moreover, even if the theory's influence in criminology did wane with the
rise of psychology and sociology as emerging social sciences in the United
States and the perspectives those disciplines brought to the study of criminality, the interest in the concept of the criminal type remained evident, as in the
work of Harvard anthropologist Earnest Hooton.[41] Hooton was a renowned
and respected scholar who was the first teacher of physical anthropology in
the United States and who made a number of valuable contributions to the
scholarly field, including *The Indians of Pecos Pueblo* (1930) and *Up from
the Ape* (1931). Hooton received his masters and doctorate in classical studies from the University of Wisconsin, but while on a Rhodes scholarship to
Oxford became disenchanted with the subject and turned to anthropology.[42]
After moving to Harvard in 1913 he taught courses in archaeology and eth-
nology, but focused his research on anthropology. His work, especially his
focus on distinct ethnic bodies, was highly influential in promoting archeolo-
gists to use skeletal materials to interrogate historical settings and relationships between people. In the late 1920s and early 1930s, he began a massive
research project studying the American criminal. Hooton believed that criminals should differ morphologically from citizens in that they should have
certain physical characteristics that a trained eye could recognize as distinct.[43]

Hooton's research culminated in the publication of two works in 1939,
Crime and the Man and *The American Criminal: An Anthropological Study,
Vol. 1: The Native White Criminal of Native Parentage*. These two books
were connected. *Crime and the Man* aimed for a general audience, while
Hooton published *The American Criminal* with a more scholarly audience
in mind. In *Crime and the Man* Hooton offered a number of strong assertions about criminals without presenting the statistical data to support those
claims, as *The American Criminal* contained the raw data that Hooton used
to reach his conclusions in the first book.[44] Perhaps as a result of those strong

assertions, though also due to Hooton's strong academic reputation, *Crime and the Man* generated a great deal of publicity, including coverage in *Time* magazine, and serves as a useful representation of his ideas about criminals and the criminal body.

At the heart of Hooton's belief is his assumption that "the behavioristic tendencies of man may be associated in some fashion with his physical characteristics."[45] Hooton's work is deeply connected to the behaviorist criminologists of the late 1800s and early 1900s, who operated under a similar assumption that physical characteristics reveal behavioristic tendencies. Like these criminologists, Hooton proposes an "organic" basis for crime, claiming that "the physical characteristics of any animal should afford some clue to the type and quality of his mental and emotional responses."[46] Although variations in the bodily makeup might not be causally related to specific behavior, he suggests one may be able to predict actions by recognizing the way in which the variations form "an indissoluble organic association."[47]

Hooton's introductory rhetoric evokes that of Lombroso decades earlier. Hooton, however, explicitly distances himself from Lombroso, critiquing him for presenting his data "in such a faulty way and in so partisan a spirit," and he takes issue with Lombroso and his followers for their assumption "that criminals are more or less of the same type the world over, irrespective of race and nationality."[48] He goes on to argue that the notion that "there are but two types of men, normal and criminal, and that these types transcend the physical differences which distinguish the various races . . . is almost too fantastic for serious consideration."[49] Nonetheless, Hooton did seem to believe that one's interiority was externally mapped onto the face or body. Hooton's project was to make sure to account for ethnicity in his comparison of criminals and civilians, so that he could accurately analyze the multiplicity of criminal types—which must, in his view, reflect the multiplicity of ethnic types.

Following the criminal anthropologists of earlier decades, Hooton looks to the role of ethnic and racial variations to understand how humans think and behave, arguing that "it would appear that racial physical differences should naturally be associated with racial psychological differences, and that the social behavior of distinct racial stocks should vary in accordance with their physiological and psychological divergences."[50] The fact that scientists have not demonstrated those differences in the ensuing decades does not, in his mind, mean that they do not exist. Instead, Hooton criticizes "the crudity and general inadequacy" of both the methods of measuring psychological differences and also the anthropological techniques used to determine racial types.[51] "Differences in racial psychology," he argues, "cannot be ascertained until we are able to select for psychological examination racial physical types."[52] In this opening, Hooton signals that he wishes to combine the best of what psychology has to offer with what he believes anthropology's sound emphasis on distinct racial typology. He believes there will be divergences in racial psychology that correspond to what he sees as the manifest physical differences between different races and ethnicities. In making such a claim, he is articulating a more sophisticated biological determinism than that proposed by earlier criminal anthropologists. At the same time, he is operating under a very similar logic that led them to assign deviance to physical difference and to correspondingly marginalize ethnicity as a physical marker.

Hooton claims to find in his research a "mountain of evidence" that separates various classes of criminals.[53] He offers fact-based and meticulously constructed data so as to account accurately for the physical appearance of criminals of all types of backgrounds and for the offenses that they committed, such as murder, burglary, and rape. He presents this data to his readers in such classifications as native- and foreign-born criminals, Old American Criminals and New American Criminals, and ethnicities that he identifies as Pure Nordic, Predominantly Nordic, Keltic, Alpine, East Baltic, Dinaric, Nordic Mediterranean, Pure Mediterranean, Nordic Alpine, or Negro. He uses these classifications as an organizational structure for his findings.

For instance, Hooton identifies the general proportions and mosaic of excess features for the Pure Nordic Old American Criminals as a narrow head and narrow face; pure blue eyes; thin eyebrows; golden, ash-blond hair with low waves; pink, ruddy skin; a short and rather broad nose; a nasal septum inclined upward; and facial prognathism absent and gonial angles not pronounced.[54] The detail is marked, and especially compelling when compared with Predominantly Nordic Old American Criminals. They, on the other hand, have a narrow face and a narrow and high forehead; lightish eyes; small ears; lightish hair that is straight; a short and narrow nose with a medium broad nasal bridge and a concavo-convex nasal profile; median eyefolds; a septum inclined upward; narrow jaws, with the jaw angles compressed; and a long and thin neck.[55] The close details in these descriptions are of great significance, for though the differences between the Pure Nordic and the Predominantly Nordic are few, they are indeed manifestly discernible. And those differences allow Hooton to structure his research in ethno-racial classifications.

Hooton graphs the tendencies between different ethnicities for committing certain crimes, comparing and ranking the numbers of men of varying ethnic descents who have committed forgery, burglary, and first-degree murder. Likewise he sets up comparisons between the numbers of crimes committed by foreign-born criminals and those by native-born men of the same ethnic background, such as Polish Austrian, Near Eastern, and Italian and Italian American. All of these are based on the detailed research that he compiled for twelve years, and all appear to be a statistically sound as a way to categorize the men who committed crimes. But ultimately Hooton is more than merely interested in creating a database for what type of man tends to commit what type of crime. He wants in some way to suggest that the physical differences act as an emblem of the behavioral differences.

The richly detailed graphs and diagrams that categorize the findings of his research—such as those for the Pure Nordic or the Predominantly Nordic Old American Criminal—group the findings into generalizations of the ethnic type so as to create a composite. However, by emphasizing the differences between these types of individuals and law-abiding citizens, Hooton creates more than a composite for the Pure or Predominantly Nordic Old American Criminal, he creates a composite of the criminal type, the very thing he claimed "too fantastic for serious consideration."[56] He slips into similar problematic methods and logical fallacies for which he had critiqued early criminal anthropologists.

Hooton claims that there are manifest physical differences between those who commit crimes and those who do not. Working within the rubric of his stated belief—that there are multiple ethnic types and therefore that multiple criminal types, based on ethnicity, need to be accounted for—he writes, "The putatively law-abiding citizen, however humble his social and economic status, is larger, superior in physique and in most anthropological character . . . [to the] . . . criminal of comparable ethnic and racial origin and drawn from approximately similar occupational levels."[57] By comparing criminals and law-abiding citizens of the same status, Hooton denies socioeconomic conditions as a cause for crime and instead looks to the biological factors that signal criminal behavior. He offers a comparison that lists a number of detailed physical attributes that differentiates the criminal from the law-abiding citizen: a thinner beard; thicker eyebrows; thinner lips; a low and sloping forehead; thinker and straighter hair; internal eyefolds; unwrinkled cheeks; compressed cheekbones and jaw angles; a slight overbite; a long, thin neck and sloping shoulders; pronounced ear protrusion; and no lip seam. The amount of detail is fascinating, of course, and suggests the level of vigilance Hooton applied to his findings. But the effect of those findings is greater than that of conferring vigilance to Hooton; they also reveal his belief that physical characteristics reveal character.

Not surprisingly, considering how anthropology (and criminology itself) had developed in the four decades or so since Lombroso, Hooton's emphasis on biological factors was a central point of contention for a number of reviewers of the book at the time. E. B. Reuter, an accomplished professor of Sociology who worked the majority of his career at the University of Iowa, was particularly critical of what he sees as Hooton's "general theoretical position [of] extreme biological determinism."[58] He called for Hooton to better deal with "the logical processes by which [he] reaches generalities" and wondered how he was able to derive "social conclusions from biological and physical measurements."[59] Ultimately, Reuter denigrated the book as "the funniest academic performance that has appeared since the invention of movable type."[60] In a bit more measured but detailed critique in *American Anthropologist*, Robert K. Merton and M. F. Ashley-Montagu similarly questioned Hooton's intentions and methods, wondering "why Hooton fastened upon a difference of a biological nature, rather than upon the many other characters of difference which are socio-economically known to exist between the civilians and the criminals, as the causative factor in criminality."[61] "The extrapolation of the 'biological' factor, to the exclusion of all others," they wrote, "may satisfy Hooton's critical sense, but it does not satisfy ours."[62]

Hooton claims early on in his treatise that "there is no necessary implication of causality—at least in the sense of a direct relationship between the physical characteristics of criminals and their antisocial conduct."[63] He situated his project, therefore, as categorizing and summarizing what the criminal looked like. However, Hooton goes on to make a broader claim for the value of and possible implications of his work. Concerning the meaning of the physical characteristics of criminals that are "in a significant degree and in a constant direction" different from those of civilians, he writes, "It is conceivable that the linkage of bodily features with mental processes may be such that the latter may be predicted from the former."[64] He does recognize that the richly detailed research discounts any ability to claim definitively a criminal type by offense. Indeed, he writes near the end of the book, "I have been at considerable pains in this investigation to demonstrate the mathematical and biological impossibility of establishing criminal types exclusively devoted to some particular kind of offense, by seeking for intricate combinations of morphological or metric peculiarities."[65] His charts cannot predict exactly what type of offense criminals will commit in advance of the crime—the highly distinct and detailed results of the evidence demonstrate that it is too difficult to render such a judgment. However, Hooton's emphasis on what he sees as physical inferiority in criminals suggests that he believes that it is possible to predict who will be a criminal, even if it is not practical to suppose that one could predict whether that criminal will be a pickpocket, a thief, a rapist, or a murderer. In fact, Hooton's categorization and summary of the racial and ethnic psychological and social differences between criminals and law-abiding citizens are meant in part to provide a scientific basis for making predictions about individuals' behavior, all on the basis of their physical appearance. Hooton moves from arguing that the physical differences signal criminal behavior to suggesting that the differences cause that behavior. It is a significant step, one that takes him away from his observation-based position of categorizing his findings into a position of postulating causes without any scientific evidence that supports his claims. Essentially, Hooton equates physical difference a priori with moral and ethical difference—a move that no amount of evidence has ever scientifically proven. We know that thin-lipped, smooth-cheeked men, with pronounced ears and sloping shoulders, an over-bite, and a low, sloping forehead are not necessarily criminals.[66]

While initial critical reception of *Crime and the Man* was mainly positive, the critique of Hooton's methodology was pronounced with the publication of *The American Criminal*, which served as the more detailed volume of data meant to accompany the former book.[67] Thomas C. McCormick, for instance, criticized Hooton for a "biased control sample" that jeopardized the validity of the data and the relevance for other subjects.[68] Frank Alexander Ross, writing in *The American Journal of Sociology* at the time, declared that "Hooton deals essentially with preponderances, pluralities, and means" and that the relevance of his types to specific individuals was not direct in any way.[69] Ross argued that it was unclear whether "Hooton himself has indisputable data, that his controls are adequate, that his statistical methods are beyond reproach, or that his deductions are the logical ones to be derived from his statistics."[70] One of the reasons that the former volume did not receive as much criticism may have been because reviewers did not have Hooton's specific data from which to evaluate his conclusions. Just as likely, however, was that the initial positive reviews were a result at least in part of Hooton's reputation and powerful influence on a generation of scholars. That influence should not too readily be discounted, just as the positive reception of *Crime and the Man* should not, as they suggest that the power of biological determinism was still quite strong in the late 1930s.

Hooton's framework of establishing racial and ethnic categories for his findings, and his categorization of the types of offenses that each ethnic type tends to commit, emphasizes ethnicity as the central means by which one must approach criminality as a concept. When Hooton goes so far as to rank the offenses committed by race and ethnic types, he highlights the role of race and ethnicity even further. In these rankings, "Old Americans," those with the oldest ancestry in America, consistently rank in the bottom half of those types most likely to commit crimes. In terms of the racial and ethnic rankings, the demonization of those who appear different is evident, especially in the emphasis in categorizing the detailed physical and morphological differences and in contending that those differences equal deviance. For Hooton, those differences are crucial, and his reaction to them makes overt his anxieties. He advocates a program in which the government would segregate paroled delinquents and set aside land for them on which they would live permanently. The territory would be closed off and supervised, but self-governed.[71] Hooton's thinking is disturbing in its ethno-racial prejudices and his assumption that all criminals come from a certain type of area and certain type of heritage:

he fails to follow the logic of his earlier assertion about the multiplicity of criminal types.

Although Hooton claims that he is merely classifying jailed criminals and compiling composites of what he has found, the rhetoric in his text belies his assertion that he is not making judgments about criminality. He suggests that criminals have been unable to adapt to their conditions, so that instead of manipulating and controlling their environment, they are "molded, distorted and enslaved" by that environment, eventually succumbing to it.[72] He writes, "It has been obvious for a long time to really scientifically-minded criminologists that the only purely environmental, non-biological means of crime prevention which has the slightest prospect of success is the training, supervision, and education of children from depressed areas and inferior stocks prior to the onset of delinquency."[73] His emphasis on "children from depressed areas and inferior stocks" reveals his racial and ethnic biases. These are the people who he claims are "molded, distorted and enslaved" by their environment.[74] Hooton assumes that individuals in these depressed areas would not be able to adapt to their conditions. How does Hooton know that the inhabitants of these areas will inevitably turn to crime, other than by their appearance? He merely assumes that those who live in those areas and are of the ethnic type more liable to commit offenses will indeed turn to crime themselves. But he consistently fails to demonstrate that physical difference is necessarily physical inferiority, let alone that physical difference necessarily leads to behavioral difference. Although it is his hope to demonstrate the validity of this claim, he can only show that there are physical differences. He does not demonstrate the assumed link between appearances and behavior that he predicts when he asserts that "the social behavior of distinct racial stocks should vary in accordance with their physiological and psychological differences" and the reason for that failure is simply because his assumptions do not hold up to intellectual inquiry.[75] His a priori judgments of character based on physical differences are baseless. His composite model of criminality owes much to the same type of biological determinism of an earlier generation and ultimately met the same critical fate.

Nonetheless, as I have suggested, the concept of a criminal type, founded on a principle of biological determinism, found its way into American popular culture in a number of ways, ranging from novels to films to comic strips. More importantly, perhaps, was the way it found its way into popular consciousness and remained there, even as scholars challenged the methodology and ideology of Lombroso and his followers, as well as Hooton. An underlying cultural logic of the criminal type was that difference was inherently threatening and that the appropriate way to construct or represent criminals is by "constructing" their bodies as different and then somehow deviant. As a strategy of representation, this was a powerful way to alleviate anxiety about criminality. The figurization of the criminal body as bestial and ethnic served to identify threats before they were realized. It also served to exclude ethnic Americans not only from political power but also from socioeconomic autonomy. Peter Stallybrass and Allon White, in *The Politics and Poetics of Transgression*, for example, note the long history of bestial representations of the lower classes as a means of exclusion from political power.[76] That strategy is apparent in the work of early American criminal anthropologists and in Hooton. However, criminalizing the body through an overexaggeration or misrepresentation of physical difference had real-world consequences for immigrants and ethnic Americans in the early decades of the twentieth century. The tropes that we can recognize in the written and visual rhetoric of the criminal body in the late nineteenth and early twentieth centuries implied that one of the ways to deal with the anxiety about crime was to inscribe the sign of criminality literally onto the criminal's face as a means of signaling the danger before it struck. This rhetoric, then, provided the public with the illusion (and most definitely the comfort) of identifying criminals and taking them out of social circulation. That "comfort," of course, could lead to severe consequences for those individuals who were identified as criminal without ever having committed a crime.

Real-life events seemed at times to justify or necessitate this rhetoric. For example, on April 28, 1919, a bomb was discovered in the mail of Ole Hanson, the mayor of Seattle who had been advocating loudly for increased public awareness of and vigilance against the dangers of political radicals in America. On April 30, the New York Post Office detained sixteen similar packages that were set to explode when they were opened. Almost twenty other bombs, in other parts of the country, were intercepted before delivery or before they were opened. One package, however, made it through to its destination, the Atlanta home of Senator Thomas Hardwick of Georgia, and was unwrapped. The explosion blew off the hands of the maid and badly injured Hardwick's wife. The mailbombs apparently comprised a plot by radicals to assassinate more than thirty of the most prominent business and political leaders in the country, including Attorney-General A. Mitchell Palmer and Secretary of Labor William B. Wilson, Supreme Court Justice Oliver W. Holmes, Jr., John D Rockefeller, and J. P. Morgan.

In an editorial on May 2 entitled "The Bomb Plot," the *New York Times* identified "Bolsheviki, anarchists, and I.W.W.'s . . . by all the indications" as the ones behind the bombs, but no individuals or groups took responsibility for the plot.[77] Nevertheless, the mailing list suggested a politically radical ideology and desire to target political and economic leaders, implying that they were out to topple the foundation of American society. The intended bombings created a distinct sense that violence threatened the stability of the country; on May 1, public reprisals against the radicals created a further feeling of upheaval and instability. In such cities as New York, Chicago, Detroit, Boston, and Cleveland, there were a number of riots in which mobs—at times using brutal means—broke up radical meetings and parades.[78] Not surprisingly, the lack of a specific culprit or group to blame for the intended bombs engendered a general anxiety about a widespread threat against America itself and manifested itself in a series of attacks on individuals and organizations that had nothing to do with the bombs.[79] Servicemen in New York, for instance, attacked the building housing *The Call*, a Socialist daily newspaper, where about 700 men, women, and children were celebrating the opening of its new offices. Insisting that the event was a meeting "of a Bolshevik nature," the men broke up the reception, destroyed the literature on hand, and drove the attendees outdoors, where they were struck and clubbed by other servicemen who were waiting outside. Focusing their fury on labor unions and on groups with Socialist or Russian connections, other servicemen went to meetings held by the Clothing Workers' Union and by the New York Joint Board of the Amalgamated Clothing Workers of America and to events at the People's House, the Russian Workers' House, and Webster Hall. The servicemen interrupted these meetings, tore up what literature they could find, and forced attendees to sing the national anthem.[80]

Following a series of further bombings in the summer of 1919, including one at the home of Attorney General A. Mitchell Palmer, Secretary of State Robert Lansing wrote in a memorandum on July 26, 1919, "It is no time to temporize or compromise; no time to be timid or undecided; no time to remain passive. We are face to face with an inveterate enemy of the present social order."[81] A nationwide strike by coal miners in the autumn of 1919 further strengthened assumptions that linked labor strife and the radical agenda and complemented assumptions about public perceptions of radicals as agitators in a class war. The Executive Committee of the National Security League, for instance, sent out a call on October 17, 1919, demanding that the American public "wake up to a realization of what is taking place. . . . The radical agitation which is menacing the foundations of our industrial life is not based upon specific grievances, but is aimed at the overthrow of American institutions and ideas just as surely as if a Bolshevist army was marching on Washington."[82] In the face of public criticism and a congressional resolution in the fall of 1919 pushing him to take action, Attorney General Palmer instituted what came to be known as the Palmer Raids of 1919–1920.[83]

The first of the major raids came on November 7, 1919. Department of Justice agents targeted the Union of Russian workers, an organization of about 4,000 Russian immigrants, in twelve cities. The raids were a travesty of civil liberties—many people were arrested without warrants, those who visited the arrested in jail were themselves arrested, and many did not receive a hearing on their arrest for weeks and even months.[84] The success of the raids was debatable. On December 21, 249 anarchists were deported by boat. But in the November raids in New York, while 650 people were arrested, only forty-three were eventually deported.[85] The next major raid began on January 2, 1920, and lasted for several days, extending up to six weeks later. Over 3,000 so-called radicals were arrested during this time and at least as many taken into custody, only to be released later; nevertheless, while officials again squashed civil liberties, the public supported Palmer's actions in the raids, regardless of the unjustifiable widespread arrests of countless immigrants who were not radicals.[86]

By the spring of 1920, Assistant Secretary of Labor Louis Post—who became Acting Secretary when Secretary Wilson fell ill—had begun to challenge Attorney General Palmer for the treatment of those arrested during the raids and for the trampling of civil liberties that had occurred in the previous months. Post agitated for the release of many of those still in custody and instigated hearings in Congress on the raids. In front of the House Committee on Rules that was investigating his response to the Red Scare, Palmer said of the alien radicals who had recently immigrated to the United States, "Out of the sly and crafty eyes of many of them leap cupidity, cruelty, insanity, and crime; from their lopsided faces, sloping brows, and misshapen features may be recognized the unmistakable criminal type."[87] In invoking the term "criminal type" and equating it with distinct physical features, Palmer gave voice to the belief in biological determinism of Lombroso, Galton, and the other early criminal anthropologists and lays bare his prejudice and anxiety about an impending threat originating in those who appear physically different than him—aligning that difference with ideological danger. His statement also made clear the distinct consequences of such a belief for those seen as different or "other" because they had what appear to be clearly marked ethnic features. Those features were seen as a sign of a threat.

Palmer's justification for why he pursued the eponymous raids is noteworthy first in the clear xenophobia in his description of the radicals' "lopsided faces, sloping brows and misshapen features." This xenophobia went hand in hand with the restrictive immigration policies that Congress adopted in the years following World War I.[88] The numbers from the Palmer Raids demonstrate that far more individuals were arrested as dangerous or seditious radicals than were warranted, but those statistics also imply the power of the anxiety that foreigners engendered in the culture. During the Red Scare, marked ethnicity came to be seen as equivalent to a threat, and ordinary immigrants were too often thus treated as criminals. In May and June 1919, following the original bombings, Congress quickly sought to institute anti-sedition laws or to rewrite laws that had been in place during the war. Although not all radicals held the same beliefs, or even pushed for the same type of change, often they were lumped together as a force from the outside who were not, as the Executive Committee of the National Security League put it, "true Americans."[89] They certainly were not treated as such, and the fear that the bombings created led the government to try to identify the perceived threat before more bombings took place. To do so, the government constructed a narrative that imagined danger all around.

In his statement to the House Committee on Rules that was investigating his response and the rationale behind it, Palmer not only articulates his own prejudices that imagine foreigners as having lopsided faces and misshapen features, but also he operates as an amateur physiognomist who possesses the expertise to decode the meaning of particular facial features. In that, we can locate how the ideas of the early criminologists seeped into the American popular consciousness when it came to discussing and identifying criminal threats. The first strategy was the exaggeration of their features as a way to assert difference from what Palmer might have identified as Native Americans or those without racial or ethnic markers. He assigns them emotional, psychological, and moral characteristics—"cupidity, cruelty, insanity, and crime"—based solely on his interpretation of what is in their "sly and crafty eyes," asserting a correspondence physical difference with moral and ideological difference. Not only does he essentialize and make uniform the appearance of the radicals—his description presumes that is how they *all* look—but he also assigns an interpretation to those physical features without actually designating how or why those "sly and crafty eyes" inherently lead to those particular conclusions. And, of course, even more foundationally, he never even makes clear why those adjectives would even apply to their particular eyes. The description, in other words, incorporates the interpretation without actually designating concrete physical characteristics.

In the particular features of the radicals, Palmer says—disregarding his own strategy of exaggerating those features and of assigning meaning to those features without actually offering any concrete description of them—we can locate the "unmistakable criminal type." That type, by the nature of those exaggerated features, is physically distinct from ordinary American citizens. By the same logic, those physical characteristics similarly become emblems of a fundamental criminality. Palmer conflates the assertion of the radicals' physical difference with their very radicalism—to look this way is to be a radical—and at the same time asserts that those characteristics were signs of criminality. For Palmer, to look like a radical *is* to be a radical *is* to be a criminal. The pseudoscientific appeal to the concept of the "criminal type" aligns Palmer's xenophobia with a rationale asserted decades before by Lombroso and other criminal anthropologists. And although that rationale had been undercut by other scholars, its place in popular culture and the popular consciousness, especially at a time of national stress and anxiety about bombings, riots, and crime, spoke to how Palmer's invocation of that rationale was something with which many of the American public could identify. Representations of that rationale in popular culture offer one way to track its cultural currency in how Americans at times harkened to xenophobia in how they imagined criminality. The immigration restrictions are another way. The rationale behind the criminal type had real-life consequences for many immigrants, and certainly for alien radicals—regardless of whether they had committed a crime. After all, the power of a priori reasoning within the concept of the criminal type—that one can identify an individual's criminality even without seeing him commit a criminal act or possibly even in advance of one—holds a great appeal as an alleviation of anxiety.[90]

Palmer's national influence began to fade in the late spring of 1920 under harsh criticism for his tactics in the raids. Following Post's attack on Palmer's rationale and his methods, a consortium of some of the most prominent attorneys in the country, including future Supreme Court Justice Felix Frankfurter, published a booklet condemning the violations of the Constitution during the raids. When Palmer's prediction that widespread radical uprisings would take place on May Day did not come to pass, he was ridiculed in the press for inciting hysteria. His bid for the presidency ended early that summer. However, the logic that Palmer articulated and acted upon did not so readily recede. It saw its culmination in the arrest and trial of Nicola Sacco and Bartolomeo Vanzetti.

In the spring of 1920, authorities in Massachusetts arrested two Italian immigrants for the robbery and murder of two men delivering the payroll of a shoe factory. The ensuing trial and conviction of Sacco and Vanzetti set off a furious controversy wherein thousands sought to save them from their eventual execution in 1927. In his opening statement at the trial, Prosecuting Attorney Williams said of the two killers, based on eyewitness reports, "They were two short men, perhaps five feet, six or seven, rather stocky, described as perhaps 140 and 160, in that vicinity; caps, dark clothes, of apparent Italian lineage."[91] That last phrase—"of Italian lineage"—stands out as the only moment in this detailed description that is uncertain. The height, weight, and clothes are determined to specific dimensions, as would be appropriate to descriptions sought by police investigating any crime. But by assigning an apparent ethnicity to the murderers as well, the prosecutor sought to capitalize on public anxieties concerning immigrants and radicals. Williams later denoted how an eyewitness noticed "an Italian with a mustache."[92] In each of these instances in his opening statement, the prosecuting attorney did not specify skin tone or anything else that might specifically signify the killers' ethnicity. He simply identified them as an ethnic type, suggesting to the jury that ethnicity itself was what lay at the heart of the identification of the men on trial.

This effort on the part of the prosecution to emphasize ethnicity to the jury was further borne out in the identification stage of the trial, during which a number of witnesses who offered identifications of the killers gave questionable descriptions. When one witness, John Faulkner, was asked by the prosecution, "What kind of looking man was [he]?", he answered, "Why, he looked like a foreigner, with a black mustache and cheek bones."[93] Another witness, Harry Dolbeare, likewise said in testimony about the same man, "He looked like a foreigner, and he had a very heavy mustache, quite dark."[94] Dolbeare also testified that all of the men involved "appeared strange to me, as strangers to the town, as a carload of foreigners. . . . That carload was a tough looking bunch."[95] Asked to describe the men in the car in terms of their looks or even the clothes they were wearing, however, Dolbeare was unable to offer anything whatsoever in terms of a description. The repeated emphasis on the appearance of the killers as "foreigners" is striking in its lack of specificity. In an echo of Palmer's statement to the House Committee on Rules, Dolbeare's testimony moves swiftly, rhetorically speaking, from strangers to foreigners to criminals, treating all three as equivalent.

Furthermore, the prosecuting attorneys, in their cross-examination of defense witnesses who claimed that the defendants were not the killers, repeatedly tried to stress ethnicity as a determining factor of identification and to downplay or contradict any attempts the witnesses made to asset their interpretation of skin complexion. A number of witnesses, including Henry Cerro, Daniel O'Neil, Wilson Dorr, and Albert Frantello, all testified that the criminals had a light complexion. In a noteworthy exchange between Frantello and District Attorney Katzmann, the district attorney sidestepped the issue of complexion and instead insisted on bringing in the issue of nationality, claiming that the witness had previously stated to a police officer that one of the killers had been Italian. Katzmann made no effort to combat the way in which the defendant had described the skin complexion of the man; instead, he sought to problematize that more concrete means of identification by raising the issue of ethnicity for the jury to consider.

The criminalization of the ethnic body that was apparent in the work of Lombroso and Hooton, in the drawings of Gould, and in the film portrayals of gangsters had real-life consequences in the trial of Sacco and Vanzetti. The witness descriptions were crucial to the conviction of the defendants, but those descriptions demonstrated a clear bias. The narrative of radical invasion and the atmosphere of hysteria that Palmer had helped to stir up in the Red Scare and the demonization of immigrants in which the ethnic body was equated with criminality informed the trial of these two men.[96] The presiding judge, Webster Thayer, in an opinion written in 1924, declared that the guilty verdict rendered by the jury in the trial had less to do with eyewitness testimony than with the "consciousness of guilt" that the defendants exhibited upon their arrest.[97] However, part of that consciousness of guilt, upon the police's approach, certainly derived from the fact that both the defendants were indeed radicals who feared, in the spring of 1920, institutional repercussions as a result of their ideological beliefs.[98] They were each armed and the police claimed that they made movements to use their guns. Upon police detention, they also lied and misled the police about their beliefs when first questioned. The defendants claimed, though, that these actions were the result of their fears about deportation or abuse by authorities. (Considering the recent Palmer Raids, that anxiety seems credibly founded.) Moreover, one of their best friends, Andrea Salsedo, had recently and inexplicably died while under arrest for his radical beliefs in New York. Sacco and Vanzetti feared a similar fate. During the trial, though, the prosecution used those actions to suggest their guilt, a strategy that buttressed their strategy of emphasizing the defendants' ethnicity to such a degree. Their history of immigration to America in the first decade of the century, when considered with their admitted radicalism, created an easy narrative for the jury to digest about the defendants as individuals who rejected an "American" way of life and who sought to threaten it. Even Judge Thayer believed them to be guilty, though he did so as much for their ideological beliefs as for the evidence that they had actually committed the crimes for which they were on trial. In an appeal for clemency filed with the Massachusetts governor, the defendants offered affidavits asserting the judge's predisposition against radicals and of his repeated statements in private to friends and colleagues during and after the trial against Sacco and Vanzetti based on their ideological positions. The appeal for clemency, though, like all their appeals, was rejected. Sacco and Vanzetti were executed on August 23, 1927.

NOTES

1. The origins of the strip had to do with Gould's desire to focus on a character dealing with the rising crime problem in urban America during the Prohibition years. His first villain was Big Boy, a character patterned after Al Capone—a well-dressed, fat, balding man with gold teeth and an ever-present cigar. Big Boy appeared in the strip for years, functioning as a representative figure of the crime boss believed to be behind much of the crime in urban America during Prohibition. The repeal of Prohibition in 1933, however, did not immediately lead to a drop in urban crime rates. In 1934, there were 1,354 cases of criminal homicide in New York alone for that single year. Following Al Capone's imprisonment in 1932, Tracy continued to fight gangsters who were now based on such headline-garnering figures as Pretty Boy Floyd, Clyde Barrow, John Dillinger, and others. Even if all of the real-life references for these characters did not originate in American cities, Gould's use of them continued to represent the crises within the city in the years following the end of Prohibition. All of them were defeated by Tracy.

Gould himself wrote of the origins of the strip, "Without a doubt, it was [the twenties] that planted the idea of DICK TRACY in my head. The revelations of fixed juries, crooked judges, bribery of public officials and cops who looked the other way showed the crying need for a strong representative of law and order who would take an eye for an eye and a tooth for a tooth. Tracy was that man." See "Chester Gould Reminisces," Dick Tracy: *The Thirties: Tommy Guns and Hard Times* (New York: Chelsea House, 1978), xi.

2. Bainbridge, John. "Chester Gould," *Life* 14 (August 1944): 43.

3. Respectively, his wife, son, daughter, brother, brother, grandson, father, and long-lost cousin. All of them, except the last two, were criminals.

4. Gould, Chester. *The Complete Dick Tracy, Volume 8: 1942–44* (San Diego, CA: IDW Publishing, 2009), 222.

5. Galewitz, Herb, ed., *The Celebrated Cases of Dick Tracy, 1931–1951* (Secaucus, NJ: Wellfleet Press, 1990), xi.

6. Galewitz, *The Celebrated Cases of Dick Tracy, 1931–1951*, xi.

7. Arthur T. Broes points out that Gould was not original in his use of the Grotesques. See Arthur T. Broes, "Dick Tracy: The Early Years," *Journal of Popular Culture* 25 (Spring 1992): 110. In his essay he quotes from Adam Gopnik's article on the comic strip *Krazy Kat* that "the practice of physiognomic distortion" had at least a 300-year history. See Adam Gopnik, "The Genius of George Herriman," *The New York Review of Books*, 12/18/1986: 20.

8. Garyn Roberts argues somewhat differently. He writes, "Chester Gould sought neither to create, perpetuate, deny, expand nor diminish popular stereotypes of the times. But he did exploit those stereotypes. Beliefs, values, and characteristics socially constructed and foisted off onto individuals and groups at this time simply made for good conventions for stories. Chester Gould's message in *Dick Tracy* was that crime did not pay; it was not that one group was morally superior to another or that some ethnic groups are more prone to crime than others." See Roberts, *Dick Tracy and American Culture: Morality and Mythology, Text and Context* (Jefferson, NC: McFarland: 1993), 79. While Roberts is aware of the ideological implications of Gould's work, it seems to me, he offers an apologia here—claiming that the Grotesques simply "made for good conventions for stories"—that is less than convincing.

9. Roberts argues, "[Gould] did not simply portray gangsters as evil; he depicted the twisted social celebration of these rogues as evil also" (Roberts, *Dick Tracy and American Culture: Morality and Mythology, Text and Context*, 5). He goes on to claim that Dick Tracy contested the appeal of the criminal for the public, in that the criminal was following the American Dream and that it was okay to do so through unconventional means (as I discuss in the first two chapters of this book). In Roberts's understanding of the strip, Gould rejects these unconventional means as socially immoral and unacceptable.

10. Smith, Shawn Michelle. *American Archives* (Princeton, NJ: Princeton University Press, 1999), 69.

11. Sekula, Allan. "The Body and the Archive," *October* 39 (Winter 1986): 3–64, 15–16.

12. For more on Lombroso and the creation of an "anatomy of deviance," see David G. Horn, *The Criminal Body: Lombroso and the Anatomy of Deviance* (New York: Routledge, 2003).

13. Nicole Hahn Rafter has identified at least eight American books published in the late nineteenth and early twentieth centuries as emerging from Lombroso's lead: McDonald's *Criminology* (1893), Boies's *Prisoners and Paupers* (1893), Henderson's *An Introduction to the Study of the Dependent, Defective, and Delinquent Classes* (1893), Eugene Talbot's *Degeneracy* (1898), Drahms's *The Criminal* (1900), W. D. McKim's *Heredity and Human Progress* (1900), G. F. Lydston's *The Diseases of Society* (1904), and Philip Parsons's *Responsibility for Crime* (1909). Havelock Ellis's *The Criminal*, a treatise written in England and about English criminals but published in 1900 in America, had further helped to popularize criminal anthropology in America.

14. Rafter, Nicole Hahn. *Creating Born Criminals* (Champaign, IL: University of Illinois Press, 1997), 112.

15. Thompson, Courtney E. *An Organ of Murder: Crime, Violence, and Phrenology in Nineteenth-Century America* (New Brunswick, NJ: Rutgers University Press, 2021), 144–145.

16. Rafter, *Creating Born Criminals*, 112.

17. Rafter, *Creating Born Criminals*, 118. Thompson points out that this is one of the distinctive elements of criminal anthropology that distinguishes it from phrenology in the late nineteenth century: whereas criminal anthropologists imagined criminals as inherently defective, phrenologists at the time believed individuals could be treated, trained, and improved. See Thompson, *An Organ of Murder: Crime, Violence, and Phrenology in Nineteenth-Century America*, 146.

18. Smith, *American Archives*, 85.

19. Sekula, "The Body in the Archive," 16.

20. There have been a number of strong recent scholarly publications on Bertillon and Galton and their legacies. Of special note are Jonathan Finn, *Capturing the Criminal Image: From Mug Shot to Surveillance Society* (Minneapolis, MN: University of Minnesota Press, 2009) and Josh Ellenbogen, *Reasoned and Unreasoned Images: The Photography of Bertillon, Galton, and Marey* (University Park, PA: Pennsylvania State University Press, 2012).

21. Smith writes of Bertillon that his work "codified a system of identification designed to measure and record the criminal body [and] was based entirely on the documentation of salient physical features." See Smith, *American Archives*, 70.

22. Sekula, "The Body in the Archive," 33. Lombroso himself endorsed Bertillonage as the most effective system of criminal identification. See Cesare Lombroso. *Crime: Its Causes and Remedies*. Translated by Henry Horton (Montclair, NJ: Patterson Smith, 1968. Originally published in 1911), 251–253.

23. Thompson notes that the "identification systems [of Bertillonage] were . . . prefigured with phrenological techniques and technologies," though she notes that the Bertillon system was better explained and understood by the general public, especially in the United States. See Thompson, *An Organ of Murder: Crime, Violence, and Phrenology in Nineteenth-Century America*, 147–149.

24. Thompson, *An Organ of Murder: Crime, Violence, and Phrenology in Nineteenth-Century America*, 152.

25. Smith writes of the composites, "They are not likenesses, material referents for individual bodies, but portraits of an abstract type, representations that supposedly reveal the 'essence' of a biologically determined group." See Smith, *American Archives*, 86–87.

26. Sekula, "The Body in the Archive," 37.

27. Sekula writes that Galton believed that his composites demonstrated "with certainty the reality of racial types. This amounted to an essentialist physical anthropology of race." See Sekula, "The Body in the Archive," 51.

28. Smith argues, "Criminals and individuals of other races might attempt to pass into the domain of white middle-class dominance, but professional middle-class observers would be able to see through their masquerades. Ultimately, then such visual technologies enabled the middle classes to imagine a stable, knowable social sphere in which their own positions and those of others would remain quite literally apparent." See Smith, *American Archives*, 93.

29. It also coexisted with currents in American culture at large in the nineteenth and twentieth centuries. For a broad-based view of the conceptualization of race and the body, see Robyn Wiegman, *American Anatomies: Theorizing Race and Gender* (Durham, NC: Duke University Press, 1995).

30. Lombroso, Cesare. *Crime: Its Causes and Remedies*. 1911. Translated by Henry Horton (Montclair, NJ: Patterson Smith, 1968), 365.

31. Lombroso, *Crime: Its Causes and Remedies*, 366–367.

32. Lombroso, *Crime: Its Causes and Remedies*, 368.

33. Leonard Savitz in his Introduction to Gina Lombroso-Ferrero's *Lombroso's Criminal Man*, writes, "In Lombroso's 'criminal anthropology' the body served as an index to an interiorized criminal essence. . . . He deemed the congenital criminal a kind of physiological throwback, a being similar to children and to 'primitive races, conflating the terms of race and criminal behavior into the same position along an imagined biological time line." See Gina Lombroso-Ferrero, *Lombroso's Criminal Man*. Glen Ridge, NJ: Patterson Smith, 1972, xii, qtd. in Smith, *American Archives*, 73–85.

34. Rafter, *Creating Born Criminals*, 127.

35. Rafter, *Creating Born Criminals*, 119. Considering one American study, Henry Boies's *Prisoners and Paupers*, Rafter writes that the photographs in the book were meant to demonstrate that "Syrians, Sicilians, and Russian Jews came from decaying stock. In neither body, mind, nor morals did they measure up to earlier, Anglo-Saxon immigrants." See Rafter, *Creating Born Criminals*, 127.

36. Lombroso, *Crime: Its Causes and Remedies*, 366–367.

37. Sekula, "The Body in the Archive," 16.

38. Asbury, Herbert. *The Gangs of New York*. 1927 (New York: Vintage, 2008), 255.

39. In *The Petrified Forest*, which came out in 1936, Humphrey Bogart plays the killer Duke Mantee with a similar physicality. Bogart plays Mantee with stiff, hunched shoulders and holds his arms quite still, not even moving them when he walks. As Muni did with Tony, Bogart portrays Duke as an ape—strong, dangerous,

not quite human. Although he is dressed in a vest and buttondown shirt, because he is on the run from the police his hair is unkempt and his five o'clock shadow is heavy. He keeps his eyes heavy and somewhat vacant. As one character says of Mantee, "What did I tell you? Look at that chin—he's a killer all right!" What separates Mantee from Tony Camonte and the hoodlums from *The Gangs of New York* is that he lacks marked ethnicity. As the same character says of Mantee, "He ain't no gangster. He's a real old-time desperado. Gangsters is foreigners and he's an American!"

40. Stallybrass, Peter and Allon White, in *The Power and Politics of Transgression* (Ithaca, NY: Cornell University Press, 1986): 132. The authors note the long history of bestial representations of the lower classes as a means of exclusion from political power.

41. I will cover psychology and sociology and their perspectives on criminality and influence on criminology in chapters 2 and 3, respectively.

42. For biographical information, I am indebted to W. S. Laughlin's appreciation of Hooton, published in *American Antiquity* 20, no. 2 (October 1954): 158–159.

43. For more of a general overview on Hooton, see Joseph Birdsell, "Some Reflections on Fifty Years in Biological Anthropology," *Annual Review of Anthropology* 16 (1987): 1–13. He writes of Hooton, "Using metrical and morphological traits he compared criminals with the general population and examined differences among criminals by crime category." See Birdsell, "Some Reflections on Fifty Years in Biological Anthropology," 3. While not everyone might be able to recognize such differences, a trained scientist who had experience reading the body morphologically should be able to discern them.

44. This strategy led to some criticism for not including the data with *Crime and the Man*. Hooton had planned to publish a second volume of *The American Criminal*, with a focus on the Negro criminal, but did not.

45. Hooton, Earnest. *Crime and the Man* (Cambridge: Harvard University Press, 1939), 5.

46. Hooton, *Crime and the Man*, 6.

47. Hooton, *Crime and the Man*, 6.

48. Hooton, *Crime and the Man*, 17; 14.

49. Hooton, *Crime and the Man*, 14. Birdsell has contended that Hooton sought to defend Lombroso against his critics, but he downplays Hooton's clear criticism of Lombroso's methods and conclusions.

50. Hooton, *Crime and the Man*, 7.

51. Hooton, *Crime and the Man*, 7.

52. Hooton, *Crime and the Man*, 6.

53. Hooton, *Crime and the Man*, 373.

54. Hooton, *Crime and the Man*, 213.

55. Hooton, *Crime and the Man*, 213.

56. Hooton, *Crime and the Man*, 14.

57. Hooton, *Crime and the Man*, 376.

58. Reuter, E.B. "Review of *Crime and the Man*," *The American Journal of Sociology* 45, no. 1 (July 1939): 123–126, 124.

59. Reuter, "Review of *Crime and the Man*," 126.
60. Reuter, "Review of *Crime and the Man*," 126.
61. Merton, Robert K. and M. F. Ashley-Montagu, "Crime and the Anthropologist," *American Anthropologist* 42, no. 3, Part 1 (July-September 1940): 384–408, 392.
62. Merton and Ashley-Montagu, "Crime and the Anthropologist," 392.
63. Hooton, *Crime and the Man*, 9.
64. Hooton, *Crime and the Man*, 9.
65. Hooton, *Crime and the Man*, 389.
66. Frank Alexander Ross, in his review of *The American Criminal*, writes that "Hooton deals essentially with preponderances, pluralities, and means" and that the relevance of his types to specific individuals is not direct in any way. See Ross, "Review of *The American Criminal*," *The American Journal of Sociology* 45, no. 3 (November 1939): 477–480, 479.

The publication of the more detailed volume of data, however, brought much harsher criticism. Ross writes that it is unclear whether "Hooton himself has indisputable data, that his controls are adequate, that his statistical methods are beyond reproach, or that his deductions are the logical ones to be derived from his statistics." See Ross, "Review of *The American Criminal*," 478. Thomas C. McCormick criticizes Hooton for a "biased control sample" that jeopardizes the validity of the data and the relevance for other subjects. See McCormick, "Review of *The American Criminal*," *American Sociological Review* 5, no. 2 (April 1940): 252–254. One of the reasons that the former volume did not receive as much criticism may have been because reviewers did not have Hooton's specific data from which to evaluate his conclusions. Just as likely, however, was that the initial positive reviews were a result at least in part of Hooton's reputation and powerful influence on a generation of scholars. That influence should not too readily be discounted, just as the positive reception of *Crime and the Man* should not, as they suggest that the power of biological determinism was still quite strong in the late 1930s.

67. See, for instance, the reviews by C. G. Woodson in *The Journal of Negro History* 24, no. 3 (July 1939): 359–360 and by Wilton Marion Krugman in *American Anthropologist* 41, no. 3 (July–September 1939): 504–509.
68. McCormick, Thomas C. "Review of *The American Criminal*." *American Sociological Review* 5, no. 2 (April 1940): 252–254, 252.
69. Ross, Frank Alexander. "Review of *The American Criminal*." *The American Journal of Sociology* 45, no. 3 (November 1939): 477–480, 479.
70. Ross, "Review of *The American Criminal*," 478.
71. While Hooton would not sterilize all of the inhabitants, believing that some future generational offspring might be "useful and capable citizens, habitual criminals who are hopeless constitutional inferiors should be permanently incarcerated and, on no account, should be allowed to breed" (392). His proposal of segregation echoes a broad advocacy for a eugenics program in the 1920s and 1930s. For current scholarship on the role and currency of eugenics in America in these decades, see June Dwyer, "Disease, Deformity, and Defiance: Writing the Language of Immigration Law and the Eugenics Movement on the Immigrant Body," *MELUS* 28 (Spring 2003): 105–122; Daylanne English, *Unnatural Selections: Eugenics in American Modernism and*

the Harlem Renaissance (Chapel Hill, NC: University of North Carolina Press, 2004); Betsy L. Nies, *Eugenic Fantasies: Racial Ideology in the Literature and Popular Culture of the 1920's* (New York: Routledge, 2002); John P. Radford, "Sterilization versus Segregation: Control of the 'Feebleminded,' 1900–1939," *Social Science and Medicine* 33, no. 4 (1991): 449–459; and Edmund Ramsden, "Social Demography and Eugenics in the Interwar United States," *Population and Development Review* 29, no. 4 (2003): 547–598.

72. Hooton, *Crime and the Man*, 387.

73. Hooton, *Crime and the Man*, 393.

74. Hooton, *Crime and the Man*, 387.

75. Hooton, *Crime and the Man*, 7.

76. *The Power and Politics of Transgression* (Ithaca, NY: Cornell University Press, 1986), 132.

77. "The Bomb Plot," *New York Times*, May 2, 1919: 11.

78. One man was killed, twelve policemen were injured, and dozens of people were hurt during the Socialist May Day celebration in Cleveland. The police employed army tanks and motor transport trucks to quell riots during the day and night. In Boston, the police's attempt to disperse an impromptu parade by radicals led to a violent battle, leaving three patrolmen and one civilian shot.

79. Radicals and those who sympathized with their cause were understandably defensive and perturbed by the wild speculation. New York City Municipal Court Justice Jacob Panken found the suggestion that the Socialist Party was responsible "absurd" and, according to the *New York Times*, declared it more likely to be the work of a "policeman or 'what is a more plausible explanation, a scheme of that peanut of a Mayor we have'" ("Soldiers and Sailors Break Up Meetings," *New York Times*, May 2, 1919: 3).

80. "Soldiers and Sailors Break Up Meetings," *New York Times*, May 2, 1919: 3.

81. "Spread of Bolshevism in the United States," July 26, 1919. The Papers of Robert Lansing, Library of Congress. Quoted in Coben, Stanley. *A Study in Nativism: The American Red Scare of 1919–1920* (New York: Irvington Publishers, 1964), 210.

82. "Says We Face Revolution," *The New York Times*, October 17, 1919: 7.

83. For more on the Raids, what led up to them and how they ended, see Louis F. Post, *The Deportations Delirium of Nineteen-Twenty* (Chicago: Charles H. Kerr, 1920), David Mitchell, *1919: Red Mirage* (New York: Macmillan, 1970), and William Preston, Jr., *Aliens and Dissenters: Federal Suppression of Radicals, 1903–1933* (Chicago, IL: University of Illinois Press, 1994).

84. Coben, Stanley. *A Study in Nativism: The American Red Scare of 1919–1920* (New York: Irvington Publishers, 1964), 219–221.

85. Robert Murray, *Red Scare: A Study in National Hysteria* (Minneapolis, MN: University of Minnesota Press, 1955), 196–197.

86. For examples of this support, see Coben, *A Study in Nativism: The American Red Scare of 1919–1920*, 227; 229.

87. House Committee on Rules, *Attorney-General A. Mitchell Palmer on Charges Made Against Department of Justice by Louis F. Post and Others* (Hearings, 66 Congress, 2 Session, 1920), 27.

88. The response to the bombings of early May and June—actions that more than likely were carried out by a small number of people—was to indict all radicals, indeed all aliens, but it also tapped into a nativism in the United States that had been brewing for decades. Over 23 million immigrants came to the United States between 1880 and 1920. There had been a number of attempts to limit immigration during those years, the most strident measures came during the 1920s and 1930s. Restrictive quotas on immigration were imposed in 1920 and 1931. In 1921, Congress sought to limit the number of immigrants to 3 percent of each national group, as represented in the 1910 census. In 1924, the National Origins Act then cut the number back to 2 percent of the 1890 census, severely limiting immigration from southeastern Europe and Russia, and fully excluding Chinese and Japanese immigrants. The rise of nativism and its underlying anxiety about the potential impact of immigrants on American ways of life were articulated but President Coolidge himself, who said in his 1923 State of the Union address, that "America must be kept American." Calvin Coolidge Presidential Foundation, "We're All in the Same Boat Now: Coolidge on Immigration," February 19, 2016, viewed on February 8, 2020.

89. "Says We Face Revolution," *The New York Times*, October 17, 1919: 7.

90. This logic continues to hold even until today, as evidenced by a recent tele-vised exchange about immigration and the national border.

On January 14, 2019, Tucker Carlson invited Mark Morgan, former chief of the United States Border Patrol, to be a guest on *Tucker Carlson Tonight*, his nightly talk show on Fox News. The topic of the segment was on illegal immigration. Following an attack on two high school students in New York City by two MS-13 gang members, Carlson focused his January 14 show on the "immigration loopholes" that enable unaccompanied minors to reside in the United States while awaiting deportation. In the interview, Morgan cited the recent judicial decision that mandated that underage illegal immigrants have to be released into the United States after a few days, "regardless of if they've been properly vetted, regardless of if they have a parent in the United States." Carlson and Morgan then blame Congress for not acting on legislation to fix this immigration policy that Morgan calls "broke" and Carlson calls "crazy." See "Tucker Carlson Tonight," 1/14/2019. https://www.youtube.com/watch?v=8KeIE6KuYus.

In speaking of MS-13 gang members, Morgan says, "When the President referred to them as animals, I said that is absolutely correct. . . . I've been to the deten-tion facilities where I've walked up to these individuals that are so-called minors, 17 or under. And I've looked at them and I've looked at their eyes, Tucker—and I've said that is a soon-to-be MS-13 gang member. It's unequivocal." Morgan rhetorically positions these gang members as "animals," invoking the history of dehumanizing criminals in order to assert a political and policy position. Moreover, in his second sentence Morgan claims he can look into the eyes of these individuals and determine they will join the MS-13 gang. The idea that he can tell what these young men will do in the future, just by looking into their eyes, is not only ludicrous, but it is also disturbing. Morgan may be an expert in his work, but he is not a fortune-teller. What makes him imagine that he can predict an individual's future merely by looking into his eyes?

In Morgan's mind, there was no doubt that their future would include the fact they would definitely join MS-13. He believes that it is inevitable that these young men will join this gang. It is, in his words, "unequivocal." He is both certain they will be gang members and also certain that it is inevitable. The sense of determinism in this is connected to his embrace of these young men as fitting his concept of the criminal type. These are not just any immigrants—these are immigrants from Central and South America. The logic of his language frames criminality as tied to a particular nationality and a particular body.

91. Osmond Fraenkel, *The Sacco-Vanzetti Case*. 1931 (New York: Russell & Russell, 1969), 36–37, 65 in original trial transcript. All further references to this text will appear with Fraenkel page number listed first, followed by the page number of the original trial transcript.

92. Fraenkel, *The Sacco-Vanzetti Case*, 40; 69.

93. Fraenkel, *The Sacco-Vanzetti Case*, 205; 426.

94. Fraenkel, *The Sacco-Vanzetti Case*, 208; 490.

95. Fraenkel, *The Sacco-Vanzetti Case*, 209; 495.

96. The issue of whether Sacco and Vanzetti were actually guilty or not has been hotly debated now for over seven decades. Of special interest to this debate are two books by Francis Russell: *Tragedy at Dedham* (New York: McGraw-Hill, 1971) and *Sacco and Vanzetti: The Case Resolved* (New York: Harper & Row, 1986). Russell believes that Sacco was indeed one of the killers and that Vanzetti was also involved, though not in the actual killing. He calls them both, in terms of their ideological beliefs, militants who were revolutionaries at heart.

97. Fraenkel, *The Sacco-Vanzetti Case*, 406.

98. For more on their radicalism, see Paul Avrich, *Sacco and Vanzetti: The Anarchist Background* (Princeton, NJ: Princeton University Press, 1991).

Chapter 2

"I Had to Have Her, If I Hung for It"

Impulse, Repression, and Repetition Compulsion

One night in the winter of 1927 in Queens, New York, Ruth Snyder pretended to fall asleep next to her husband Albert and then snuck into an adjoining room where her lover, Judd Gray, drunkenly waited for her. They returned together to the master bedroom where Albert was sleeping in the married couple's bed. As he lay on the bed, asleep and inert, the lovers smashed a sash weight against his head, whereupon he awoke with a yell and struggled against his attackers. They overpowered him, however, and struck him repeatedly with the weight until he was unconscious. Later they strangled him with a wire, unnecessarily as it turned out, because Albert Snyder was already dead. Gray left to travel upstate to Syracuse to establish an alibi, while Ruth Snyder called the police and pretended to have been victim to an intruder who had killed her husband. The police, however, quickly saw through her threadbare story and convinced her to confess. Judd Gray was immediately arrested and confessed as well.

The press gave extensive coverage to the capture of the killers, their trial, and the death sentence that each received. It turned out that Ruth had convinced her husband to take out a life insurance policy and then forged Albert's signature on an addendum that paid extra if the insured died by an unexpected act of violence. Not surprisingly, this became fodder for the press and the story became one of the main tabloid narratives of the year, making both Gray and Snyder notorious celebrities. Before and after the conviction, Ruth Snyder wrote feature articles for a number of newspapers, including the *New York Evening Journal*, the *New York Evening Post*, the *New York World*, and the *New York Daily Mirror*. These articles ultimately culminated in an autobiography, *Ruth Snyder's Own True Story*. While on death row, Gray too wrote an autobiography, *Doomed Ship*, published posthumously in 1928.

59

It would have been hard to predict what happened with the two. Ruth was an attractive young housewife with a nice home in a respectable and safe community. Judd Gray was a successful salesman with a wife and family of his own. Their lives, from outward appearances, seemed happy and content. What then had led them to the moment on January 28, 1928, when they each sat alone in the electric chair facing a small audience of onlookers, executed for the murder of a man who had done no harm to either of them? (See Figure 2.1.)

Not surprisingly, each defendant blamed the other for the murder. Snyder claimed during the trial that she was in the bathroom at the time of the attack on her husband and her attempts to stop Gray were met with resistance, which caused her to faint.[1] Gray, in turn, did not deny his role in the actual killing as much as he claimed that he was under the sway of her influence, against which he could offer no resistance. It is this claim that I will take up in this chapter: that he was unable to control what he was doing and that he acted not as a willing executioner but as a man who acted without agency or intent. In

Figure 2.1   Ruth Snyder and Judd Gray. *Source*: John Frost Newspapers/Alamy Stock Photo.

Doomed Ship, Gray does admit to the crime, but he also subtly suggests that he should not be blamed, even as he declares his guilt.

Gray asserts that he is writing in order to educate the public about how easy it is to slip into duplicity:

> Indeed I am not writing this as an excuse for my sins or misdeeds. I am not writing it even for understanding—I have in my mind one purpose only—that of showing how possible it is to fall into anything—how impossible it is to hurdle life conventions—that the way to salvage life after practicing duplicity is to confess our sins.[2]

However, his "confession" is a curious one. He takes the stance of the penitent seeking absolution, and yet he repeatedly seeks to mitigate his own responsibility for the crime. He claims that Ruth had convinced him that her husband beat her and abused her and that he had threatened further harm to her in the future. Gray positions himself as the gallant knight in shining armor coming to the defense of the maiden in danger. But this knight does not want to be seen as a hero but rather as a victim. He writes, "And I put no blame on [Ruth] in my confession, except to say that it was due to her that I was party to it, which is true, although it in no way relieves me of any guilt."[3] This is a tricky sentence—he assigns responsibility to Ruth, asserting that she made him "party" to the crime, but he also accepts a share of the blame. He says later, "I am willing to accept every bit of the guilt that is mine."[4] But how much is his? His is the sole voice of the autobiography, and therefore "every bit of the guilt that is mine" can only be understood in how he represents the story. The "case history" that he offers in the guise of educating the public in fact seems to be his attempt to offer into evidence how he was under Ruth Snyder's influence, how he was prey to his own impulses, and how he had little control over his actions.

Throughout *Doomed Ship*, Gray asserts over and over that he was not in his right mind during the time leading up to murder, beginning with the first time he kissed and then slept with Ruth: "our lips met—love—madness rather."[5] In this telling phrase he constructs an image of passion that equates his love of Ruth with insanity: his love for her and what he did because of it, the murder, was a function of and a result of his "madness." Eventually, he suggests that he lost all concern for his own well-being, that something had taken hold of him and destroyed his real self: "I did not much care what happened—the real me seemed dead anyway. . . . I was positive that I was mad. A grotesque and horrible madness had burned me away and left but a loathsome and malignant ghost."[6] Gray's autobiography is designed to raise questions of accountability. If he was not his real self, if he had been impaired in his judgment by madness and his desire for Ruth and his inability to resist her, and if we can recognize the complicated set of factors that had led him to commit this crime, then how can we see him as responsible for his actions? How can we blame him, hold him accountable, and judge him guilty?

Gray's repeated references to "madness" places his narrative of criminality in a different context than that of the previous chapter. Instead of understanding Gray as emblematic of a criminal type, we need to situate his representation of his madness more appropriately within the realm of psychology, psychiatry, and mental health care. These disciplines were not new to the United States in the 1920s. In fact, they had been present in different forms for over 100 years. For instance, lunatic—or insane—asylums first appeared in the American colonies in the mid-to-late 1700s, built upon principles and practices well known in Europe. The establishment of state asylums in the United States began in 1850 and many state hospitals were built in the next few decades, along with institutions designed to care for the intellectually disabled, though the terminology of the 1800s and early 1900s included such terms as "mental aliens," "feeble-minded," "imbeciles," and "idiots."[7] Two of the nineteenth-century developments in methods of diagnoses were mental chronometry, which measured the speed of mental processes, and mental testing, which measured intelligence.[8] By the early 1900s, these methods to determine the intellectually disabled were widely in use by professional (or clinical) psychologists and continued for decades, becoming common practice.

Much of the effort to treat patients in these institutions was intended to be humanitarian and based on moral principles. Indeed, this approach was rooted in what is often referred to as Scottish commonsense psychology, which had a Christian and moral foundation, and was the predominant influence on American psychology for much of the nineteenth century.[9] Of course, as we know, these institutions did not always adopt a humanitarian approach. Many institutions—meant to either treat and aid patients or imprison them for past actions—did not always prioritize care for the individual foremost in their practices. For instance, based on his twelve years of running the Vineland Training School for Feeble-Minded Girls and Boys, the prominent psychologist H. H. Goddard sought to establish an empirical equation between criminals and "imbeciles" or "morons." In a 1914 study of the causes and consequences of "feeble-mindedness," he suggested that "feeble-minded" offenders are victims of their own biology and predestined to bad behavior and argued that "the so-called criminal type is merely a type of feeble-mindedness."[10] His interest in the offenders seemed less about care, then, and more about preventing them from doing harm to others.[11] Goddard first demonstrated his interest in the link between criminals and "imbeciles" with the publication of *The Kallikak Family: A Study in the Heredity of Feeble-Mindedness* in 1912 and then reached its apex with his 1915 publication of *The Criminal Imbecile: An Analysis of Three*

Remarkable Murder Cases.[12] As is evident in his thinking, although the discipline in which Goddard operated was different than that of criminal anthropology, the logic of biological determinism was still quite prevalent.

One of the logical concerns of the determinism at the heart of the concept of the criminal type was that it implied there was little to do to combat it. Criminal anthropologists sought to identify—through classification—the physical typology connected to crime, but their methods received heavy criticism. Similarly, with "feeble-mindedness," Goddard recognized that there was little he could do to change those who might have a predisposition to crime and untoward behavior and so early in his career he embraced eugenics as a potential solution. As mentioned above, Goddard did not rely on racial or ethnic classifications in and of themselves for determining who might be a potential problem, but instead focused on IQ exams as the best way to identify potential threats.[13] Primarily he advocated segregating the "feeble-minded" from the general population as a means by which we could contain the criminal potential of those who inherited "feeble-mindedness."[14]

Of course, although he could appeal to the rhetoric of madness as something beyond his control, Judd Gray could not persuasively cloak himself as an "idiot" or an "imbecile" or as "feeble-minded." Nothing in his background allowed for that. Nonetheless, he did seek in his autobiography to construct a narrative of psychological determinism, to construct a rhetorical strategy that utilized the language of contemporary psychology to more effectively admit his actions while still denying his agency. In order to explain his participation in the murder, he shifts the blame for his moral weaknesses to Ruth but also to other targets as well. For instance, he writes that he had been drinking heavily for months before the murder. "I was living on alcohol then," he writes, insisting that his reliance on alcohol impaired his judgment, reaching its apotheosis with his drunkenness on the night of the murder.[15] His portrait of his impaired judgment complements another assertion—that was not in his "mind" during the months leading up to the murder. Although he was diagnosed as mentally sane at the time of the trial, he denies his ability to recognize what he was doing: "I can only think neither of us was aware of what we were doing. Regardless of what the alienists say I know I was not the person I formerly was, nor am I today."[16] Three selves are represented here: a former self who would have resisted Ruth and the temptations that led eventually to the crime, a present self who can recognize the horror of the crime but is still not the same as he once was, and a third self who existed during the time of the madness. Gray writes as if a juggling act had taken place inside his psyche, with his insane half consistently asserting itself:

In fact, there almost seemed two persons inside my skin—one constantly striving to act normal—the other constantly doing foolish things. Such as shaving

two or three times in the morning, looking for things I had already dressed
myself in, turning on the water in the boiler, as I did at home, and leaving it to
flood the cellar.[17]

He perceives these moments as symbols before the fact that he was "foolish" or insane, and he groups his actions during the killing as part of that same
pattern of behavior. He acts, in essence as his own psychologist, presenting
his own case to the reader and also interpreting and assigning meaning to his
behavior for us.

Nonetheless, although these moments do tap into a rhetoric of insanity meant to mitigate his responsibility, his primary strategy is to present
himself to the reader as a pawn of Ruth's, unable to resist her charm and
beauty: "That I proved to a be a weak and worthless weapon in her hands
is true—had I been of better material never could she have molded me so
readily."[18] He employs this rhetoric of the unmanly man with no control over
his woman. He writes, "Why I never had manhood enough to warn [Ruth's
husband] by an anonymous letter or strength enough to prevail upon her I do
not know."[19] Even though he is cognizant that the planning of the murder is
wrong, he claims that he is powerless to right that wrong and in his language
of not having enough "manhood" evokes impotence. Moreover, he presents
that lack of agency as a state of not being in his right state of "mind": "If I
had possessed any mind at all I certainly would have followed the intuitive
wrong that was being evidenced in my very soul and would come out like a
man and told her so."[20] He is "not a man" he implies, because he is unable to
resist his desire for her, a desire that he "was only half-heartedly, impotently,
combating."[21] His desire for her is here curiously—and perhaps ironically—
identified as "impotence," suggesting that she acted as something of a siren
for Gray, luring him into danger. He does not "possess his mind" and his
impotence puts her in the position of strength.

Gray represents his lack of control over his own sexual impulses, moreover, as reason not to blame him for the murder. He continually focuses not
upon his own motivations but upon his inability to resist Ruth's will. He
offers as testimony his willingness to allow her to test poisons upon him in
order to measure their effects. He writes, "It gave Ruth the supremacy in any
suggestion and forced the complete abdication of my will and judgment."[22]
First, he was unable to resist her sexually. Here he presents himself as having
abdicated all agency to her. He is under her control, victim of a sort of sexual
determinism. His impotence to resist her sexually mutates into an impotence
to resist her very will and he becomes little more than a tool of her making.
In this framework, Ruth has used her power over him to essentially turn him
into a slave to her wish to kill her husband.

He asserts that before his relationship with Ruth Snyder he was—much as he is at the time of the writing of the autobiography—an innocent and law-abiding citizen. Her influence and his inability to resist her brought about the madness and the creation of another self who engaged in a pattern of infidelity, excessive drinking, forgetfulness, and "foolish" behavior that ultimately led to murder: "It must be true—the fact that if we come in contact with a personality continuously we assimilate a share of their character or characteristics."[23] He poses Ruth as the figure with agency in this scenario, imposing her character on him so that he "assimilated" her homicidal impulse into his own being, if only for a short time.

Gray wants to be judged in terms of the selves that held sway before and after his relationship with Ruth: the deeply religious, faithful, and loyal man who was brought low by forces beyond his control and who deeply regrets his actions during his "madness." In his autobiography he wants not only to express the many mitigating factors that influenced him, but also to be judged according to those factors. All in all, he looks to assign responsibility for the murder to his drinking, to his madness, to Ruth Snyder—anywhere but to himself. He has two obvious motives for why he would kill Albert Snyder: to have Ruth to himself but also the insurance claim that he and Ruth could then share. But he refuses to entertain the thought that he might be truly guilty. In constructing his own case history for the reader, he writes over and over that no matter what happened he is not at fault, he had no intention to kill, it wasn't really him. In delineating those mitigations, Gray places all blame for his actions on another self, a part of him over which he could not gain control. We might call that "part" his unconscious.

In 1917, William Healy, a British American neurologist and psychiatrist who was a pioneer of psychoanalysis in the United States, wrote in *Mental Conflicts and Misconduct* of a division of self in young criminals that echoes Gray's assertion of multiple selves operating during the last years of his life: "We find that some misdoers do not, in their misconduct, appear to be in the least carrying out their keenest desires. Their actions are forced, as it were, by something in themselves, not of themselves."[24] Healy does not identify or name this "something," but in his use of the language of "force" there is the implication that the "something" is beyond the individual's control. Moreover, Healy goes on to claim that the behavior has nothing to do with want or desire, that "the effect of the conduct in question is not in any ordinary sense pleasurable to the misdoers, nor do they regard it as such . . . it seems as if one of its most noteworthy characteristics is the curious absence of any idea of pleasure to be derived from it."[25] Healy's conclusions suggest that there is little sense of choice in the behavior of these individuals, that they are led by impulses or instincts that are not under their control, let alone of their choosing. In these passages Healy articulates a concept closely in line with Sigmund Freud's notion of the unconscious.[26]

Freud did not introduce the idea of the unconscious. Others—including Gottfried Wilhelm Leibniz, Johann Friedrich Herbart, Hermann von Helmholtz, Arthur Schopenhauer, and Friedrich Nietzsche—had posited that there were motivations and processes that individuals might not be aware of that were driving their behavior. Certainly, though, none had developed as rich a theory of the unconscious as Freud. And of course, none had dedicated most of their careers to revising the workings and manifestations of the unconscious and ultimately seeking to apply those operations not only to human behavior but also to religion and culture. At its heart, Freud's work focused on how consciousness operated as a cloak for primal instincts it did not want to uncover or reveal. The human ego, using one of his own terms, was not in control. In Freud's conception, the primal instincts or drives of sex and death were in fact what drove most of what individuals do and, in relation to his patients, were at the heart of the neuroses that most people suffered from.

Freud was controversial for most of his career, and only in part because he was so obsessed with sex.[27] In fact, Havelock Ellis in England and Richard Krafft-Ebing in Germany were also very much focused on sexual practices. However, many contemporary psychologists rejected Freud's work as unscientific because of his reliance on the interpretation of symbols—symbols which were not inherently figurative or symbolic until determined as such, subjectively, by the psychoanalyst, and symbols which were often interpreted to be focused on the sex drive and nothing else.[28] Freud argued that the sex drive is biological and universal, in that it is neither species- nor culture-specific, but others argued that individuals can have multiple motivations for behavior—even if those motivations are in fact unconscious. Still, for Freud, the sex drive was foundational to neurosis because other primal motivations—food, self-preservation, and so on—were essential for survival and could not be redirected. Only the sex drive, in Freud's estimation, could be displaced into something else, something that might be healthy but also might become a perversion or neurosis.

In his early articulation of how the mind works, Freud imagined it as a multilayered system where the unconscious shapes thoughts and behaviors.[29] All people have some desires that we cannot consciously accept. We repress these or keep them unconscious, although that means they remain active because we do not actually deal with them through conscious scrutiny. Those unconscious desires continually seek access and expression and in certain moments—dreams, fantasies, jokes, slips of the tongue—those unconscious drives can become manifest. Through psychoanalysis, the patient can work to scrutinize those desires with the help of the psychoanalyst who can help the patient decode and decipher the symbolic representations of the desires and move the patient away from neuroses and perversions and toward healthy relationships. The process, in essence, provides an unmasking of the unconscious, especially and primarily of the sexual instincts and desires of the specific individual. Part of that process had to do with understanding the sexual development of the individual from the childhood stages through adult sexuality, the development of which could lead to perversions—where a single component of the sex instinct is privileged over others—or neuroses—where a patient's inability to rectify an aspect of his or her sexuality overwhelms that individual and is translated into symptoms. These then can lead to sublimations, repressions, and unhealthy behavioral choices.

Judd Gray's attempts to portray himself as under an influence of sexual impulses and insanity beyond his control reflect a rhetoric associated with Freudian psychoanalysis and demonstrate its impact on how Americans were thinking about crime and criminality in the early twentieth century. In his 1933 treatise, *Crimes and Criminals*, William A. White—a psychoanalyst and the administrator for St. Elizabeth's, the federal hospital for the insane in Washington, DC—discusses the logic that psychoanalysis brings to man's attempts to understand human behavior:

> ack of every event of a psychological nature there can found other events out of which it grew and which give it meaning, in other words what is usually called a cause, and . . . no psychic event happens with such a background or without the possibility of finding such antecedent factors . . . it does not rest within the province of the whim of the actor what he shall do or say under a given set of circumstances, that if a longitudinal section of the conduct of any individual be studied carefully it will be seen that the entire series of acts constituting this section follow one another logically and in accordance with a definite, prescribed plan.[30]

The work of psychoanalysis, he says, is about taking the time to account for both the actor and the act and to distinguish between them. Moving toward an "appreciation of the individuality of the actor rather than an exclusive consideration of the act," White suggests, better allows us to identify causes, ascertain any precedents for the actions, and better situate the context in and through which the individual acted.[31] These are the crucial factors within psychoanalysis and the dynamics of much of its appeal. Judd Gray's use of the language of psychoanalysis points to its emerging role within American culture.

The logical nature of cause and effect that served as its foundation afforded psychoanalysis, in the first decades of the twentieth century, some of the authority of empirical science and led it to greater acceptance in the United

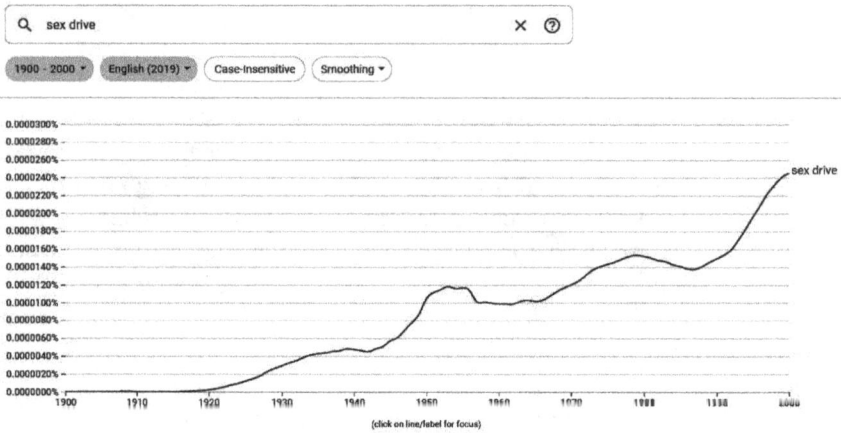

Figure 2.2 Ngram of Uses of "Sex Drive." *Source*: Figure created by author based on Google Ngram Viewer, http://books.google.com/ngrams.

States, especially in the public eye. The psychoanalytic movement enjoyed rising visibility in the United States following Freud's highly influential series of lectures at Clark University in 1909. While eleven articles on Freud and psychoanalysis were published in national magazines between 1910 and 1914, three times as many appeared in the next four years; moreover, articles had begun to appear in the mass circulation women's magazines and major newspapers and a number of young intellectuals and artists—including Max Eastman, Floyd Dell, and Mabel Dodge Luhan—were writing on and publicly embracing psychoanalysis as a science and undergoing therapy themselves.[32] These writers were treated by such well-known psychoanalysts as White, Smith Ely Jelliffe, and A. A. Brill. The influence of their work and theories, through the embrace of other physicians, psychologists, journalists, and intellectuals correspondingly spread into the broader American culture. Indeed, consider the jump in the use of the term "sex drive" in American English in the following chart (See Figure 2.2.).

Freud's ideas had clearly gained significant cultural currency and the steep rise in 1920s and beyond in the use of terms such as "Oedipal Complex," "libido," and even "psychoanalysis" speak to the reach of what Freud was proposing in his work.

Gray's autobiography serves as an example how psychology and specifically psychoanalysis had an influence on how criminality was imagined by the general public in the twentieth century. Psychoanalysis gave a language to criminality that occurred when an individual lacked agency over his own actions. In Freud's conception, the idea of an id run amok took hold as a type of determinism that the individual could not escape.[33] It also implied a potential mitigation of individual guilt and responsibility. As the discipline became more professionalized and as psychoanalysis became both more well known and accepted in the public sphere, the representation of motive in criminal narratives both real and fictional became more focused on impulses that individuals could not seemingly control, repressed emotions, and compulsive and violent behavior. This representation of motive as primary within the crime narrative operated differently than the logic of biological determinism that was built into the concept of the criminal type, which was based on race and ethnicity as determining factors in criminal behavior.

The rise of the genres of literary realism and naturalism in the late nineteenth and early twentieth centuries brought with them frequent representations of crime and criminality that had psychological themes, especially of note in the novels of Frank Norris, John Dos Passos, and John Steinbeck. In Dos Passos's sprawling *Manhattan Transfer*, for instance, Bud Korpenning grows up in rural New York state on a farm and faces constant physical and emotional abuse from his father, who cannot control his frustration at the family's inability to make their farm economically feasible and who takes that frustration out on Bud. Eventually tiring of the abuse, Bud kills his father and escapes to New York where he tries to find work. Haunted by the murder and unable to find a steady job, Bud eventually leaps to his death off of the Brooklyn Bridge. In Norris's *McTeague*, Frank Norris similarly represents the effects of economic hardship on one's psychological state. The titular character suffers the betrayal of his once-best friend and loses his dental practice, thereafter sliding inexorably into poverty and desperation, eventually brutally killing his wife for the money she has been hoarding as gold coins. McTeague's rage about how fate has worked against him is a violent assertion of will against the conditions of poverty and contingency and—as with Bud Korpenning in Dos Passos's novel—exemplifies the value of White's psychoanalytic approach of distinguishing between the act and the actor. In *The Grapes of Wrath*, Steinbeck similarly represents Tom Joad's criminality as reactionary rather than predatory. At a dance in Oklahoma, Tom uses a shovel to hit and kill a man who had stuck him with a knife. Seven years later, in California, Tom watches as a police officer kills his friend Jim Casy and responds by beating the officer with a club, partly out of retribution for the death of Casy but also out of fear for his own safety. Steinbeck presents both of these killings as somewhat mitigated by the psychological desire for self-preservation as a response to extremely heightened feelings of fear within moments of great violence. In each of these narratives—*Manhattan Transfer*, *McTeague*, and *The Grapes of Wrath*—crime is portrayed as an outgrowth of an individual's psychological response to emotions, conditions, and forces that feel well beyond that individual's control.[34]

While Norris, Dos Passos, and Steinbeck—along with other writers such as Nathanael West, Richard Wright, and Horace McCoy—used the genres of realism and naturalism to dramatize individual psychological responses to feelings of powerlessness, Theodore Dreiser explored the cultural influence of psychology and psychoanalysis more directly in his use of characterization and figurative language, especially in terms of his representations of the unconscious. For instance, the defining moment of drama in *Sister Carrie*, I would argue, occurs when Hurstwood checks the office safe before he closes up for the night, as he does every night in his role as the manager of Fitzgerald and Moy's. Hurstwood is in a moment of crisis as he tends to the details of his job, as his wife has discovered his affair with the young actress Carrie Meeber and has filed for divorce. On this night, for the first time in his experience, he finds the safe unlocked. He decides to check the money drawers, although he "did not know why he wished to look in there."[35] This notion of "not knowing" or conscious will is repeated throughout the next series of events. As he looks at the money, "a voice in his ear" tells him, "Count them."[36] This voice then directs him onward. "Why don't I shut the safe?" his mind said to itself, lingering. "What makes me pause here?" For answer there came the strangest words: "Did you ever have ten thousand dollars in ready money?"[37]

That voice in his ear is his own, but in this moment of decision, Hurstwood's mind is somehow separate from his self, disembodied. He removes to his office to ponder the situation and a voice says, "The safe is open. There is just the least little crack in it. The lock has not been sprung.'"[38] Still, he stops himself, considering the situation and its implications. He puts the money back and takes it out a number of times. He is paralyzed in indecision, caught between his unconscious desire for the money and how it could provide for a future with his new beloved and his fear of doing wrong by stealing the money.[39]

It is here, in that moment of split-selfhood, that fate intervenes: "While the money was in his hand the lock clicked. It had sprung! Did he do it? He grabbed at the knob and pulled vigorously. It had closed."[40] Dreiser's representation of Hurstwood's internal struggle between leaving the money or taking it, as emblematized by the "voice," succeeds in taking the reader inside Hurstwood's psychological landscape. At this crucial moment he dramatizes the ways that the unconscious can rear and assert a desire that isn't always under the control of the conscious self. Once the safe closes, Hurstwood becomes "a man of action" and actualizes the plan to take the money and escape with Carrie. The disembodied voice that drove him to consider the crime becomes fully embodied in the actions he then takes and his unconscious desire becomes manifest.

In *An American Tragedy*, Dreiser returns to the figurization of the unconscious through a disembodied voice at a moment of extreme tension and crucial decision-making. Clyde Griffiths is in love with the wealthy Sondra Finchley but also attached to the factory worker Roberta Alden, his fiancée who he has impregnated. Clyde has been trying to convince Roberta to give up the child—or, perhaps more importantly, him. While Roberta still loves him, he now only desires Sondra and Roberta poses an obstacle blocking the social and economic advancement that will come with a marriage to Sondra. He concocts a plan to kill Roberta on a boating expedition in such a way that it appears to be an accident. As he rows with Roberta, Clyde struggles with the emotional weight of his plan of action. Like Hurstwood in Dreiser's previous novel, Clyde dithers back and forth about what to do, seemingly deciding to abort the plan when he accidentally hits her with his oar and topples her out of the boat. As Roberta call to him for help, Clyde hears what Dreiser calls an "Efrit," a genie, speaking in his ear: "You might save her. But again you might not! . . . Wait—wait—ignore the pity of that appeal."[41] Clyde does not drown her by holding her head underwater or through any action that he takes. He instead swims away from her. The Efrit then tells him "that this has been done for you."[42] Dreiser's use of the passive voice suggests that Clyde is not the agent of death but the beneficiary of it. But, of course, the Efrit operates figuratively and narratively as the disembodied voice of Clyde's unconscious, much as with what happened with Hurstwood in the office with the open safe.[43] Hurstwood only left with the money after the lock of the safe had somehow locked shut. Clyde did not directly murder Roberta—the blow to the head was an accident—but he does allow her to die through his decision not to save her. With both characters, their inactions—*not* putting the money back and *not* helping the drowning young woman—represent their deepest unconscious wishes and both also constitute criminal choices.

Dreiser's novels serve as examples of how the interest in the unconscious went beyond the discipline of psychology and seeped into broader American culture. With his use of disembodied voices and selves, Dreiser dramatizes how the individual mind can deal with moments of great strain and stress by essentially separating from itself as a way to cope with a desire that it rationally and morally cannot justify. Of course, the followers and advocates of literary naturalism were deeply invested in exploring notions of power and individual agency within the dynamics of forces that the individual had no control over.[44] That could take the form of racial, ethnic, or gender restrictions; socioeconomic hardship; familial abuse; bad luck; or even—as I have tried to show here with Dreiser's work—internal and unconscious desires that the individual could not tamp down.[45] In their frequent representations of criminal behavior within these dynamics, moreover, naturalists not only explored conceptions of individual agency and contingency, but they also dramatized how difficult it is to assign responsibility and guilt to crime. Do we blame Bud Korpenning or Tom Joad for their crimes (or even McTeague himself?) once we recognize the conditions under which they acted? Do we recognize the ways in which Hurstwood and Clyde acted out of an unconscious desire that they were not able to resist—and, if so, do we blame them for what happened?[46]

It is within this literary and cultural milieu that we should place Judd Gray's *Doomed Ship* and his willingness "to accept every bit of guilt that is [his]." However, to see how the literary representation of the unconscious and the ways in which psychoanalysis seeped into American culture—and with it how criminality became understood to be, in part, beyond the individual's control—we need to examine the work of a different writer. That writer is James M. Cain, who used the story of Ruth Snyder and Judd Gray to write not one but two novels that enjoyed wide critical and commercial success and who explored with much great efficacy the concepts of guilt and responsibility within the divided criminal self.

At the conclusion of Cain's 1934 novel, *The Postman Always Rings Twice*, Frank Chambers sits on death row, wondering what has happened to him and how he has arrived at this end. Waiting for his execution, he considers whether he could have unconsciously meant to kill Cora—his wife and the pregnant mother of his child—in the car crash that took her life and for which he was convicted of murder. He wonders whether the crash, which he claims was accidental, could have been something other than an accident, something he did purposefully:

> There's a guy in No. 7 that murdered his brother, and says he didn't really do it, his subconscious did it. I asked him what that meant, and he says you got two selves, one that you know about the other that you don't know about, because it's subconscious. It shook me up. Did I really do it? God almighty, I can't believe that! I didn't do it! I loved her so, I tell you, that I would have died for her! To hell with the subconscious. I don't believe it. It's just a lot of hooey that this guy thought up so he could fool the judge. You know what you're doing, and you do it. I didn't do it, I know that. That's what I'm going to tell her, if I ever see her again.[47]

The language that the death row inmates use for individual motivation refers specifically to the psychology of the unconscious, with the caveat that "subconscious" was and is a frequent misnomer for "unconscious." Although

Frank Chambers doesn't know anything about Freud's work—about the sex and death drives; about repression; about the development of the id, the ego, or the superego—he does recognize the implications of a discipline that probes the individual's motivations for behavior. Freud's work calls into question how much control the individual has over his own actions, whether the accident that occurred while Frank was driving was in fact a manifestation of his inner desire to kill Cora. And Frank's desperation in asserting his love for Cora and in denying any desire to hurt her implies that the question of self-control is one that is very much on his mind.

In *Beyond the Pleasure Principle* and then *The Ego and the Id*, both published in the early 1920s, Freud extends his thinking about sexuality and instinctual drives beyond what I have addressed above. In *Beyond the Pleasure Principle*, Freud suggests that the individual tries to engage in behavior that can satisfy sexual impulses, but that this satisfaction is only temporary and so must be repeated, culminating in what he called a "repetition compulsion." The tension that results from this repeated compulsion is only resolved through death. Freud linked the self-preserving ego instincts and the sexual instincts, calling them life instincts, Eros, in opposition to the death instinct, Thanatos. Freud thereby represents the mind as a site of struggle between these drives, with each acting to repress the other in different ways, including acts of aggression against others as a redirection of a death wish for the self. In *The Ego and the Id*, Freud establishes a structural conception of the unconscious, with a scheme that is fully separate from the structure of the conscious mind, where the struggle of the instincts takes place. It is here—in this formulation of an unconscious mind fully separate from the conscious mind, and in this formulation where sexual impulses and life instincts do battle with death instincts within the individual—that we can return to *The Postman Always Rings Twice* and have a sense of what Frank Chambers is articulating as he waits for his execution on death row. Ultimately, Frank Chambers' terror at the possibility that he may have wanted to unconsciously harm Cora serves as an especially desperate articulation of his fear of what he might desire, what he might be capable of, and what he can't seem to control.

Frank Chambers is a drifter at the beginning of the novel and Cora is the wife of Nick Papadakis, the owner of a roadside diner in rural California. Frank, the first-person narrator of the novel, stops at the diner for a meal and Nick takes a liking to him and offers Frank a job there, working on cars at the filling station attached to the diner. He tells Nick that he has a few offers to mull over but then Cain describes Frank's first sight of Cora:

> Then I saw her. She had been out back, in the kitchen, but she came in to gather
> up my dishes. Except for the shape, she really wasn't any raving beauty, but she

had a sulky look to her, and her lips stuck out in a way that made me want to mash them in for her.[48]

Frank takes the job, because from "the filling station I could just get a good view of the kitchen."[49] Frank's attraction to Cora is immediate and powerful. That night Frank tries to eat a meal but has to rush outside to vomit: "I let everything come up. It was like hell the lunch, or the potatoes, or the wine. I wanted that woman so bad I couldn't even keep anything on my stomach."[50]

From the beginning, Cain configures Frank's attraction as something beyond his control, but he also conflates that desire with violence. When he first sees her he wants to "mash [Cora's lips] in for her," suggesting not only that he wants to kiss her passionately, but that he also wants to hit her and to hurt her. In his first conversation with her, later that day, he comes close to her and makes an advance that she rejects: "I went out. I had what I wanted. I had socked one in under her guard, and socked it deep, so it hurt. From now on, it would be business between her and me. She might not say yes, but she wouldn't stall me. She knew what I meant, and she knew I had her number."[51] The language of "sock[ing her] in under her guard, so it hurt" is aggressive and connotes boxing or fighting. His desire for violence is then made manifest the next day, when they kiss for the first time:

I took her in my arms and mashed my mouth up against hers. . . . "Bite me! Bite me!"
I bit her. I sunk my teeth into her lips so deep I could feel the blood spurt into my mouth. It was running down her neck when I carried her upstairs.[52]

Lust and violence commingle in their first sexual experience and Frank's desire to hurt Cora meets a match in her apparent masochism. Their deeply physical relationship stands in contrast to how Nick thinks of Cora. While Frank calls her a "hell cat," Nick imagines her as nothing more than his "little white dove." Cora doesn't want to be a peaceful, little white bird, though.

Cora convinces Frank to collaborate to murder Nick so that they can be together, and after one failed attempt they succeed in killing him in what looks like a car accident that the other two survive. They arrange themselves in the wreckage for when the police arrive:

I began to fool with her blouse, to bust the buttons, so she would look banged up. She was looking at me, and her eyes didn't look blue, they looked black. I could feel her breath coming fast. Then it stopped, and she leaned real close to me.

"Rip me! Rip me!"

I ripped her. I shoved my hand in her blouse and jerked. She was wide open, from her throat to her belly.[53]

The milieu of the scene, with the destroyed car and Nick's corpse, bespeaks of destruction and the consequence of violence but the language of the narration is brutal in a different way—Cora doesn't tell Frank to rip her blouse, but to rip *her*. It's not her blouse that is wide open, but Cora herself. The disjunction between these two—between the clothes and the body—serves as a displacement of Frank's desire to do bodily harm to her, and indeed of Cora's own desire for that to take place. The scene then continues, with sexual desire becoming fully conflated with physical violence:

I hauled off and hit her in the eye as hard as I could. She went down. She was right down there at my feet, her eyes shining, her breasts trembling, drawn up in tight points, and pointing right up at me. She was down there, and the breath was roaring in the back of my throat like I was some kind of an animal, and my tongue was all swelled up in my mouth, and blood pounding in it.

"Yes! Yes, Frank, yes!"

Next thing I knew, I was down there with her, and we were staring in each other's eyes, and locked in each other's arms, and straining to get closer. Hell could have opened for me then, and it wouldn't have made any difference. I had to have her, if I hung for it.

I had her.[54]

In saying, "I had to have her, if I hung for it," Frank gives voice to the compulsive desire that leads him to danger and actually correctly predicts his own ultimate ending.[55] This moment is, of course, the culmination of the conflation of sex and violence and of sex and death in the novel. Frank is unable to resist his sexual drive, especially in how he has blurred the lines between sex and violence. Having sex with Cora after killing Nick—indeed, in front of Nick's corpse while they wait for the police to arrive at the scene—is something he cannot resist, regardless of the dangers involved.

This scene works as a direct dramatization of Freud's notion of the repetition compulsion—the desire for violence and sex that Frank first felt upon seeing Cora and then acted upon in biting her lip. Ultimately that compulsion again manifested itself after Frank killed Cora's husband and felt the need to have sex with her at the scene. The language of compulsion is clear when he says he "had to have her." Of course, he didn't *have* to, but he *wanted* to, and it felt like a necessity. It was an impulse he couldn't manage, and it was a repetition of everything he felt about her since he first wanted to "mash her lips in." The conflation of his desires and the struggle to successfully negotiate his different impulses are more than he can carry out. He might love her, but how that love manifests itself is not what he imagines it to be.

That manifestation comes to its culmination after Cora gets pregnant and they get married at City Hall. Afterward, they go to the beach because Cora wants to go swimming, but in the water she says, "Frank, I feel funny inside."[56] Fearing a potential miscarriage, she has Frank tow her in to the shore so they can head to the hospital. Frank struggles in the water with Cora: "When you hurry in the water you're sunk. I got bottom, though, after a while, and then I took her in my arms and rushed her through the surf."[57] The use of language in this scene is noteworthy in how it operates in two ways at the same time. Frank is offering a literal description of how he sank under the water while towing Cora until his feet hit the bottom. Once he touched down, though, he was able to move forward with her in his arms and get her to the car. In these same sentences, though, Cain is offering the reader a figurative description of Frank's psyche. Much like the same ways that his use of the idiom "if I hung for it" is both literal and figurative, Cain's use of "sunk" and hitting the "bottom" evoke Frank's state of mind.

The night before, Frank had said to Cora, "We're chained to each other, Cora. We thought we were on top of a mountain. That wasn't it. It's on top of us, and that's where it's been ever since that night [we killed Nick]."[58] The conflation of sex and violence shifts when Cora becomes pregnant. Now she is a maternal figure and not a sexual object. While swimming and floating in the water, she mentions that her breasts are getting bigger with her pregnancy. "It's a new life for us both, Frank" she says to him.[59] However, Frank does not want a new life. He wants what he had. As he tows her in, he feels "sunk" and that he has reached "bottom." After he gets her to the car and heads to the hospital in Santa Monica, they get stuck behind a slow-moving truck. Unable to pass on the driver's side, Frank tries to get by the truck on the right: "I pulled out to the right and stepped on it. She screamed. I never saw the culvert wall. There was a crash, and everything went black."[60] Frank awakens in the car to "the awfulness of what [he] heard": the sound of Cora's blood spilling across the hood of the car, "like rain on a tin roof."[61] She is dead.

The language in the crash scene is notably different than Frank's usual narration. These four declarative sentences lack Frank's usual flair, with no use of idiomatic language, nor double entendre. The narration, one might say, lacks *Frank*. His usual personality as the narrator is missing and of course, the fifth sentence lacks a first-person agent. Frank narrates the accident as if a crash just happened. What he does not include is that his decision to pass on the right was the deciding factor in causing the accident: "there was a crash" implies that, even as the driver, he was a passive bystander to what happened, as opposed to the one who steered the car into the culvert wall. Cain's use of sentence structure and language once again demonstrates Frank's psychology. He killed her, but does not want to accept responsibility. Once Cora no longer represented a sexual desire for him, once she became pregnant with his child, Frank no longer wanted her in the same way. The violence that was always conflated with desire here becomes mere violence. The repetition compulsion reaches its inevitable conclusion, in Cora's death.

After he is convicted of murder for Cora's death, Frank ends his narration on death row, awaiting execution, and there Cain completes his portrayal of psychological impulse and the denial of accountability that echoes Gray's authorial strategy in *Doomed Ship*. Frank says,

> There's a guy in No. 7 that murdered his brother, and says he didn't really do it, his subconscious did it. I asked him what that meant, and he says you got two selves, one that you know about the other that you don't know about, because it's subconscious. It shook me up. Did I really do it? God almighty, I can't believe that! I didn't do it! I loved her so, I tell you, that I would have died for her! To hell with the subconscious. I don't believe it. It's just a lot of hooey that this guy thought up so he could fool the judge. You know what you're doing, and you do it. I didn't do it, I know that. That's what I'm going to tell her, if I ever see her again.[62]

Cain's direct invocation of Freud's psychological theories makes evident that his novel is meant to dramatize the ways that criminality in American culture is framed within certain linguistic tropes and rhetorics. Frank's insistence on his innocence and his rejection of the "subconscious" and hidden intentions does not so much dissuade readers from his guilt as it does to only further bring it to our attention. Like Gray, he seeks to disassociate responsibility from actions—"I didn't do it!"—and insist that conscious intentions, as opposed to impulses or drives, are all that matter when it comes to criminality.

The Postman Always Rings Twice, published in 1934, was a phenomenal commercial success, with a screen adaptation released in 1946 and over a million copies sold by 1950. In his next book, *Double Indemnity*, serialized in *Liberty Magazine* in 1936 and ultimately published as one of three novellas in 1943, Cain again utilized Freudian notions of foundational drives and instincts as central to his characters' motivations. In a plot again inspired by the Snyder-Gray story, Walter Huff is an insurance agent who sells supplemental accident insurance to Phyllis Nirdlinger for her husband. Phyllis seduces Walter and convinces him to help her kill her husband for the money, which they do, but then face an investigation headed by a claim manager at the insurance company. Walter and Phyllis turn on each other and both attempt to kill the other. The novel ends with them both on a ship headed toward Mexico, agreeing to commit suicide together by jumping overboard at the same time. The novel, like *Postman*, is a first-person narrative of lust, betrayal, and murder. Walter, like Frank Chambers (and Judd Gray), is driven by a deep sexual desire for a woman who he cannot resist even when he knows that she is dangerous and that a sexual relationship with her is a bad idea. Indeed, when he first meets her in her house, he notes her attractive figure, using a term that clearly is intentional on Cain's part in its double entendre allusion: "Under those blue pajamas was a shape to set a man nuts."[63] And go "nuts" for her is exactly what he does, as his physical dalliance with her, and more seriously his participation in the murder, demonstrates.

In this novel, though, Cain explores not only the motivations of his male protagonist but also the motivations of his femme fatale. Phyllis obviously kills her husband for the money, but that is not the only reason. As Walter discovers, Phyllis has killed before—a previous husband, that husband's first wife, and a child. Again, some of that was for material gain—money and property—but Phyllis has not only killed for these reasons. She has also killed seven other children and acquired property only through two of them. It turns out that Phyllis is what we could classify as a psychopath. Freud himself wrote of crime, in 1928, that "two traits are essential in a criminal: boundless egoism and a strong destructive urge. Common to both of these and a necessary condition for their expression is absence of love, lack of appreciation for (human) objects."[64]

Cain, as we saw in *Postman*, was invested in dramatizing (and monetizing) Freud's ideas and portrayed Phyllis as someone cast straight out of *Beyond the Pleasure Principle*. In one suggestive scene in the novel, Phyllis's stepdaughter Lola relates to Walter what she saw in a moment when she encountered Phyllis in private:

> I came in on her, in her bedroom, with some kind of foolish red silk thing on her, that looked like a shroud or something, with her face all smeared up with white powder and red lipstick, with a dagger in her hand, making faces at herself in front of a mirror.[65]

On one level, this scene seems to capture Phyllis playacting a part as a murderess, dramatically and sensationally overdressed as an envoy from death itself. On another level, however, this scene also reads as a reenactment of a previous moment, a repetition of one of her previous murders. Indeed, the many murders themselves—often with little to gain except for the pleasure of the act—serve as a type of repetition compulsion. Freud writes in *Beyond the Pleasure Principle* that although stimuli originate both externally and internally through our instinctual drives, the psyche protects itself from outer stimuli, allowing the instincts that emanate from within to dominate and take precedence. For Freud, the psyche differentiates between our two greatest instincts, pleasure and pain, by constructing barriers against pain, refusing to recognize the internal as a site for pain stimuli and transferring its conception of the origin of the pain from the internal to the external. Freud posits trauma as the means through which external stimuli is conceived as having internal origins. In a case of trauma, all psychic barriers break down, "provok[ing] a very extensive disturbance in the workings of the energy of the organism, and [setting] in motion every kind of protective measure."[66] Trauma, therefore, leads to a breakdown of how the system operates, for the psyche no longer is able to displace pain as a stimulus originating outside of itself and therefore both pleasure and pain are perceived as internal drives.

Cain constructs Phyllis as an embodiment of this dynamic. For her, pleasure, satisfaction, pain, and death are all bound together. In Freud's terms, her desire to repeatedly place herself into dangerous and deadly situations offers "no contradiction of the pleasure-principle: it is evident that the repetition, the rediscovery of identity, is itself a source of pleasure."[67] At the end of the novel, Phyllis appears on the steamship dressed in the same outfit that Lola had seen her wearing earlier. Walter describes her as looking "like what came aboard the ship to shoot dice for souls in the Rime of the Ancient Mariner."[68] Whereas the figure that Phyllis embodied in the earlier scene was something of an envoy for death, at the end of the novel her presentation of self in the same outfit is now matrimonial. Just before she appears in this outfit, she had told Walter, "The time has come [f]or me to meet my bridegroom. The only one I ever loved. One night I'll drop off the stern of the ship. Then, little by little I'll feel his icy fingers creeping into my heart."[69] Phyllis's language of marriage and love in this conversation, combined with the object of that love—death itself—evocatively and fantastically illustrates how she imagines pleasure and pain, sex and death, as of a piece. As a sendoff, a final statement on her life, she articulates the very conflation of Freud's two foundational instincts.

As dramatizations of Freud's ideas, Cain's novels enjoyed great commercial and critical success and further embedded those concepts into American culture. Indeed, the portrait of criminality arising from impulse, repression, and repetition compulsion became a staple of American crime narratives for decades—from *In Cold Blood* and *Silence of the Lambs* to the films of Hitchcock and De Palma. A significant part of this is due to Cain's skillful narrative approach. Because Walter narrates the novel and because he only has a very limited perspective on Phyllis and knows so very little of her background, we never receive a history of Phyllis that would better help us understand her actions. Like Frank Chambers, she conflates pleasure and pain but—also like Frank—we don't ever fully know why. This, of course, is a signature strategy of Cain's—to represent the criminal in a Freudian light without having to do the work of explication of the behavior. In that way, his stories can be both salacious and sensational without having to engage in the intellectual rigor that a psychoanalyst would have to bring to the therapeutic situation. Cain was therefore able to capitalize on the more fantastic elements of these stories of lust and murder without dragging an audience into a lecture hall. That formula led to a highly successful career and an approach that writers and filmmakers have adopted for the past ninety years.

Of course, the conception of criminality arising from impulse and repression was not limited to the realms of literature and film; it also, not surprisingly, had a conspicuous place within the American justice system. Perhaps the foremost example of the influence of psychoanalysis and Freudian notions of the unconscious occurred in the trial of Nathan Leopold and Richard Loeb, who were arrested and then convicted for the kidnapping and murder of Bobby Franks on May 21, 1924. The defendants knew Franks as a fourteen-year-old boy who lived and attended school in their neighborhood in Chicago, and they lured him into their car that afternoon with an offer of a ride home. Inside the car, they struck Franks in the head with a chisel, knocking him unconscious, asphyxiated him with a gag, and later dumped his dead body in a culvert. The body was discovered before Franks's father had paid the defendants' demand for a ransom of $10,000. Due to a number of clues that the two had left, the defendants were soon arrested by the police for the crimes of kidnapping and murder. Recognizing the strength of the case that the state had compiled against them, Leopold and Loeb soon confessed their guilt.

When Franks's body was first discovered, the brutality of the crime immediately captured the attention of the press and the murder garnered headlines all around the city. But when Leopold and Loeb were arrested and subsequently tried for the crime, the attention paid to the case absolutely exploded. The national and even international press converged on Chicago to transcribe the events of the trial as they occurred that summer and those events were front page news not only in Chicago but also all over the country and even overseas. The point of interest for the press, and for the public in general, was why Leopold and Loeb, both of whom came from wealthy and prestigious families, would commit such a crime. What could be their possible motive?

In the summer of 1924, Nathan Leopold was nineteen years old and set to begin his second year of law school. Richard Loeb was eighteen and had also already graduated from college and completed a year of graduate school. They were both academic prodigies who seemed to have tremendous careers ahead of them. Neither of the young men needed the money they would have received for the ransom, with each benefiting from a generous allowance from his parents, and there seemed to be no material motive for the crime. At the same time, they did not claim to be insane. They were unlikely killers.

Figure 2.3 Nathan Leopold (Left) and Richard Loeb. *Source*: Underwood & Underwood/ Corbis. George Rinhart/Corbis Historical/Getty Images.

They were successful, highly intelligent, respected, and wealthy; on the surface, they did not appear in any way to pose a threat. What reason would they have to kill anyone? (See Figure 2.3.)

In their trial, the defense team, led by Clarence Darrow, surprised the prosecution by switching their pleas to guilty for both the kidnapping and the murder. This tactic was decided upon as their best chance to avoid the death penalty. The trial, therefore, was technically a sentencing hearing and became a forum on whether these two admitted murderers should be allowed to live. The defense team's argument centered on two elements. First was their age—as boys, not yet of age, they should not receive the penalty handed down, by tradition, only to those at least twenty-one years of age. Second was their state of mind—Leopold and Loeb, the defense argued, were mentally diseased. Although they were not legally insane, although they could separate right from wrong, they could not resist the impulses that compelled them to murder Bobby Franks. They were driven to assert their self-perceived superiority and felt completely apathetic about taking someone's life. The defense team's assertion of disease was suggestive in that it did not offer justification or an excuse for the crime, but instead sought only to explain its origin and suggest that there may be a mitigating factor when it came to their responsibility for the crime.

Darrow focused on the defendants' psychological development during their upbringing. Both boys had been supervised by strict governesses who physically and emotionally punished them for indiscretions and who sexually abused them as adolescents. As a result of that abuse, Darrow argued, the two boys had each developed malfunctions in their nervous and glandular systems that impaired their ability to make moral judgments and therefore on how they viewed right and wrong.

The defense lawyers were well aware of contemporary advances in psychological theory and they put these advances to use in their defense. This included the work of psychoanalysts but also that of biological theorists. Darrow himself was aligned with the biological school. He had written in 1922 of the biological causes of crime, focusing on

> ductless glands . . . [that empty secretions into the blood] acting like fuel in an engine [to] prepare it to respond to the directions to fight or flee any type of action. . . . It is only within a few years that biologists have had any idea of the use of these ductless glands or of their importance in the function of life. Very often these glands are diseased, and always they are more or less imperfect; but in whatever condition they are, the machine responds to their flow.[70]

Proponents of the biological school, similarly to the psychoanalytic school, argued that transgressive behavior derived from impulses within select individuals. Edwin Sutherland, in his highly influential *Principles of Criminology*, first published in 1924, writes, "The approach from the point of view of personality cannot be sharply differentiated from the biological theories."[71] The difference between the two, of course, is that the biological theorists focused their thinking on the physiological organism, not the psychological self, that comprises the individual.[72] These theorists recognized that mental disorders may be a cause for crimes committed by individuals, but they argued that those disorders had an origin not in a psychological response to stimuli but a physical one.

Although biological theorists often looked to physiological heredity and inherited mental traits as the roots of physical deficiencies, their postulations on the influence of the glandular system offer their most compellingly empirical argument about the ways in which an individual might be biologically disposed to crime, whether he wants to commit that act or not.[73] Focusing on the chemical dynamics of the human body—"the ductless glands or endocrines . . . [that] are the chemical factories of the body"—biological theorists identified the key glands as the pituitary, the pineal, the thyroid, the parathyroids, the suprarenals, the sex glands, the liver, and the pancreas and suggested that "the disorder of any one of the important glands is almost certain to derange the others."[74] They cited the relationship between the nervous system and the glandular system as a critical one in understanding how impulses can stimulate activity in the glands and can lead to abnormal behavior. Emotional shocks and traumas, therefore, can cause the glands to overreact and continual stress can lead to permanent disorders of the glands. The individual's response to impulses, according to this school of thought, is drastically affected by the biological responses of the glandular and nervous systems.

In compiling his team of experts for the defense, Darrow relied on biological theorists with whom he was intellectually aligned, but also sought out key figures in the American psychoanalytical community. The psychiatrists and psychologists who interviewed Leopold and Loeb were some of the most eminent not only in Chicago but also in the country. They worked as two teams: Harold Hulbert and Karl Bowman, a psychiatrist in private practice and a lecturer at Harvard, respectively, conducted an extensive physical and psychiatric examination that gave special consideration to the psychiatric and physical histories of Leopold and Loeb; the second team, comprised of nationally renowned experts such as Drs. William Healy, William A. White, Bernard Glueck, and Ralph Hamill, conducted an examination of the defendants that focused much more on psychoanalytic issues. Both teams presented reports to the defense lawyers, though the defense only introduced the Bowman-Hulbert Report into evidence in the trial. The other doctors, however, did offer testimony in the important penalty phase.

In light of their work on criminality, psychoanalytic theory, and trauma, White and Healy's presence on the defense team signaled Darrow's interest in using the sentencing hearing to propose the argument that mitigating psychological factors effected the defendants' actions. In *Crimes and Criminals*, White notes how external factors have influence over an individual's actions, writing that "man never acts solely as an individual nor solely as a member of society but always as both."[75] The social processes that the individual finds himself a part of represent the influences "from without" that White posits can and do affect an individual's behavior. Using a logic that emphasizes personal trauma as a possible origin of crime, White considers the relationship between what individuals experience and their reactions to those stimuli as critical to understanding criminal behavior. He cites two causes for why individuals might commit a crime: the desire to compensate for deprivations they suffered as a child or the desire to enact revenge on a parent who has been particularly harsh on the child. Both of these causes share experiential and reactional elements: individuals have a history that shapes them, both in what happened and in how they responded and continue to respond to what happened. White writes, "These illustrations show how criminal acts which may appear on the surface to be quite senseless are, as a matter of fact, conditioned by very definite experiences in earlier life."[76]

White's suggestion of the importance of childhood in determining later behavior not only echoes Freud, but it also concurs with the position of Healy, who had earlier stressed the psychological reaction to social processes in *Mental Conflicts and Misconduct.* Healy most strenuously emphasizes the critical role played by the child/parent relationship in determining behavioral development:

> The basis for much prevention of mental conflicts is to be found in close confidential revelations between parents and children . . . we find that even in families supposed to be well cared for there is often little or no knowledge of [what children are doing, whom they are meeting, what they are seeing and hearing, and as much as possible of what they are thinking] which lead[s] to the troubles with which we are dealing.[77]

Such a lack of communication creates a need for the child to look elsewhere than the family for role models of behavior and greatly increases the feeling of seclusion in the child. Healy writes, "These misdoers with moral conflicts never had any one near to them, particularly in family life, who supplied opportunities for sympathetic confidences."[78] The crimes that these individuals commit could represent either an actual or a symbolic striking back at those who failed to emotionally provide for the child, a means through which the individual responds to a prior trauma. Whether these actions are the result of conditions of an early life or a reaction to it or whether they are a result of or response to a present situation, what Freud, White, Healy, and others who stressed social processes in their psychoanalytic work imply is that the criminal—while the perpetrator of the act—might in fact be considered a victim of circumstances whether from within or without. Impulse and instincts may guide the criminal's behavior regardless of any sense of pleasure or desire, and he might not be able to modify that behavior, whether he wants to or not.

In conducting case histories of Leopold and Loeb, the psychiatric and psychological experts found, in their respective reports, elements of trauma that suggested possible explanations for the defendants' actions, including the death of Leopold's mother at sixteen and Loeb's problematic relationship with his iron-willed governess. Bowman and Hulbert found a "profound attachment" between Loeb and his governess, despite the fact that Loeb deemed her overly strict and that "he could escape detection and punishment by lying."[79] Bowman and Hulbert criticize the governess's role in Loeb's upbringing, writing, "She effeminized him and would not allow him to mix enough with other boys. She would not overlook some of his faults, and was too quick in her punishment. He, therefore, built up the habit of lying, without compunction and with increasing skill."[80]

In his memoirs, *Life Plus 99 Years*, Nathan Leopold, who also had a problematic relationship with his governess, which included a strong sexual component, identified Loeb's relationship to his governess as central to his friend's character and central to why he killed Bobby Franks:

> Dick's basic motive, I think, must be sought in his basic personality—in what he was, in how he had been conditioned. Primarily, I think, it was a kind of revolt—an overreaction against the strictness of his governess who had had charge of him until he was fifteen. A basic feeling of inferiority, maybe; a desire to show that he could do things and bring them to a successful end on his own.[81]

Loeb, in essence, had something to prove, something about himself that he could only demonstrate by proving his own genius, something inspired by this relationship and against which he felt compelled to act in some way. Leopold, in turn, provided Loeb with a forum for his ideas and schemes, offering encouragement and even assistance.

The defendants had committed a series of minor crimes before the Franks's kidnapping and murder, including vandalizing building and automobiles, looting a house, and setting fire to an abandoned building. Loeb was fascinated with crime. He was an avid reader of detective stories and narrative accounts of the lives of notorious criminals, and he was fully intrigued by the machinations of detection and capture. The crime spree that he embarked upon with Leopold was a manifestation of this fascination and his opportunity to experience it for himself. Crime offered him a means of expressing his most deeply felt self and experiencing his fundamental desires, regardless of the consequences. Leopold, however, had a vastly different motive for his actions. In his memoirs, he tries to pinpoint the reason for his participation:

> My motive, so far as I can be said to have one, was to please Dick. Just that—incredible as it sounds. I thought so much of the guy that I was willing to do anything—even commit murder—if he wanted it bad enough. And he wanted to do this—very badly indeed. . . . [H]is friendship was necessary to me—terribly necessary.[82]

Leopold did not seem to be overtly violent. He writes, "For the commission of the crime itself, I had no enthusiasm. Indeed, I had a feeling of deep repugnance."[83] His motivation was his infatuation, or love, for Richard Loeb. While he was "undersized, round-shouldered and had rather bulging eyes," Loeb was an athletic and handsome teenager.[84] Leopold thought of Loeb as something of a Nietzschean superman, highly intelligent, attractive, and physically superior. There was a "compact" between the two—in exchange for Leopold's participation in Loeb's crimes, Loeb would agree to have sex with him. Each, then, had his wishes fulfilled through this arrangement and each proceeded with the series of crimes with no regard for the consequences of others, culminating in the murder of the fourteen-year-old Franks.

Of course, not everyone would respond to the traumas of their youth in such a violent way. Both reports suggest—as the Joint Report of Drs. White, Healy, Glueck, and Hamill put it—that "their criminal activities were the outgrowth of an unique coming-together of two peculiarly maladjusted adolescents, each of whom brought into the relationship a long-standing background of abnormal mental life."[85] The brutal slaying of Bobby Franks, then, derived from what these two boys were able to offer one another, from how each satisfied the other's needs.

The Joint Report refers to Loeb as "an individual with a pathological mental life, who is driven in his actions by the compulsive force of his abnormally twisted life of phantasy [sic] and imagination."[86] The same report deems Leopold, in turn, "a special abnormal type, the paranoid psychopathic personality."[87] In their estimation, Leopold believed that his own desires outweighed all other considerations: "His ego is all-important, right or wrong, his desires and will being the only determinants of his conduct."[88] Therefore, Leopold matched up well with Loeb, who the reports suggest possessed a "pathological moral obtuseness."[89] They both believed that they were superior and that notions of right and wrong did not apply to them, that they needed to consider only the satisfaction of their desires and impulses.[90]

The Bowman-Hulbert Report, however, gives a more detailed examination of the defendants and offers a broader portrait of what the two defendants offered one another. For each of the two, the doctors conducted family, academic, sexual, and physical histories; a physical examination; and a psychiatric study and interpretation. For Richard Loeb, besides the section on his governess, the doctors also stressed his early development and criminal fantasies and his delinquencies as an adolescent. Bowman and Hulbert state that Loeb "has always had a marked feeling of inferiority."[91] Much of this resulted from physical frailty as a child, something that he grew to compensate for by creating fantasies in which he had strength, cleverness, and great intelligence:

> Up to the age of nine he was inferior physically, being rather frail. He was not allowed to play freely with other boys in strenuous outdoor games. As a result he tended to spend a good deal of time by himself thinking over his unsatisfactory life of reality and constructing a world of phantasy [sic], in which he occupied a dominant role and in which his emotional life was satisfied.[92]

These fantasies grew to focus on criminal acts of which he was the mastermind. Of special importance for Bowman and Hulbert was that in his fantasies "there is no instance of his performing a crime alone, where there was no one to appreciate his skill."[93] Loeb needed an audience to derive full satisfaction for his deeds, to feel that he was indeed not inferior.

After he grew stronger physically, he noticed a different physical defect that "prevented his feeling on equal terms with other boys. That was his delayed maturity and his lack of sexual potency."[94] The physical exam had revealed a lack of a secretion from the sexual glands that corresponded with Loeb's lack of sexual urges. Moreover, the continued feeling of inferiority led him to value especially highly the thrill he received from committing crimes without punishment, for the secret knowledge offered him something that others did not have. He felt superior in those moments. Eventually, of course, his friendship with Leopold provided him not only with the opportunity for admiration in that he had an audience for his crimes but with the thrill of feeling superior, for Leopold conceived of Loeb in these very terms.

As a child and adolescent, Leopold, like Loeb, had often conceived of himself as inferior to others. He had a number of health problems that led to this feeling, including, Bowman and Hulbert write, "the very definite disorder of the control of his heart and blood-vessels. . . . He probably has Bright's Disease. He certainly has cardio-renal disease."[95] Leopold turned both to his exceptional intellect to satisfy his emotional needs, and also, like Loeb, to a fantasy world. His fantasies, though, most often revolved around a king-slave scenario, in which he would sometimes identify with one role and sometimes the other, though he usually preferred that of slave.

The fantasies had a marked sexual component. His sex urge was strong. Bowman and Hulbert note in their physical examination of Leopold physical disorders in the pituitary and pineal glands that usually carry with them "a disorder of the increased function of the sex glands."[96] They attribute this disorder to a great extent to a governess who "exposed herself indecently" to him at an early age and who had such an influence on him that "he was never able to emancipate himself from her erroneous teachings and mistakes."[97] The king-slave fantasies, in which Leopold was able to find emotional fulfillment, also offered sexual gratification. These fantasies gave Leopold such satisfaction that "he would prefer to actually play the role of slave to some one whom he regarded as his superior, than he would to be independent, or take the role of superiority."[98] In Loeb, Leopold found someone in real life who he could conceive of as his superior. He gradually fit Loeb into his king-slave fantasy. Such was the makings of the "Compact" between them, with disastrous consequences. In their analysis of Leopold, Bowman and Hulbert write, "The phantasies [*sic*] when confused with realities, are definite, irresistible impulses."[99] Leopold was willing to do anything, even to kill, to satisfy those impulses.

After twelve days of deliberation, Cook County Circuit Court Judge John R. Caverly decided to hand down life sentences to the two defendants. Darrow had delivered a rousing 12-hour speech at the conclusion of the hearing, arguing against the immoral and unethical punishments of the American justice system, especially that of the death penalty, but also repeatedly hammering home the youth of the defendants. In articulating his ruling from the bench, Caverly suggested that the age of the Leopold and Loeb, as well as legal precedent, guided his thinking. Nonetheless, the extensive press coverage—local, national, and international—from the beginning of the kidnapping to the end of the sentencing brought forward the concepts of impulse and repression and the language of psychology and psychoanalysis to "explain" crime in a fundamentally different way than that of criminal anthropology and the concept of the criminal type, as articulated in the first chapter.[100] Although the latter also had tremendous sway in American popular culture, the intense interest in the trials and sentencing of Leopold and Loeb and Gray and Snyder and the extensive commercial success of the novels of James Cain demonstrate the cultural interest in the ideas about criminality that these latter narratives dramatized.

Psychology was not new to America in the 1920s and 1930s. Nor were notions of insanity. However, Freud's notion of the unconscious—the "subconscious" to Frank Chambers—was new and the possibilities of the power of impulse, the dangers of repression, and the trope of repetition compulsion were all fresh and compelling to the American imagination of the early twentieth century. And, of course, with their elements of sex, betrayal, lust, perversion, and death, these stories were sensationalized, fantastic, and alluring to an American public. However, these narratives did not supersede ones that highlighted the criminal type; instead, they operated alongside of them. What they had in common was a deep interest in individuals who were not fully in control of their actions—whether because of biological determination or because of psychological trauma and neuroses. Both threads highlight individuals who do not seem to live with full agency in their choices, though that lack of free will is represented in differing ways.

One of the central variations, though, in the two different conceptions of criminality is that the narrative of impulse holds open the possibility that a type of intervention can change the seeming inevitability of the criminal act. Freud himself believed wholeheartedly in the value of psychoanalysis, in the hard work of therapy, and the intervention of the analyst to help the individual move from neurosis to healthy thoughts and relationships. Cain's imagining of Frank Chambers and Phyllis Nirdlinger does not seem to hold any possibility of them seeking help, of course, but perhaps if Ruth Snyder and her husband—or Judd Gray and his wife—had sought help with their marriages then the terrible murder in Queens in the winter of 1927 would not have taken place. Leopold and Loeb both were psychologically damaged young men, for a variety of reasons, but psychological therapy may have helped steer them toward better outcomes. But these real people did not get the intervention they needed, and the consequences of that were disastrous for all involved. As we move in the next chapter, toward the rise of sociology and the role of environmental determinism in criminal behavior, we will find a group of scholars who make intervention the hallmark of their work, leading to much more positive results for the individuals involved and also for the greater community.

NOTES

1. John Kobler, ed. *The Trial of Ruth Snyder and John Gray* (Garden City, NY: Doubleday, Doran & Co., 1938), 220.

2. Gray, Judd. *Doomed Ship* (New York: Horace Liveright, 1928), 154–155.

3. Gray, *Doomed Ship*, 203.

4. Gray, *Doomed Ship*, 207.

5. Gray, *Doomed Ship*, 82.

6. Gray, *Doomed Ship*, 200.

7. In a presentation to the American Association of the Feeble-Minded, H. H. Goddard proposed classifying individuals with intellectual disability. Using standard IQ exams, Goddard suggested that those with a score of 51–70 be called morons, those 26–50 be called imbeciles, and those with a score of 0–25 be called idiots. These terms became standard in the field. In this chapter I will continue to use these terms, as they were the language of the time period, but I will continue to place them in quotation marks to signify that they are terms of the past and not the present day.

8. These methods had their roots in France, Germany, and Britain—the latter of which came from Sir Francis Galton, who was in part the subject of attention in the first chapter for his development of composite photography and his application of that technology for criminological purposes.

9. In the early 1870s, under the influence of the New Psychology arising from Germany, Charles Saunders Peirce and William James led a change toward what came to be known as the new American psychology that moved away from Clinical Psychology to an applied science more rooted in the laboratory. Peirce and James articulated a new American philosophy, pragmatism, that ultimately led to James's 1890 publication of *Principles of Psychology*. Interested in not only behavior but also consciousness itself, James combined in this book his philosophical background with a physiological interest to explore both a cerebralist conception of consciousness with a belief in the behavioral efficacy of consciousness that ultimately led to his articulation of a future for psychology as an applied discipline in the natural sciences. His work was central in using the university system to further professionalize the discipline in the United States—although, to be fair, he was not the only one who

did so. While he had opened an informal psychological laboratory at Harvard in 1875 and then in 1885 established an official psychological laboratory there, the first in the United States, faculty at both Princeton and Yale were offering courses in psychology in the 1880s and George Trumbull Ladd of Yale had published the influential *Elements of Physiological Psychology* in 1887. However, it was really G. Stanley Hall, a student of James, who truly professionalized the discipline, establishing the *American Journal of Psychology* in 1887 and helping to organize the founding of the American Psychological Association in 1892. By that time, laboratories were present at the aforementioned universities, as well as at the University of Pennsylvania, Columbia, and Hall's institute, Johns Hopkins University.

10. Goddard, H.H. *Feeble-Mindedness: Its Causes and Consequences* (New York: Macmillan, 1914), 8. Qtd. in Rafter, *Creating Born Criminals*, 140.

11. It is important to note that Goddard was a complicated figure. For instance, in relation to his assertions of a relation between feeble-mindedness and blame, he believed that a criminal's intellectual disability should limit his criminal responsibility, because that individual had no control over the effects of that disability on his actions. He was also something of a pioneer when it came to working with the intellectually disabled and highly respected in the field. As noted above, he was the head of Vineland, an institution committed to serving the intellectually disabled, for over a decade and published widely on educational components of working with this population, including his 1914 book *School Training of Defective Children*. Finally, he actively advocated for the creation of what we now call Special Education for the deaf, blind, and intellectually disabled children.

12. *The Kallikak Family* focused on the descendants that a soldier from the 1700s had sired through an extramarital affair with a feeble-minded woman. The results of that affair—the offspring that followed, through a number of generations—were a populous group of distantly related criminals. Goddard proposed that their criminality was a result of their shared genetic disposition toward feeble-mindedness. Capturing the public's interest in criminality in a way that mirrored the public fascination with the concept of the criminal type, Goddard's book became a wide commercial success. Soon after publication of *The Kallikak Family*, however, critics attacked the book for errors that Goddard had made in his research methods. After careful consideration over the next many years, Goddard eventually disavowed the book.

13. For more on Goddard's use of intelligence testing and its relation to his embrace of eugenics, see Leila Zenderland, *Measuring Minds: Henry Herbert Goddard and the Origins of American Intelligence Testing*. Cambridge: Cambridge University Press, 1998.

14. Eugenics, however, while repeatedly having flashes of popular support in the American twentieth century, never gained widespread support as a policy solution for feeble-mindedness, much as it had not for those identified through racial and ethnic markers as the criminal type.

15. Gray, *Doomed Ship*, 200.

16. Gray, *Doomed Ship*, 211.

17. Gray, *Doomed Ship*, 190–191.

18. Gray, *Doomed Ship*, 182.

19. Gray, *Doomed Ship*, 190.

20. Gray, *Doomed Ship*, 195.

21. Gray, *Doomed Ship*, 95.

22. Gray, *Doomed Ship*, 152.

23. Gray, *Doomed Ship*, 183.

24. Healy, William. *Mental Conflicts and Misconduct* (Boston, MA: Little Brown & Co., 1917), 17.

25. Healy, *Mental Conflicts and Misconduct*, 17.

26. After finishing his medical degree with a specialization in gynecology, Healy became interested in neurology and eventually psychoanalysis. He identified himself, ultimately, as a psychiatrist and therapist, spending most of his career working with juvenile delinquents in child guidance clinics. He published *Structure and Meaning of Psychoanalysis* in 1931.

27. Some psychologists—those who focused on the psychology of consciousness—rejected his work because they did not believe in the concept of the unconscious. Others—behaviorists—rejected it because they did not believe in the existence of the mind. Many rejected it because of Freud's reliance on his own clinical cases and the lack of verifiable data. It was, in essence, an untestable theory. Without experiment and laboratory confirmation, many psychologists rejected psychoanalysis because it had no real scientific objectivity. Accordingly, for many, it could not be viewed as actual rigorous science.

28. Although Freud argued that the sex drive is biological and universal, in that it is neither species- nor culture-specific, others argued that individuals can have multiple motivations for behavior—even if those motivations are in fact unconscious.

29. In 1923's *The Ego and the Id* he revised this "topography" of the mind into something more sophisticated and structural, with three distinct mental systems: the id, the ego, and the superego.

30. White, William A. *Crimes and Criminals* (New York: Farrar & Rinehart, 1933), 24.

31. White, *Crimes and Criminals*, 120. White was well known and deeply respected in his work. He held a number of prestigious national positions, serving as the president of the American Psychopathological Society in 1922, of the American Psychiatric Association in 1924–1925, and of the American Psychoanalytical Society in 1928.

32. Nathan G. Hale, Jr., *Freud and the Americans: The Beginnings of Psychoanalysis in the United States, 1876–1917* (New York: Oxford University Press, 1971): 397–398.

33. Except, perhaps, through psychoanalysis—though the individual would have to seek such therapy out.

34. Two early critics who had a great deal of influence on the literary criticism of naturalism were Lars Ahnebrink, in *The Beginnings of Naturalism in American Fiction*, published in 1950, and Charles Child Walcutt, with *American Literary Naturalism: A Divided Stream*, published in 1956. However, Richard Lehan and Donald Pizer are the foundational critics of naturalism whose work came to dominate

critical discourse on realism and naturalism in the late 1960s, 1970s, and early 1980s. See Pizer, *Realism and Naturalism in Nineteenth Century America*, published in 1967, and Lehan, *Theodore Dreiser: His World and His Novels*, published in 1969.

35. Dreiser, Theodore, *Sister Carrie*. 1900 (New York: Norton Critical Edition, 1991), 190.

36. Dreiser, *Sister Carrie*, 191.

37. Dreiser, *Sister Carrie*, 191.

38. Dreiser, *Sister Carrie*, 192.

39. The rise of the New Americanists in the 1980s and 1990s brought a keen critical interest in how socioeconomic and marketplace dynamics took aesthetic shape in literary naturalism. In *Form and History in American Literary Naturalism*, June Howard positions naturalism as a literature of decline that is derived from the representation of class conflicts and anxieties. Walter Benn Michaels—in *The Gold Standard and the Logic of Naturalism*—and Mark Seltzer in *Bodies and Machines*—both sought to place American literary naturalism with the nineteenth- and twentieth-century discourses of the social and aesthetic conflicts that the novelists were representing, especially the conflict of the economic marketplace.

40. Dreiser, *Sister Carrie*, 193.

41. Dreiser, Theodore. *An American Tragedy*. 1925 (New York: Signet, 1981), 493.

42. Dreiser, *An American Tragedy*, 493.

43. In *Determined Fictions*, Lee Clark Mitchell specifically focuses on elements of language and style as literary representations of determinism, seeking to distance himself from the broader cultural landscapes of much of the New Americanist critics.

44. In 1994, Paul Civiello positioned himself against the New Americanists and their focus on the historical moment, arguing that naturalism operated as a narrative mode aligned with historical processes and concerned "with a central post-Darwinian crisis: the collapse of humanity's conception of an order in the material world, an order that had formerly imbued that world with meaning" (2). See *American Literary Naturalism and Its Twentieth-Century Transformations*.

45. Recent critical work has sought to move somewhat beyond the critical focus on determinism and focuses more on how these literary texts were directly engaged in the political and cultural issues of their day. For example, see John Dudley, *A Man's Game: Masculinity and the Anti-Aesthetics of American Literary Naturalism* and Jennifer Fleissner, *Women, Compulsion, Modernity: The Moment of American Naturalism*, both published in 2004, and Ira Wells, *Fighting Words: Polemics and Social Change in Literary Naturalism*, published in 2013.

46. Anita Loos, in her brilliant satire *Gentlemen Prefer Blondes*, includes a passage that specifically points to this cultural interest in crime and agency. Loos's protagonist, Lorelei, recalls her time in Little Rock and her affair with her boss. When Lorelei discovers that he was sleeping with other women as well, she goes to visit him at his apartment:

> I mean one evening when I went to pay a call on him at his apartment, I found a girl there who really was famous all over Little Rock for not being nice. So when I found out that

girls like paid calls on Mr. Jennings I had quite a bad case of histerics and my mind was really a blank and when I came out of it, it seems that I had a revolver in my hand and it seems that the revolver had shot Mr. Jennings. (32)

Loos skillfully constructs this narration to exploit the notion of the split self and crime: Lorelei's "histerics" lead to a moment of unconsciousness when "another self" seems to take over while her "mind was really a blank." More to the point, moreover, Loos's construction of that last phrase—"the revolver had shot Mr. Jennings"—wonderfully illustrates the way that Lorelei deflects responsibility for the shooting from her and directly—somehow—to the gun itself. She didn't shoot him, the gun did. That displacement brilliantly illustrates and satirizes how naturalists' literary figurations of the unconscious operate to shift agency and culpability for the criminal act from the individual to something beyond his or her control.

47. Cain, James. *The Postman Always Rings Twice*. 1934 (New York: Vintage, 1992), 116.

48. Cain, *The Postman Always Rings Twice*, 4.

49. Cain, *The Postman Always Rings Twice*, 4.

50. Cain, *The Postman Always Rings Twice*, 9.

51. Cain, *The Postman Always Rings Twice*, 7.

52. Cain, *The Postman Always Rings Twice*, 11.

53. Cain, *The Postman Always Rings Twice*, 46.

54. Cain, *The Postman Always Rings Twice*, 46.

55. This is a recurring motif in Cain's work. In his novel *Serenade*, the protagonist, an opera singer, is a bisexual man who loses his voice every time he engages in gay sex, but who cannot seem to help repeating doing so, even though it leads to career ruin.

56. Cain, *The Postman Always Rings Twice*, 111.

57. Cain, *The Postman Always Rings Twice*, 112.

58. Cain, *The Postman Always Rings Twice*, 108.

59. Cain, *The Postman Always Rings Twice*, 111.

60. Cain, *The Postman Always Rings Twice*, 112.

61. Cain, *The Postman Always Rings Twice*, 112.

62. Cain, *The Postman Always Rings Twice*, 116.

63. Cain, James M. *Double Indemnity*. 1943 (New York: Vintage, 1989), 7.

64. "Dostoevsky and Parricide," 178. This text is an introductory article to a German scholarly collection on Dostoevsky's *The Brothers Karamazov*, published in 1928: *Die Urgestalt der Brьder Karamasoff*, ed. W.L. Komarowitsch (Munich: Piper Verlag, 1928). A translation of Freud's text can be located in *Standard Edition*, XXI: 177–194. This passage quoted in J. Reid Meloy, "A Psychoanalytic View of the Psychopath." (2008). San Diego Psychoanalytic Society and Institute. Retrieved from http://www.yorku.ca/rweisman/courses/sosc6890/pdf/meloypaper-psychopathy.pdf

65. Cain, *Double Indemnity*, 84.

66. Sigmund Freud, *Beyond the Pleasure Principle*, translated and edited by James Strachey (New York: W.W. Norton & Company, 1989, originally translated in 1961, originally published by Freud in 1920): 158.

67. Freud, *Beyond the Pleasure Principle*, 158.

68. Cain, *Double Indemnity*, 114–115.

69. Cain, *Double Indemnity*, 114.

70. Darrow quoted in Irving Stone, *Clarence Darrow for the Defense* (Garden City: Country Life Press, 1941), 203.

71. Sutherland, Edwin. *Principles of Criminology* (Chicago: University of Chicago Press, 1924), 55.

72. Ernest Bryant Hoag and Edward Williams, representative psychiatrists of the biological school who worked in the courts in Los Angeles, write in their 1923 treatise, *Crime, Abnormal Minds and the Law*: "Much which now passes as a purely mental disorder has in reality a *physical basis* and before a diagnosis of feeblemindedness can be made, one must usually have access to various factors as the ductless glands, various infection, disorders of *metabolism*, accidents, and numerous other physical conditions" (author's emphasis). Ernest Bryant Hoag and Edward Huntington Williams, *Crime, Abnormal Minds and the Law* (Indianapolis, IN: The Bobbs-Merrill Company, 1923): 57.

73. The biological theorists Max Schlapp and Edward Smith are striking specific in their explanation of biological malfunctions that lead to criminal behavior, offering a full accounting of the glandular system that begins at the level of the cell: "The fundamental point, once more, is that the minute cells become disturbed or diseased and that from this small focus of trouble the disturbance of the whole body spreads out." See Max G. Schlapp and Edward H. Smith, *The New Criminology* (New York: Boni and Liveright, 1928), 86. Schlapp and Smith, like Hoag and Williams, were psychiatrists who worked within the criminal justice system. They detailed the workings of disturbed or diseased cells and the ways in which the body was affected: "The blood and lymph form the media or environment of the human cell, the surroundings in which it lives, the bringers of its nourishment. . . . Speaking broadly, if the imbalance of the blood and lymph chemistry manifests itself in early life, the cells are likely to form badly; if the trouble comes along after maturity, they work badly" (Schlapp and Smith, *The New Criminology*, 87–88).

Regarding the imbalance, regardless of when it occurs, it leads to abnormal cell performance and that consequently culminates in behavioral issues.

74. Schlapp, Max G. and Edward H. Smith, *The New Criminology* (New York: Boni and Liveright, 1928), 88.

75. White, *Crimes and Criminals*, 15.

76. White, *Crimes and Criminals*, 28.

77. Healy, *Mental Conflicts and Misconduct*, 71–72.

78. Healy, *Mental Conflicts and Misconduct*, 71–72.

79. Maureen McKernan, *The Amazing Crime and Trial of Leopold and Loeb* (Chicago: The Plymouth Court Press, 1924), 87. McKernan's account of the trial provides both the Bowman-Hulbert Report and the Joint Report of Drs. White, Healy, Glueck, and Hamill, "in full, except for the unprintable matter" (82). The details of the sexual relationship between the defendants are suppressed from publication; I am, however, interested more in the fact of that relationship and how it constituted

a "compact" between them than I am in the actual details of the sexual acts between them. All further references to the reports in this text will cite McKernan.

80. McKernan, *The Amazing Crime and Trial of Leopold and Loeb*, 88–89.

81. Leopold, Nathan. *Life Plus 99 Years* (New York: Doubleday, 1958), 50.

82. Leopold, *Life Plus 99 Years*, 49–50.

83. Leopold, *Life Plus 99 Years*, 49.

84. Francis X. Busch, *Prisoners at the Bar*, from the Notable American Trials Series. (Indianapolis, IN: The Bobbs-Merrill Company, 1952), 167.

85. McKernan, *The Amazing Crime and Trial of Leopold and Loeb*, 142.

86. McKernan, *The Amazing Crime and Trial of Leopold and Loeb*, 163.

87. McKernan, *The Amazing Crime and Trial of Leopold and Loeb*, 155.

88. McKernan, *The Amazing Crime and Trial of Leopold and Loeb*, 143.

89. McKernan, *The Amazing Crime and Trial of Leopold and Loeb*, 159.

90. The Joint Report was most likely not introduced into the trial because Drs. White, Healy, Glueck, and Hamill questioned whether the defendants possessed at the time of the murder a "normal 'sense of right and wrong,'" a claim that would call for a plea of innocence due to insanity, a pleas that Darrow and the defense lawyers did not want to make out of fear that they would lose and the defendants would definitely face the death penalty. The prosecution, nevertheless, strenuously objected that Darrow and the defense team were effectively pleading insanity during the penalty phase with his line of defense and Darrow was indeed limited in his abilities to introduce all of the witnesses that he had planned.

91. McKernan, *The Amazing Crime and Trial of Leopold and Loeb*, 105.

92. McKernan, *The Amazing Crime and Trial of Leopold and Loeb*, 105.

93. McKernan, *The Amazing Crime and Trial of Leopold and Loeb*, 92.

94. McKernan, *The Amazing Crime and Trial of Leopold and Loeb*, 105–106.

95. McKernan, *The Amazing Crime and Trial of Leopold and Loeb*, 137–138.

96. McKernan, *The Amazing Crime and Trial of Leopold and Loeb*, 138.

97. McKernan, *The Amazing Crime and Trial of Leopold and Loeb*, 110; 111.

98. McKernan, *The Amazing Crime and Trial of Leopold and Loeb*, 122.

99. McKernan, *The Amazing Crime and Trial of Leopold and Loeb*, 123.

100. Paula S. Fass is perhaps *the* authoritative voice on the press coverage of the trial. See Paula S. Fass, "Making and Remaking an Event: The Leopold and Loeb Case in American Culture," *The Journal of American History* 80, no. 3 (December 1993): 919–951.

Chapter 3

Reforming the "Bad" Boy

Juvenile Delinquency, Intervention, and Choice

In 1938, Spencer Tracy starred in *Boys Town*, a film about Father Flanagan—a real-life priest dedicated to reforming juvenile delinquents—who years earlier had founded the actual Boys Town outside of Omaha, Nebraska. With Mickey Rooney costarring as Whitey Marsh, a stubborn boy reluctant to give up his errant ways, the film was a commercial and critical success. Tracy won the Academy Award for his lead performance and spent most of his speech speaking about the actual Father Flanagan and his work. Boys Town itself was and continues to be a village intended to care for and educate at-risk children. The village includes a school, dormitories, and administrative buildings and the boys themselves elect a mayor and council to participate in the oversight of the village. Throughout the film, Flanagan repeatedly offers a refrain that succinctly sums up the ethos of his work: "There's no such thing as a bad boy, I'm sure of that (See Figure 3.1.)."[1] This statement reflects his belief that everyone has the potential to make good decisions, so long as they can imagine those choices as possible. Flanagan's plan for helping the boys consisted of cultivating their potential by offering them the "proper" living arrangements that would enable them to imagine those choices. With the creation of Boys Town, he provided them with new environmental conditions in which they could demonstrate that they were, in fact, "good boys." By the end of the film, Whitey learns that his connections to the criminal world hinder his ability to make smart choices and he embraces the ideology of Boys Town. The film ends with his election as mayor.

As I demonstrate in the second chapter, the notion that criminals are made, not born, had currency in American culture by the time *Boys Town* was produced. However, the connection between environmental conditions and criminality was different than that of the perceived biological and psychological influences on individual behavior. Certainly, the idea of an environmental

97

Page 98, Chapter 3.

Figure 3.1   Spencer Tracy as Father Flanagan in *Boys Town*. *Source*: Taurog, Norman. 1938. *Boys Town*. United States: Metro-Goldwyn-Mayer.

determinism was similar in conceiving of juvenile delinquency as originating somewhere outside of the individual's control, but as *Boys Town* sought to dramatize, that sense of determinism need not be totalizing. Built into the "made not born" construct is a belief that individuals are not inherently bad or evil, but that instead they turn to bad decisions because of circumstances that might be environmental or psychological and a product of a type of trauma or neurosis over which the individual has no control. Regardless, if a criminal can be made, logic would have it that we might be able to intervene to help him make better decisions or to make sure that the individual never went down a bad path in the first place. The construct of environmental determinism, as articulated by Father Flanagan and others at the time, wasn't fully deterministic. Similarly to the potential impact of psychoanalysis and therapy for those individuals who dealt with psychological and mental health issues, the potential to intervene in the situations that impacted the young men who were juvenile delinquents provided the possibility that criminals could be deterred from crime before they actually ever became criminals. Criminality was thereby not imagined as inherent—there was "no such thing as a bad boy."

Father Flanagan's belief in the innate goodness of these boys and in the possibility of their redemption parallels the approach of a group of sociologists in the 1920s and 1930s who were likewise engaged in work to reform and rethink how best to deal with juvenile delinquency and other contemporary issues of crime and poverty in urban America. Those scholars—known as the Chicago School of Sociology—sought to demonstrate that adolescents could indeed make wiser and healthier choices if they had the opportunity to operate in different conditions. In this chapter I will examine the work of these sociologists and how they imagined criminality as a result of an environmental milieu. I will consider how those ideas corresponded to film representations of juvenile delinquency. In so doing, I will articulate how this idea of criminality—because it has within it the possibility of an individual learning to make better choices—differs from that of the previous two chapters in how it imagines the primacy of determinism over free will. To begin to explore this, I will first consider the work of the Chicago School.

With its appointment of Albion Small as head professor, the University of Chicago founded the first Sociology Department in the United States in 1892. Small was a leading force in the establishment of sociology in the United States, publishing the first textbook in the discipline in 1894, helping found the American Sociological Association, and instituting and serving as the editor of the *American Journal of Sociology* for thirty years.

He also brought into his department an illustrious group of colleagues, including W. I. Thomas, Robert Park, and Ernest Burgess. In 1921, Park and Burgess co-authored the highly influential textbook, *Introduction to the Science of Sociology*, and during the next decade or so oversaw the training of students who collectively, along with colleagues at the University and beyond, became known as the Chicago School of Sociology, with an influence that lasted through the mid-twentieth century.[2] While Small, Thomas, and George Vincent led the first generation, Park, Burgess, Ellsworth Faris, and William Fielding Ogburn headed the second generation and they produced a number of important graduate students, some of whom went on to form the third generation of Chicago sociologists.[3]

The influence on the Sociology Department on other scholars at the University of Chicago—Jane Addams, Thorstein Veblen, John Dewey, and George Mead—is apparent in the department's attention to issues of class and its frequent emphasis on the conjoining of theory and research, especially with its focus on scientific research that emphasized social conditions and realities. From the department's founding, Small sought to treat the city of Chicago as a social laboratory that provided a great many potential research avenues for students and scholars. The second generation reinforced this approach. Park's greatest influence in the program was in the classroom and in his oversight of graduate work. Along with Burgess, he emphasized the value of studying urban issues in a systematic manner as a means of training sociologists and teaching them to theorize solutions to those problems.[4] During the 1920s and 1930s, faculty and graduate students at the University of Chicago instituted a series of studies and published a number of treatises that espoused the belief that human behavior was determined by social structures and the influence of the surrounding physical environment. Some of these books included Nels Anderson's *The Hobo* (1923), Frederick Thrasher's *The Gang* (1927), Louis Wirth's *The Ghetto* (1928), and Harvey Warren Zorbaugh's *The Gold Coast and Slum* (1929), each of which focused on neighborhoods and people in their home city and taken collectively represent a lasting contribution to the discipline. Under the supervision of Park and Burgess, Martin Bulmer writes, these scholars embraced field research that moved away from the survey research previously emphasized by sociologists, and instead utilized "observational methods drawn from journalism and anthropology [and that] were designed to lay bare social processes in a way not hitherto achieved by social scientists."[5]

The social processes that the Chicago School detailed had to do with how these neighborhoods and communities actually operate in terms of what it means to live in them as individuals. In *The City*, published in 1925, Park, Burgess, and Roderick McKenzie articulate the underlying theory of their approach:

> There are forces at work within the limits of the urban community—within the limits of any natural area of human habitation, in fact, which tend to bring about an orderly and typical grouping of its population and institutions. The science which seeks to isolate these factors and to describe the typical constellations of persons and institutions which the cooperation forces produce, is what we call human, as distinguished from plant and animal, ecology.[6]

This notion of human ecology—or social ecology, as it came to be known—was the force that Park and Burgess and their colleagues sought to unravel or decode.[7] For them, the work of the sociologist was to recognize that individuals do not exist in a vacuum but instead act according to the context in which they live. Park asserted a relationship between the environment and human behavior that took place within that environment, writing, "The fact is . . . that the city is rooted in the habits and customs of the people who inhabit it. The consequence is that the city possesses a moral as well as a physical organization, and these two mutually interact in characteristic ways to mold and modify one another."[8] This conception of "a moral as well as a physical organization," which mutually interact, is especially revealing. His notion of social ecology centered on how one's environment could have a major influence over how an individual would fare socially, economically, and morally. When that environment works well it has a positive effect on the individual's worldview. However, when that environment is "toxic" or "disorganized," it has a deleterious effect and leads to worse behavior by those living in those conditions. He writes, "It is probably the breaking down of local attachments and the weakening of the restraints and inhibitions of [those who commit crime], under the influence of the urban environment, which are largely responsible for the increase of vice and crime in great cities."[9] The interpretation of criminal behavior here is focused less on individual choices than it is on the social ecology of the city—the "breaking down of local attachments and weakening of restraints and inhibitions" and the influence of the urban environment. For Park and Burgess and their students, individuals who commit crime are a product of poor social processes that exist in "disorganized" environments.

With its emphasis on urban sociology and contemporary social problems, and with its integration of theory and ethnographic fieldwork, the Chicago School had a tremendous impact on how scholars and laymen thought about crime and criminals. The mentorship of Park and Burgess and the scholarship of Thrasher, Wirth, and Zorbaugh laid the groundwork for a series of books written and edited by Clifford Shaw that argued that juvenile delinquency derives from social disorganization in particular communities that limits the ability of boys to make healthy decisions. The conditions of their environment served to circumscribe their sense of individual agency and led them to believe that they had little choice over what became of them. The sense of determinism in this theory of criminality is somewhat acute; however, Shaw contended that sociology has a role to play in helping the boys through an intervention that demonstrated to them that they did indeed have agency. By addressing the social disorganization of these communities and moving the delinquents to a healthier social ecology, Shaw argued that sociology could directly address the problem of juvenile delinquency. The influence of Shaw's work was widespread enough to reach beyond academia and public policy, extending to the representation of juvenile delinquency in popular culture in films such as *Angels with Dirty Faces* and, of course, *Boys Town*. These films, echoing the underlying principle of Shaw's work, dramatize the value of a positive intervention that, through positive role modeling, could help delinquents recognize and make better choices. And, in so doing, these films, like Shaw's work, complicated the concept of criminality in terms of issues of agency and contingency.

Writing in *The City*, in a chapter entitled "Community Organization and Juvenile Delinquency," Park expresses a belief in a contingent individual agency. He writes, "The sources of our actions are, no doubt, in the organic impulses of the individual man; but actual conduct is determined more or less by public opinion, by custom, and by a code which exists outside of us in the family, in the neighborhood, and in the community."[10] By emphasizing the influence of these factors—public opinion, customs, and codes—that exist externally to the individual, Park posits a logic of crime akin to environmental determinism in its mitigation of individual agency. He goes on to argue that what we already know about the intimate relations between the individual and the community makes it clear that delinquency is not primarily a problem of the individual, but of the group. Any effort to reeducate and reform the delinquent individual will consist very largely in finding for him an environment, a group in which he can live, and live not merely in the physical or biological sense of the word, but live in the social and in the sociological sense. That means finding a place where he can have not only free expression of his energies and native impulses, but a place where he can find a vocation and be free to formulate a plan of life which will enable him to realize in some adequate way all the fundamental wishes that, in some form or another, every individual seeks to realize, and must realize, in order to have a wholesome and reasonably happy existence.[11]

In Park's view, juvenile delinquents are raised in environments that lead them to imagine few possibilities for advancement or success. Of course they turn to crime—it's essentially what they have been trained to do by the custom and mores in those environments. Park's belief that those who grow up in troubled environments develop limited notions of what options are available to them informed his work as a scholar and a teacher. He instilled in his students the idea that the fundamental work that they were called to do was to approach this issue in a methodical and analytical manner.[12] They were to study social problems, analyze them, form hypotheses about what to do to improve the problem, and test those hypotheses out in practice. Underlying this approach was his belief that social scientists need not only catalog problems but also propose solutions to those problems. Park and his colleagues believed that they could offer useful interventions for individuals in these conditions. That work, as he notes in the above passage, means helping those individuals locate "a place where [they] can find a vocation and be free to formulate a plan of life which will enable [them] to realize in some adequate way all the fundamental wishes that, in some form or another, every individual seeks to realize, and must realize, in order to have a wholesome and reasonably happy existence." The intervention that Park and his colleagues advocated was to shift these young men into different conditions where they can better recognize alternative choices that could lead to better lives.

The foundational assumption of the Chicago School was that the conditions of the individual's environment have a direct impact on his moral development. Louis Wirth, in *The Ghetto*, articulated it thus: "If students of human nature have learned to be cautious about any one thing more than another in recent years, it is to be cautious about attributing the character of a people and of an individual to human nature without a scrutiny of the historical experiences of the group or the individual."[13] Seeking to understand human nature through a study of an individual or a group without placing that individual or

Figure 3.2   An Illustration from Harvey Warren Zorbaugh, *The Gold Coast and the Slum. Source*: Hanna Holborn Gray Special Collections Research Center, University of Chicago Library.

the group in a broader context, in other words, can only lead to broad generalizations that will, no doubt, lead to mischaracterizations if not misunderstandings of human nature. The specific context is paramount. In thinking about the ghetto, his subject of study, Wirth states, "The institution of the ghetto is not only the record of a historical people; it is a manifestation of human nature and a specific social order."[14] Indeed, the relationship between social life and human nature is central, in Wirth's mind, to understanding human behavior. He writes, "If we knew the full life history of a single individual in his social setting, we would probably know most of what is worth knowing about social life and human nature."[15] What is key in the understanding of human nature, in this framework, is the relationship between the individual and his social setting (See Figure 3.2.).

What does this privileging of the social context—what the Chicago School called the "social ecology" of a space—look like in practice? A good place to consider this may be the work of another student of the Chicago School, Harvey Warren Zorbaugh, in his study, *The Gold Coast and the Slum*, which focused on Chicago's Near North Side—a fascinating geographical area that included some of the wealthiest and poorest parts of urban Chicago in close proximity to one another. Zorbaugh's book focuses on three main areas of the Near North Side: the slum, the rooming-house world, and the Gold Coast, and he carefully lays out the different ways each of these areas operate, especially in relation to how individuals act in these spaces. Of the rooming-house world, with its lack of community-mindedness and rootlessness, he writes that it "is a world of political indifference, of laxity of conventional standards, of personal and social disorganization."[16] In such an environment, the individual's "social contacts are more or less completely cut off. His wishes are thwarted; he finds in the rooming-house neither security, response, nor recognition."[17] Finally, Zorbaugh concludes, the individual in this setting is faced with three choices:

> The emotional tensions of thwarted wishes force the person to act somehow in this situation. His behavior may take one of three directions: He may find himself unable to cope with the situation, and attempt to withdraw from it. This withdrawal frequently takes the form of suicide. . . . Or, again, the person may build up an ideal or dream world in which are satisfied the wishes that find no realization in the harsher life without. . . . Or perhaps a substitution is made, and the person finds satisfaction for his thwarted wishes in symbols which represent old associations, or lavishes his affection on a dog or a parrot.[18]

The overwhelming isolation of the environment, in Zorbaugh's view, leaves the individual with few options. The individuals here can find no viable out, no route to success.

For Zorbaugh, this worldview derives not only from poverty but also from a set of social codes that exist in that environment that reinforce the individual's sense of limitations. He writes about the slum:

> It is apparent that the slum is more than an economic phenomenon. The slum is a sociological phenomenon as well. Based upon a segregation within the economic processes, it nevertheless displays characteristic attitudes, characteristic social patterns which differentiate it from adjoining areas. And it is this aspect of slum life that is especially significant from the standpoint of community organization. The slum sets its mark upon those who dwell in it, gives them attitudes and behavior problems peculiar to itself.[19]

The defining characteristic of the slum—indeed of each part of the overall area of study—is less an economic situation than a sociological one. As a sociologist, Zorbaugh privileges "attitudes and behavior problems" above economic factors. He ascribes the living conditions as the cause of those attitudes and problems and minimizes how much he assigns cause to the actual economic factors that are at the root of the institutionalization of the slum as a geographic area. This is how he—and Park and the others in the Chicago School—comes to see a relationship between sociological conditions and moral development and to articulate a type of fatalistic determinism in how they imagine that relationship. In seeking to understand those problems and attitudes, or more importantly what type of behavior they lead to, Zorbaugh comes back to the foundation of his training in social ecology. He writes,

> Taking into consideration the segregated nature of the population of the cheap lodging-house, with its mobility and anonymity and its lack of group life, common social definitions, and public opinion, and taking into consideration the social patterns that grow out of the cultural conflicts of the life of the foreign colony, it is not surprising that the slum is a world of unconventional behavior, delinquency, and crime.[20]

In this moment of summing up—of noting the issues of segregation, of isolation and anonymity, of a lack of common social customs—Zorbaugh contextualizes his conclusion that crime is a natural or organic outgrowth of the social conditions of the slum. The environment that one lives in creates the conditions for a set of particular behaviors. Regardless of whether a neighborhood has distinctive social customs that create a social organization, or if it lacks the common customs that unite the community and therefore lead to social disorganization—for Zorbaugh each outcome is a product of the conditions of the space.

Thrasher's work in *The Gang* was influential in helping the sociologists understand the role of social disorganization. According to Robert E. L. Faris, Thrasher found the "phenomenon of gang formation a natural sociological development."[21] Thrasher argues that gangs "constitute merely one of many symptoms of the more or less general disorganization" of the early twentieth-century American city, with its booming economic development and large numbers of immigrants.[22] "Life is in constant ferment physically, economically, and culturally," he writes. "Rapid change and enormous movement have tended to prevent the development of a consistent social code supported by all members of the community. . . . The result is a high degree of disorganization, manifesting itself in vice, crime, political corruption, and other social maladies."[23] Simply put, Thrasher argued that "the community forces that curb illegal behavior were weak or inoperative in these areas of the city."[24] In this type of situation, gangs "not only find an environment favorable to their development, but their life and activities are colored by the disorganization they find there."[25] The gang establishes its own set of codes, filling in the vacuum that exists and providing a type of structure to which these young men are attracted. That individuals gravitate to it, for Thrasher, can be no surprise.[26]

In the eyes of these sociologists, at the least the environment can delimit what one can imagine in terms of behavioral choices. Within the social disorganization of the poor communities of contemporary Chicago, gang life and juvenile delinquency were the organic product of a lack of social codes and networks that steered young men toward education, work, and wise decision-making. But this construction of social ecology also provides a type of blueprint for how sociologists could change that behavior—either by changing the environment or by removing the individual to a new one. As a central element of their methodology, Thrasher, Wirth, Zorbaugh, and others in the Chicago School researched and compiled firsthand accounts of life in the neighborhoods they were surveying and then published selections from these accounts to give details to their broader analyses and to make vivid the types of claims the sociologists made about life on the socioeconomic margins. These accounts were powerful ways to give voice to those men and women who lived in these spaces and the sociologists promoted the value of these "life histories" as valuable pieces of evidence and data for their work. Indeed, in addition to their treatises on the relation between the sociological structure of the city and crime, members of the Chicago School published three "life histories" of individuals: *The Jack-Roller*, *The Natural History of a Delinquent Career*, and *Brothers in Crime*, all overseen by Clifford Shaw and focused on individual criminals with whom Shaw collaborated in the writing (Stanley in *The Jack-Roller*, Sidney in *The Natural History of a Delinquent Career*, and the Martin brothers in *Brothers in Crime*). At the heart of these books were first-person narrations that detailed the boys' backgrounds and their stories of crime and attempts to become productive citizens. Shaw, along with Burgess, buttressed these narrations with reflections on the stories and research on the particularities of neighborhoods and institutions and on juvenile delinquency itself. These books dramatized the theories that Shaw and his colleagues proposed about the fundamental influence of the environment on an individuals' development and testified to how these individuals saw very few options available to them in terms of locating a means of successful negotiation of modern urban life.[27] They also offered an argument that intervention in that environment could produce potential solutions to social ills such as juvenile delinquency and recidivism.

All three books in the series share a common organization—first, Shaw offers introductory materials, then the criminal gives his account of his life, and finally Burgess provides a set of summaries and discussions. This framework enables Shaw, as editor, to present the story as an argument about delinquency and intervention. The introductory material includes the history of behavior as a child and the social and cultural background, all of which include a history of arrests, of the family, and of peer relationships. As Shaw writes in *The Natural History of a Delinquent Career*, he views delinquency "not as an isolated act, but in relation to the mental and physical condition of the offender, the whole sequence of events in his life, and the social and cultural situations in which his delinquent behavior occurred."[28] In advance of the narrative itself are also his considerations of the socioeconomic conditions under which Sidney grew up, including poverty rates, delinquency rates and locations, and the criminal records of peers. For instance, he notes, "Everywhere throughout the neighborhood is evidence of the inferior economic status of the inhabitants Rents and family income are universally low."[29] A few paragraphs later, he suggests, "The successive changes in the composition of the population, the disintegration of the lien cultures, the diffusion of divergent cultural standards and the gradual industrialization of the area have resulted in a dissolution of the neighborhood culture and organization."[30] The impact of these social and cultural conditions is paramount to how Shaw wants his reader to understand and react to the stories of these young men and their criminal careers.[31]

Of special import were the events in the child's early years that may have shaped the child's behavior:

> The study of case histories has indicated that very frequently the delinquent behavior of older offenders may be traced back to experiences and influences which have occurred very early in life. In many of these cases it is possible to describe the continuous process involved in the formation and fixation of the delinquent-behavior trend. In the search for factors contributing to delinquency in a given case, it is desirable, therefore, to secure as complete a picture of the successive events in the life of the offenders as possible.[32]

For instance, in *The Jack-Roller*, Shaw notes that Stanley has a record that shows a clear sequence of behavior problems, from truancy and petty stealing at six years old to jack-rolling and burglary as an adolescent, establishing a progression of crimes.[33] Shaw delves into Stanley's family background, as he does with Sidney in *The Natural History of a Delinquent Career* and the Martin brothers in *Brothers in Crime*. The histories of these oft-broken families—with their economic struggles, their rough housing conditions, and their alcohol abuse—are an integral element in the schema. In addition, Shaw frequently includes maps of the city that highlight the home addresses of delinquents and the precincts in which delinquency most frequently occurs. All of this information is presented as data that chronicles the urban conditions in which these individual stories take place. Moreover, that data in turn contextualizes the choices that the individual boys make into a life of crime.

For instance, in *The Jack-Roller*, Shaw and Burgess suggest that Stanley did not have full control over his development and that instead his personality took form under a very particular social ecology. According to Burgess, Shaw identified the "prevalence of [petty stealing, shoplifting, and sex practices] among the children" in his neighborhood and determined that there was a "community spirit and background which would not only tolerate, but even foster, delinquent practices among the younger boys in the neighborhood."[34] He also saw the continual family conflicts as related to his delinquency and also to his "failure to make an adjustment in his own home at the time of his parole from the various correctional institutions to which he was committed."[35] Finally, aspects of Stanley's personality—including "attitudes of persecution, suspicion, resistance to discipline and authority, self-justification, and a definite tendency to excuse his misconduct by means of self-pity, fatalism, and by placing the blame on other persons"—clearly were part of his problem in making good decisions.[36] Ultimately, Burgess proclaims that "Stanley, not more than anyone else, is neither to be praised nor blamed for his personality traits. They were formed for him before he gained conscious control of his destiny. The point to be grasped is that the formation of the personality pattern is a natural product of forces in the constitution of the individual and in his childhood situation."[37]

That "childhood situation" under which Stanley grew up are the conditions, as in the other life histories, of urban Chicago in the first decades of the twentieth century: a space of highly divided socioeconomic opportunities, as Zorbaugh and Park and Burgess had already made quite clear in their own work. Shaw and Burgess argue that "the personality pattern" of delinquents such as Stanley, Sidney, the Martin brothers and countless others are "a natural product" of particular young men from particular backgrounds, who respond to those conditions with despair and a deep feeling of helplessness. They are not arguing that all young men from the ghetto are going to become criminals. Instead, they are suggesting that some young men in those conditions will respond negatively—and predictably—to their situation and turn to crime with little sense that they have other options. These books put a human face on the theory of social ecology that the Chicago School was enumerating and demonstrate that environmental conditions can have a primary impact on how some individuals come to perceive the world and imagine possibilities for their lives.

Shaw writes in the first chapter of *The Jack-Roller*, the first in the series, "The unique feature of [life histories] is that they are recorded in the first person, in the boy's own words, and not translated into the language of the person investigating the case."[38] This allows readers of the narrative to understand "the personal attitudes, feelings, and interests of the child; in other words, it shows how he conceives his role in relation to other persons and the interpretations which he makes of the situations in which he lives."[39] Life histories, then, should provide a specific representation of how the criminal thinks about his own actions, with a particular approach that the criminal employs to represent his behavior. Shaw argues that these stories provide three distinct pieces of information: "1) the point of view of the delinquent; 2) the social and cultural situation to which the delinquent is responsive; and 3) the sequence of past experiences and situations in the life of the delinquent."[40] The distinct point of view, of course, means that the "social and cultural situation" is interpreted solely through the subjective position of the criminal and that the sequence that he includes again is subject to his own understanding and memory of what has happened in his life.

In their narratives, the storytellers all rely on a set of tropes that positions them, perhaps not surprisingly, as victims of forces beyond their control. Stanley, in *The Jack-Roller*, sees the source of his problems as the death of his mother and his father's subsequent remarriage: "As far back as I can remember, my life was filled with sorrow and misery. The cause was my stepmother, who nagged me, beat me, insulted me, and drove me out of my own home."[41] In Stanley's view, this woman prioritized her biological children over her stepchildren, favoring them at meals and beating the stepchildren for their misdeeds, as well as making them do all of the difficult work around the house.[42] This eventually led to Stanley's repeated absences from home and delinquency. Living there is clearly untenable in his mind, but Stanley likewise sees other spaces as also oppressive. He says of living in a reform school, "I thought how miserable I was, always under pressure and watched and trailed. I was like a wild animal, hunted and pursued, captured and caged, punished and beaten. My life was not my own, to be lived like other boys, free and happy."[43] In writing of his time in prison, a few years later, he uses a similar rhetoric of a lack of agency and the image of a caged animal:

I was like a dog in a cage, and there had always been someone to torture me. For seven years I had been going out of one jail into another. Why? Because I was a victim of circumstances. Why couldn't I have had a kind mother, instead of a hell-cat of a stepmother; a father to teach me; a home full of comfort, where I'd gladly go instead of being in the shadow of fear of going home to eat supper. Why? Just because Fate had it in for me.[44]

Stanley is representative of the other subjects of the life histories in the series. He sees himself as a victim of circumstances, someone who just never got his opportunity. As he says as he faces the prospect of another incarceration, again for robbery, "Why couldn't the world give me an even break just once?" (134). In Stanley's mind, he doesn't make choices so much as life makes choices for him.

Stanley believes that only certain members of society are free to make choices. The strongest evocation of his perspective takes place in a poem that he includes, entitled "Life's Circumstances." In the poem he describes a world where individuals are subject to fate and are weak victims in the face of forces more powerful than they are, writing at one point, "We are nothing but straws/In this strife-swept world."[45] Relying on imagery of powerful storms and overwhelming seas that "surround" individuals, he constructs a metaphor of fate "weaving" a spider's web and "hold[ing] sway" over its "victims."[46] At the end of the poem, however, Stanley suggests that "the man with the gold" has more control over his circumstances than the poor, making clear his view that money and class status are a means toward agency.[47] Overall, the poem calls to mind some of the worst traits of American literary naturalism that work too hard to connect an impassive natural world with man's declining fate, but it also evocatively demonstrates Stanley's belief that individuals on the socioeconomic margins have little control over what happens to them. Of his own potential for success, he later writes, "As a boy in St. Charles I had gone crazy about Alger's books, and wanted to be one of his heroes and go out into the world and make a fortune honestly, but now, bah! I learned that that was a lot of poppycock. My only chance to make a fortune was to steal it."[48] Horatio Alger's stories of self-making, derived in part from Ben Franklin's notion that economic success and moral virtue are linked, offered readers the belief that the marginalized can improve their lives through wise and moral choices. However, even in this moment, when he actually seems to recognize that he is making a choice—albeit, an illegal one—Stanley still positions this as something that he *has* to do, as his "only chance." Along with his metaphors of entrapment and his insistence that he just can't catch a break, his language suggests that Stanley sees his life of crime as something he has little actual choice in. In clear contrast to what Alger suggests in those books that he seemed to enjoy so much as a child, Stanley positions crime as his only option and criminality the inevitable result of the conditions under which he grew up.

One of the central problems with individual narratives is the impulse to generalize from the particular—to treat the one story as indicative and prescriptive for all in similar situations. Shaw is quite aware of this logical fallacy and goes to great lengths to demonstrate that he is not seeking to suggest that all children in these environments will become delinquents. In the opening chapter of *The Jack-Roller*, Shaw argues that "the delinquent behavior of the child cannot be understood and examined apart from the cultural and social context in which it occurred."[49] But, he goes on to say that through the life history, "it is possible to study not only the traditions, customs, and moral standards of neighborhoods, institutions, families, gangs, and play groups, but the manner in which these cultural factors become incorporated into the behavior trends of the child."[50] While social context is a crucial element in the overall story, the personal narrative offers readers the chance to see how the individual "incorporated" those factors into his own, or, at the least, offers readers the chance to see how he believes they affected his life. Shaw points out that "it is desired that his story will reflect his own personal attitudes and interpretations, for it is just these personal factors which are so important to

the study and treatment of the case. Thus, rationalizations, fabrications, prejudices, exaggerations are quite as valuable as objective descriptions, provided,
of course that these reactions be properly identified and classified."[51] Shaw
makes clear that he is cognizant of "rationalizations, fabrications, prejudices,
and exaggerations" that each subject makes, and that their particular perspectives on their own past should not be taken at face value. Indeed, Shaw
did not merely allow the subjects of the life histories to offer their stories
unfiltered; instead he endeavored to check the subject's story against family
histories, official records of arrests, and medical and psychological reports.
Nonetheless, Shaw did not dismiss those "rationalizations, fabrications, prejudices, and exaggerations" as mere falsehoods but instead tried to recognize
their value in terms of what they revealed about the subjects' own beliefs
about their own lack of agency.

Shaw addresses the subjective viewpoint in his introduction because he is
aware of its limitations and its lack of reliability. He critiques a number of
popular criminal autobiographies published in the first decades of the twentieth century, including Jack Black's *You Can't Win* (1926) and Ernest Booth's
Stealing Through Life (1929), because they lack any evidence that would
corroborate the narrator's claims. He argues, "The value of these documents
. . . is greatly diminished because of the lack of supplementary case material which might serve as a check on the authenticity of the story and afford
a basis for a more reliable interpretation of the experiences and situations
described in the documents."[52] Shaw, like the other members of the Chicago
School, was less an editor than a social scientist who was offering these
stories as case studies that would allow readers to recognize a problem and
to see the value of the treatment he prescribed. Shaw argues that the publication of the life histories should be accompanied by family histories; medical,
psychiatric, and psychological findings; descriptions of relationships; and
"any other verifiable material which may throw light upon the personality
and actual experiences of the delinquent in question."[53] The value of all this
material, for Shaw, is in helping the reader evaluate and interpret the personal
document "more accurately."

For Shaw, to interpret "more accurately" means to understand the influence
of the environment and the ways that social ecology takes hold of an individual story. In the opening sections of each life history, wherein he lays out
the context for each particular story and how it fits into the greater scheme of
life in Chicago, Shaw presents each protagonist's choice of crime as virtually
organic, as an outgrowth of the conditions in which they found themselves.
In these sections Shaw himself not surprisingly employs the rhetoric of social
ecology that I identified in Zorbaugh and Thrasher. That rhetoric, though,
becomes a central element in the subjects' own narration of their lives, as they
similarly embrace a cause-and-effect logic tied to the ideology of the Chicago

School. For instance, the manner in which Stanley tells his story—not only rhetorically but also structurally—follows the pattern that Shaw lays out in explaining the effects of social ecology. In his narrative, Stanley privileges particular actions leading to specific consequences—such as mistreatment at home leading to leaving home and then leading to his taking up petty crime—mirroring the logic of social ecology that argues that particular conditions lead individuals to imagine only limited choices for themselves. Ultimately, the books read less as narratives and more as arguments, based on individual stories but buttressed by hard contextual evidence.

In the words of Lester Kurtz, Shaw and Burgess's work "marked the beginning of effort in the United States to construct theories of the sociology of delinquency on a foundation of empirical research."[54] In claiming that "few scholars would dispute the centrality [of their work]," Kurtz recognizes the value of this emphasis on empiricism as a correlation to the subjectivity of the life histories.[55] That approach, as I have demonstrated, was foundational to the work of Park and the leaders of the Chicago School and these books that Shaw oversaw do important work in helping us understand delinquency more complexly. Similarly, Martin Bulmer suggests that Shaw imagined the life history providing "a source of hypotheses which could then be tested by further case histories and statistical analysis. Shaw, like Ernest Burgess, saw life history and quantitative methods as complementary."[56] Bulmer goes on to say, "The life history was an impressive demonstration of the importance of social (as well as individual) factors in delinquency, in the interplay between a person's environment and that person's own individual personality."[57] The idea of complementary research—of the subjective balanced by the empirical—allowed Shaw to more clearly illustrate how multiple factors influenced the subjects' development and behavior. The environmental factors of the family and neighborhood have a deep impact on the juvenile, in the conception of Shaw, but that impact is not necessarily summative. Instead, that influence is more about what the juvenile imagines as possible and what he imagines as out of his control. The factors do not lock him into a particular fate, though they can lead him to feel that way and delimit what he imagines as options.[58] The distinction is crucial, for it allows for a type of sociological intervention that will broaden the juvenile's view of possible behavioral choices.

The self-consciousness about verifiability and the value of the life history as data that Shaw displays in the opening chapter of the first volume of this series, I have tried to show, is palpable, and yet understandable when we consider that he was a social scientist striving to demonstrate the empirical value of what reads as clearly subjective material. He knows that there are those who "seriously question its value for the purpose of scientific generalization because of its subjective and non-quantitative character." Nevertheless, he asserts, "it seems to be true that there are many aspects of delinquency which are not, for the present at least, susceptible to treatment by formal statistical methods."[59] For Shaw and the members of the Chicago School, the publication of these volumes is not to titillate or to entertain, but instead to inform and to formulate hypotheses for criminal behavior:

> Life-history data have theoretical as well as therapeutic value. They not only serve as a means of making preliminary explorations and orientations in relation to specific problems in the field of criminological research but afford a basis for the formulation of hypotheses with reference to the causal factors involved in the development of delinquent-behavior patterns. The validity of these hypotheses may in turn be tested by the comparative study of other detailed case histories and by formal methods of statistical analyses.[60]

Again, the implied idea here is that the life histories have value when they can be put to use in considering the problem at hand and developing ideas for potential treatment and solutions.

From the opening volume of the series, Shaw explicitly asserts that the value of the type of life history that he offers is "not only for research into the factors contributing to delinquent conduct, but also for the more practical purposes of social treatment."[61] Those practical purposes are twofold: individually, for the subject himself, and generally, for others who live in similar conditions. Shaw is not concerned that the subject's narrations will have little claim to objectivity (or even veracity); he writes, "it is desired that his story will reflect his own personal attitudes and interpretations, for it is just these personal factors which are so important in the study and treatment of the case."[62] The subject's perception of the events of his life and how he sequences those events will provide the professionals working with him the keys to helping him recognize potential dangers and pitfalls and ultimately make better choices. Moreover, by emphasizing that these life histories have "practical purposes for social treatment," Shaw is arguing that the stories of these individuals have the potential to point the way to changing the conditions in the very environment that held such great sway over these individuals.

When we consider the events of *The Jack-Roller* from the perspective of what it demonstrates about engaging actively in the problem of delinquency, we can recognize that Shaw's primary goal was to help Stanley change his environment, which in turn helped Stanley change his outlook. Stanley moved in with a foster home in one of the nondelinquent communities of the city, with a "family in which the relationships were sympathetic and informal."[63] Tied to this was helping Stanley make contacts with groups of young people his age in the vicinity of his new home, away from the temptations of his old neighborhood. As Shaw admits, "The development of relationships in these

conventional groups was a gradual process and entailed profound readjust-
ment of his interests and philosophy of life."[64] But these did eventually take
hold and supplant his old and more negative relationships with friends and
family. The final step was more difficult, entailing vocational guidance. Shaw
set Stanley up with a number of different job possibilities, a number of which
he did well in, but also from which he quit or was fired for behavioral issues.
Eventually, after two years, Shaw secured him a position as a salesman, at
which he was successful and satisfied. He never returned to crime and he
grew to become a well-adjusted, contributing member of his community with
a job and a wife and children. The intervention was timely and it was successful. Shaw's theorizing of the disorganization in Stanley's life as the cause of
his worldview led him to place Stanley in an environment with stronger and
more stable social codes and behaviors. Changing Stanley's environment, at
least as presented in *The Jack-Roller*, was essential to his transition to a more
conventional and successful life.

Of course, things do not always go so well. In his summary of Sidney's
story, in *The Natural History of a Delinquent Career*, Shaw writes that
because he lived in one of the "most deteriorated and disorganized sections" of Chicago, "Sidney had very little access to the cultural heritages of
conventional society and he was not subject to the constructive and restrain-
ing influences which surround the child in the more highly integrated and
conventional residential neighborhoods of the city."[65] Starting at about six
years old, Sidney palled around with older boys, skipping school and engaging in petty theft. As he grew up he consistently aligned himself with older
boys in gangs and took active part in their crimes, especially with shoplifting
and robbery. Eventually, he advanced to greater instances of burglary and
finally to rape. Although he had a long arrest record and a history in reform
schools and detention homes, he became a violent and dangerous criminal.
Shaw notes that "the usual formal methods of treatment—special supervision,
probation, repeated incarcerations in correctional institutions, and parole—
failed to check the development of Sidney's career in delinquency," but he
argues that there was never "any definite attempt to understand the nature
of Sidney's delinquency or to formulate a plan of treatment adapted to his
particular needs."[66]

The book itself, then, operates as a call for greater engagement in treating
the problem, for a greater focus on the conditions that led to the behavior
and not the symptoms or result of that problem, that is, delinquency and ultimately violent crime. In Shaw's mind and in the minds of the other researchers and writers within the Chicago School, the treatment should focus not
on the reformatory institution or the prison but instead on the environmental
factors that have such a great influence on the individuals and lead them into
their criminal behavior. Intervention, on an institutional or societal or even

individual level, has the potential to lead to improved conditions and greater options (either real or even imagined) for the people who live in those conditions. Through these books and through his research, Shaw sought to provide the inspiration and motivation for local residents, groups, and governments to acknowledge and begin to develop solutions for the social problems of their neighborhoods. Moving from identification of the environmental factors that lead children astray to the desire to resolve or at least to mitigate them, Shaw described potential treatment and intervention that could move individuals from contingency to agency. This remains, in many ways, his great achievement.

In articulating the impact of conditions on individuals, the Chicago School appeared to embrace an environmental determinism that was, ultimately, more complex than it first appeared. For these scholars, that "determinism" was neither totalizing nor nullifying of agency. Instead, what the theory of social ecology posited was that conditions led particular individuals to the perception of limited options. This is distinct from whether those options were indeed circumscribed. The belief that they were was powerful enough, as we can see with some of the life histories that Shaw published. Indeed, a primary representation of that belief was Stanley's overwrought poem of an indifferent and cold natural world that crushes its "victims" similarly to how social forces crush the powerless. The Chicago School did not ascribe that type of power to the environment of urban Chicago and they did not argue that conditions dictated a criminal future for those that lived there, but they did detail the correlations between conditions and crime. Moreover, they advocated for an active intervention that focused on those conditions that led to those perceptions of limited agency and an intervention that would help those individuals recognize their own ability to make healthy choices. In so doing, they did not solve the problem of juvenile delinquency, nor those of urban blight and crime within the American city. However, they did articulate a theory of criminality that suggested that, if the individual was making poor choices, perhaps we can help him to make better ones? That maybe this isn't fate or fortune, but something we can engage and improve upon?

The Chicago School's endorsement of engaged responses to social conditions was echoed in a number of popular crime narratives in the early decades of the twentieth century in the United States. Foremost among these are the gangster films from the late 1930s and early 1940s that focused on the issues of juvenile delinquency. The "Golden Age" of gangster films took place more in the late 1920s and early 1930s and included such films as *Scarface* and *Little Caesar*. These films proved to be powerful learning opportunities for a number of iconic actors and directors, including James Cagney, Humphrey Bogart, Edgar G. Robinson, Howard Hawks, and William Wellman. Following the passage of the Hays Production Code, however, gangster films in the 1930s began to focus less on the gangster and more on those seeking to capture him, as a way to more specifically promote crime as a social ill.[67] Correspondingly, audiences began to see more films with FBI and Treasury agents and actors like Cagney and Bogart began to demonstrate that they could play the good guy in these films as well as the bad guy. By the end of the decade, inspired in part by the success of the 1935 Pulitzer Prize-winning play *Dead End*, and the subsequent film in 1937 of the same name, crime films took a new turn, toward narratives that often dramatized the issues of juvenile delinquency. These films illustrate the traction within popular culture of the concept of criminality that is the highlight of the Chicago School—the concept of criminality as a choice, though one that emerges from a belief in a circumscribed agency.

Dead End and *Crime School* were the first two films starring the Dead End Kids, the cadre of actors who had performed in the original play and then moved to Hollywood. The Dead End Kids went on to star in dozens of films under this name and others, including the Little Tough Guys, the East Side Kids, and ultimately the Bowery Boys.[68] Some of these films enjoyed commercial success, others less so. The group was predated by the collection of children known as Our Gang—or the Little Rascals—who had starred in over 200 short films between the early 1920s and early 1940s.[69] Whereas the Our Gang films were almost always comedic, starring a diverse group of boys and girls, the Dead End Kids began as actors in serious dramas—although over time they moved from characterizations of streetwise young toughs toward characters who were tough only as a veneer, but were essentially likable and posed little danger toward society. Although the Our Gang films had helped establish a market for films that showed children in a naturalistic—if comedic—light, the films with the Dead End Kids demonstrated that there was a market for films that examined the more serious plight at kids at risk in difficult urban situations.[70]

Perhaps their most well-known film was *Angels with Dirty Faces*, starring Jimmy Cagney, Humphrey Bogart, and Pat O'Brien, which focuses on the rise of Rocky Sullivan from petty thief to big-time player in the city crime syndicate.[71] Much of the film juxtaposes Rocky's criminal enterprises with scenes of his interaction with old neighborhood friends and a group of young men who idolize him. Rocky serves as a mentor for these young men, often frustratingly so for Father Jerry Connolly, the local parish priest who is hoping to inspire them to move away from the temptations of crime. Father Connolly is also an old friend of Rocky. Indeed, Jerry was with him when Rocky was first arrested and placed in reform school. Director Michael Curtiz offers a damning montage at that moment in the film, showing Rocky's ensuing fall into crime—from petty larceny to assault and battery to arrests for bootlegging and eventually manslaughter, with corresponding stays in the state reformatory and eventually the state penitentiary. This montage illustrates what Rocky's girlfriend, Laury, says to Father Connolly late in the film, "It's not his fault, Father. He was just a kid who made a mistake and got sent to reform school. They made a criminal out of him. But he's not bad, not really bad. You know that." He responds, "I'm not blaming Rocky for what he is today. But for the grace of God there go I."[72]

Rocky has little opportunity to learn any other way of life; his institutionalization led to him learning more about crime and limited his ability to imagine that he could create a future outside of it. In *Inventing the Public Enemy*, his excellent study of the gangster in American culture, David Ruth writes of *Angels with Dirty Faces* (along with *Dead End Kids*), that these films "inverted genre conventions and explored the environmental roots of criminality. These sympathetic portrayals of helpless men and women caught up in circumstances beyond their control perhaps offered consolation to audiences struggling with the incomprehensible forces of an economy in chaos."[73] The film repeatedly illustrates Rocky's loyalty, generosity, and sense of community spirit, while at the same time suggesting that events have conspired against his locating any possibility for a life within legal boundaries. Rocky's circumscription, in fact, becomes the very means through which Father Connolly seeks to help the neighborhood kids move toward a different model of success.

The young gang—played by the Dead End Kids—admire Rocky and treat him as a hero. After Rocky is arrested for murder near the end of the film, Curtiz employs another revealing montage that illustrates how the kids see their mentor. In a series of clips, Curtiz shows the boys reading newspaper headlines and stories about Rocky and making such comments as, "That dope of a governor is so scared of Rocky he's appointing a special prosecutor," "They can't build no house that will hold Rocky," and eventually "He'll show those mugs how to die in a big way." Throughout Rocky's arrest, conviction, and sentencing, the boys remain loyal to him. Perhaps it's not surprising, considering that Rocky offers a charismatic model—he dresses well, hangs around nightclubs, garners press attention, and seems rather invincible to them. After they help him, he presents them with a wad of money as thanks. They promptly skip a planned basketball outing with Father Connolly and buy flashy suits and head to a poolroom to play pool and bet on shots, mimicking Rocky. Father Connolly finds them there and asks them, "What makes you think that hanging around poolrooms spending this kind of money with a lot of hoodlums is going to get you anything but jail?" And that is what is at stake in this film—the future of these kids (See Figure 3.3.).

The film sets up two contrasting models of behavior for them, one represented by Father Connolly and the other by Rocky. But Rocky is not a stock character. He has a number of good qualities and he wants to support Father

Figure 3.3 Jimmy Cagney as Rocky Sullivan, along with the Dead End Kids, in *Angels with Dirty Faces*. *Source*: Curtiz, Michael. 1938. *Angels with Dirty Faces*. United States: Warner Brothers.

Connolly in his endeavors in the neighborhood. He tries to give him money, anonymously, for a new youth recreation center, but Father Connolly rejects it. In doing so he articulates the terms of the battle:

> Supposing I take the money, kid myself that it's a means to an end. But it isn't. Never will be. Inside the center, the boys will be clean and outside they'll be surrounded by the same rotten corruption, crime, and criminals. Yes, yourself included. Criminals on all sides for my boys to look up to and revere and respect and admire and imitate. What earthly good is it for me to teach that honesty is the best policy when all around they see dishonesty is the better policy? The hoodlum or gangster is looked up to with the same respect or the popular hero. . . . Yes, you have my boys too. Whatever I teach them, you show me up. You show them the easiest way. The quickest way is with a racket or a gun. . . . Soapy and those kids, give them a break, will you? Don't offer them any more money. Don't encourage them to admire you.

Father Connolly wants the recreation center so that he can reach out to these boys and others like them, kids who need positive mentors who can model good decision-making and the type of behavior and choices that will lead to success. Yet, at the same time, Father Connolly is not naïve. He realizes that, to many kids, crime appears to offer a viable means to success. He wants to find a way to save them from the type of choices that will lead them down this path. It's too late to do this for Rocky, he's well aware. He says at one point, "I'd do anything for [Rocky], anything in the world to help him. I'd give my life if I thought it'd do any good. But it wouldn't. You see, there's all those other kids, hundreds of them, in the streets and bad environments who I don't want to see grow up like Rocky did. I can't sacrifice them for Rocky. You see, they have lives too. I can't throw them away, I can't." The system that was meant to reform Rocky made a career criminal out of him. Instead of institutionalizing kids in that system and seeing the same thing happen to them, Father Connolly wants to create a new possibility, outside of crime and outside of the current system meant to deter crime.

For Jerry, the intervention that "saved him" came after Rocky's original arrest. While Rocky was placed in reform school, Jerry moved in a different direction, ultimately becoming a priest. He is not looking to convince the kids to become priests, of course, but rather he is suggesting that there may be other institutions that can offer young men guidance. For him, it was the church. He hopes in this case that it can be the recreation center and a reformed city where the criminal syndicate does not control business or the government. Whereas Rocky could not locate other models or imagine other options once he was placed in reform school, Jerry could and he wants the present-day kids to recognize that there are other paths to success. This all comes to a head when he visits Rocky on death row, as Rocky awaits his execution. While Rocky plans to die courageously, showing everyone that he is not afraid, Jerry asks him to do something selfless—to pretend to be scared so that the kids ultimately see him as a failed model and will turn in a different direction.

> I want you to let them down. You see, you've been a hero to those kids and hundreds of others all through your life. And now you're going to be a glorified hero in death and I want to prevent that, Rocky. They've got to despise your memory. They've got to be ashamed of you. . . . I know what I'm asking. And the reason I'm asking is because being kids together sort of gave me the idea that you might like to join hands with me and save some of those other boys from ending up here, thousands of hero-worshipping kids all over the country. . . . I can't reach all of those boys, it's impossible to do without your help, Rocky.

The fulfillment of Jerry's intervention can only happen if the boys back in the neighborhood and the "thousands of hero-worshipping kids all over the country" reject Rocky and other criminals as viable models. In this meta-moment, Father Connolly is speaking not only to Rocky but also to all of the other filmic representations of criminals, the characters portrayed in so many films by Cagney, Bogart, Robinson, Paul Muni, and others.[74] While the Hays Code had legislated a particular type of representation of criminality, *Angels with Dirty Faces* does something much deeper—it calls for a verisimilitude in the representation of criminality, arguing that films need to stop glorifying crime as a likely path to success and to stop representing it as the only available option that is available for young men like the Dead End Kids.[75]

Rocky, in the end, accedes to Father Connolly's wish, pretending to be scared as he is executed, and Father Connolly returns to the crestfallen boys at the end and leads them to the recreation center.[76] Although Rocky had not been able to pursue other options outside of crime once he was placed in the system, he does realize that he has the ability to enable others to imagine something else, as Jerry has asked of him. The film, while ostensibly a story strictly about what happens to Rocky, is ultimately focused on what might happen to these other children—these potential angels with dirty faces—and what they might become. The film dramatizes the questions of Shaw and Park and others in the Chicago School: how can we help young men avoid the same fate as Rocky (and Stanley and Sidney and others)?[77] It ends on an optimistic note, suggesting that environmental determinism need not be a fait accompli, that juvenile delinquency does not necessarily lead only to a lifetime of criminality, that positive intervention can play a seminal role in helping these young men recognize different and better choices, and that their lives are redeemable.

The same year that *Angels with Dirty Faces* came out, 1938, also saw the premiere of another film about juvenile delinquents, a film that garnered even greater commercial and critical success: *Boys Town*, with which I began this chapter, with Spencer Tracy portraying Father Flanagan, the priest who founded the actual Boys Town in Nebraska. Tracy's Father Flanagan is rhetorically quite similar to O'Brien's Father Connolly: both of them articulate a clear faith that young men can make good choices given the opportunity and the proper conditions. Flanagan's repeated mantra—"There's no such thing as a bad boy, I'm sure of that"—is an articulation of his belief that everyone has the potential to make good decisions. He takes it as his personal mission to help the juvenile delinquents he works with to realize that they have choices and to imagine the value in choosing healthy ones. In this film, unlike in *Angels with Dirty Faces*, the issue at stake in the narrative has less to do with proper role models and more to do with empowering the young men. Through Father Flanagan's intervention, the boys learn how to be successful citizens who contribute to their communities.

The film highlights his motivation in the opening scene, when Father Flanagan visits Dan Farrow on death row as he waits for his execution. They are joined in the cell by the judge, a reporter, and the warden, who says that

Farrow "wants to admit his debt to the state." Farrow, though, rejects this rhetoric:

> Is that what all this is about? You're gonna take my life because I owe the state something? When I was a kid, twelve years old, my mother died. Did I go on the cuff to the state for the gutters I slept in, is that it? . . . Where was the state when a lonely, starving kid cried himself to sleep in a flophouse with a bunch of drunks, tramps, and hobos? Is that when this debt started? The only pals I had were the kids in the alley. I had to be tough to string along. Just before we got out of the state's arms, the reformatory, we made up a gang—six of us, and pals. We bet our lives across the board and we let them ride. . . . Get this. One friend. One friend when I was twelve years old and I don't stand here like this.[78]

Farrow's rejection of a "debt" is powerfully—if a bit melodramatically—stated here. What type of debt do these figures imagine he owes? As he says at one point, "when I went in [to the reformatory] copping a loaf of bread was the job, when I came out I could rob a bank." As with Rocky Sullivan, as with so many juvenile delinquents, Dan Farrow's criminality is a product of the reformatory. The very institution designed to punish him for his first misdeeds and to reform his bad behavior instead taught him that he has few options in life other than crime.

Farrow's speech haunts Father Flanagan as he returns from the execution. As he sits on the train, he hears Farrow's words repeated in his head, "Twelve years old. One friend. Starving kid. Never had a chance. Reformatory." These are the words that, upon his return home, drive him to come up with a different type of intervention than what the state has offered boys like Farrow at age twelve. Upon his return home, Flanagan witnesses a wild street melee among a group of children. The brawl quickly gets out of control and the police arrive to clean the scene up, though not before one of the children breaks Mr. Morris's store window. Father Flanagan heads back to the refuge he runs for homeless men. He tells the men that it was too late for him to help Dan Farrow. He continues, "I guess it's too late to do very much for you. I'm afraid you're satisfied with something to eat and a place to sleep." Instead he decides to put his energies into helping a group of boys who have no home, boys like Tommy and Skinny, whose mother isn't present in their lives in any way. In court, he notes, "Your honor, these boys were arrested this morning. It's now 3:30. Has anybody come forward to say one good word for them? Father, mother, uncle, sister, anybody?" He argues that rather than sending the boys to the reformatory, the judge should "place them in my charge. I'll give them a home, I'll see to their schooling, and I'll guarantee their good conduct." With the permission of the judge and his bishop, he sets up a residential home for these boys and begins to take in others as well. He has a new mission—to give these boys a chance before they grow into the older men "satisfied with something to eat and a place to sleep."

He founds "Father Flanagan's Home for Boys" for five boys and then brings in more—ten, twenty, fifty—before he realizes he needs to create a much larger institution, a virtual town where the boys can live and thrive. He buys 200 acres where he can build a town with "gardens, dormitories, a gymnasium, classrooms." His intention is to offer these boys a different path than that of the streets or the justice system, an alternative institution to the reformatory that is detailed in the life histories of the Chicago School or the one that taught Rocky Sullivan how to become a career criminal.[79] He wants to empower them by creating a "town for boys, run by boys." There they can learn how to make proper, healthy, life-affirming decisions that benefit themselves and others in their community. There, they can have, as he tells Mr. Morris, "the chance to live a nice, decent life out in the open where they belong."[80]

Twice in the film, Father Flanagan sits down with the major publisher in the town, Mr. Hargraves, to discuss his efforts and those conversations provide the context for much of the issues at play in the establishment of Boys Town. Hargraves tells Flanagan, "There's a feeling in official circles that you're setting up a tacit criticism of things as they are . . . [and] boys like that get their chances in institutions." Flanagan agrees with the idea that his is a criticism of the current institutionalization of the delinquents but fiercely contends that Hargraves is ignoring the evidence of what happens to young boys put into those institutions that Hargraves supports: "You have a string of newspapers. You get reports on human derelicts, you know the percentage of boys who survive institutions. You must know, you above all men. And you have no right to hinder me in helping children!" As Father Flanagan sees it, the state has failed in helping children and his approach is successful, as he repeatedly tells those who doubt him and his methods. And, again, at the heart of this position is his belief that "there is no such thing as a bad boy." Rather than condemning and punishing these boys, he is suggesting, we need only offer them an alternative to the choices they have been making and they will make better decisions. "One friend," Dan Farrow suggested, was all he needed. Father Flanagan vows to be that friend.

Flanagan appeals to private citizens and businesses for financial support for his work with the argument that what they spend to help him will be actually be less than what they would lose should these boys evolve into full-fledged criminals in their community. His goal is to help the boys grow instead into "useful" citizens who can contribute to their communities. He states at one point that "every boy who becomes a good American citizen is worth $10,000 to the state. That's a fact. I have good authority for it." Good citizens pay taxes, they create jobs, they participate in the working of the government and private industry. Criminals cost private citizens and cost the state when it comes to institutionalizing them in reformatories or jails. Father Flanagan makes an economic argument here that is persuasive to many in the film, but there are ideological undertones to what he does as well. His work suggests that the boys can change, that they are not necessarily fated to a life of crime based on poor early decisions or because of the conditions in which they were raised. Changing those conditions can lead to better behavior. Intervention has value and merely institutionalizing juvenile delinquents is not the type of intervention that leads to changed behavior, as Dan Farrow pointed out at the beginning of the film.

In his speeches and actions, Father Flanagan parallels the work of Shaw, who advocated for an intervention that sought to change the conditions that led to juvenile delinquency as opposed to an intervention that amounted punishing bad choices. At Boys Town, the boys themselves determine how the town operates. They do the actual construction of the buildings, plant the gardens, teach classes, oversee the local branch of the post office, play baseball games, and even elect a mayor. There is work to do and a town to run and Father Flanagan gives them the autonomy to make decisions about what they want to do individually and as a community. They operate on the honor system, which demonstrates to them the value of their word and their reputation. This system is a tremendous success, in that the boys learn what it means to be a good and useful citizen. They can then take those lessons with them after they leave and repatriate into the broader community outside of Boys Town. Their daily commitments to making the town work in big and small ways—from sweeping floors and serving breakfast to overseeing a budget and determining future directions for the town—the boys come to recognize the level of their own agency and they learn how to utilize that agency to make smart, healthy, and wise decisions.

The conflict that pushes the film's narrative forward takes shape in the story of Whitey Marsh, a young delinquent portrayed by Mickey Rooney. Whitey looks up to his brother, Joe Marsh, who is a gang leader, and he tries to emulate Joe as much as possible. When we first meet him, he is running a card game and taking money off of a group of compatriots. Joe has been arrested and has asked to meet Father Flanagan before he goes to jail. In the meeting, Joe tells Father Flanagan that Whitey isn't cut out for crime, that he just isn't tough enough for a criminal career. Joe wants him to go to Boys Town so that he can straighten out and he sends Father Flanagan to collect Whitey and take him in. Whitey resists Father Flanagan and the ethos of Boys Town, though. Instead of cooperating with others, he tries to manipulate and control them. He's a hard case and he makes things difficult for many of the other boys, let alone for Father Flanagan, who has taken on Whitey as a special project. He's not interested in the alternative that Father Flanagan's intervention offers. He seems unable—or unwilling—to learn how to put his own agency to good use. He has no real friends. By trying to manipulate the other kids, Whitey exerts control but to what end? He is only imagining his options to be about mastering a situation and taking advantage of others. He does not know how to be in a moment where he isn't trying to work some sort of scheme. This comes to a head when he meets up with Joe after Joe escapes and robs a bank. Whitey is shot during the robbery and resists giving away his brother to the authorities. Instead, he steals away and joins Joe and his confederates, who then turn on Joe and Whitey. In this moment, Whitey realizes that he may not have had the control he had imagined and that he has put himself into a perilous situation. But all of the boys of Boys Town, along with Father Flanagan, converge on the hideout and overwhelm the bank robbers, rescuing Whitey and his brother, dramatically illustrating the power of the community that works together. The film ends, months later, with the unanimous selection of Whitey as the new mayor of Boys Town. He accepts, barely able to speak through his tears, grateful for what he has become and for what Boys Town has shown him.

Whitey comes to recognize that the choices he has been making in his life repeatedly lead him into danger. He cannot move forward until he learns to reject his brother Joe as a model and to embrace an idea of agency that is tied to responsibility and community. This is the lesson of *Boys Town*—that we do have choices and options and that the decisions we make have an impact on those around us, people we care about, people in our community. The film, like *Angels with Dirty Faces*, succinctly dramatizes the work of the Chicago School of Sociology. It locates a way—similarly to the life narratives—to humanize the theories of Park and Burgess and Shaw that suggest that social ecology has a tangible impact on the individual's chances for success. These scholars did not posit a strict environmental determinism that dictates that poor kids from difficult urban environments are doomed to failure because of social conditions. Instead, they found that those conditions lead the individual to too readily believe that he doesn't have any real options or choices other than crime as a means of getting ahead. The distinction is crucial: it's the difference between believing in a totalizing determinism and a powerful influence that can only be overcome through help and positive influences. That help is the type of intervention that Shaw advocated for and the type of intervention that the two priests in the two films offer the young men. The films suggest that these boys can make good choices if only they can recognize them as good and as positive. Indeed, if only the boys can recognize, like Stanley, that they do have agency and can actually make choices.

How much agency does an individual actually possess? This has been a fundamental question of modern American culture and the figure of the criminal has been especially useful in considering it. The members of the

Chicago School of Sociology uncovered in their research a way of thinking about criminality that was somewhat antithetical to the anthropologists and psychologists considered in the previous two chapters. To Robert Park and his students, with their belief in the power of social ecology to influence young men, the criminal was, in essence, made and not born. This framing of criminality as a by-product of environmental determinism suggests that individuals had few options to turn to in order to make ends meet or to advance socioeconomically. Moreover, the individual's perceptions of the conditions are as deeply powerful as the conditions themselves: for the juvenile delinquents discussed in this chapter, the inability to perceive alternatives in the life histories is difficult to overcome. Clifford Shaw believed he could demonstrate to young men like Stanley how to overcome the influence of negative social conditions by resituating him into a healthier environment. At first both Stanley and Sidney fail to see that they do not have to return to their old neighborhoods after their releases from the reformatory or from jail, but they do because they can't seem to imagine *not* returning there or not returning to the type of lifestyle of gambling and drinking that they partook in earlier in their lives. It is only with intervention that Stanley learns to do so. Father Flanagan's belief in the value of the juvenile delinquents that he worked with and their redemptive possibilities produces a model of criminality that emerges out of poor choices rather than inevitability. It is only with his continued support that Whitey eventually learns to move away from his older brother as a model and to embrace what is happening at Boys Town.

The previous two chapters have laid out models of criminality in the Modern age that derived from the concepts of a mitigated and contingent agency. The concept of the criminal type assumes that there is something fundamentally "wrong" with the criminal, something biological that is not within the control of the individual and ultimately deterministic.[81] And although the model of criminality that emerges from unchecked impulse holds out hope that the individual may make healthy decisions with an intervention of psychoanalysis or therapy, this model operates on the belief that this individual represents a danger without direct intervention because of something internally (in this case psychologically) "wrong" with that individual. The Chicago School's conception of social ecology and its link to criminality is different from both of these models—in the first case because it is not wholly deterministic in the same way that biological determinism is, and in the second case because it locates the source of the origin of criminality not within the individual but within the environment in which the individual lives and was raised. The value of the life histories and the juvenile delinquent films of the late 1930s is in their suggestion that an individual's perceptions of a contingent agency and limited behavioral choices might be overcome by active mentoring and the presentation of alternatives to what seems like a fated life. The interventions of Shaw—and, in the films, of Fathers Connelly and Flanagan—offer hope and a sense of possibility for individuals who before then just did not imagine a future outside of what they saw around them in their neighborhoods and communities. The success of the interventions in the life histories and in the films, however, suggests that individuals could recognize that they did actually have options.

When we imagine that individuals have choices and that they need not necessarily choose a life of crime, we also begin to imagine that those individuals need to take responsibility for the crimes they may choose to commit.[82] This is the lesson that Whitey learns in *Boys Town*, that he has a responsibility to the other kids in his community and that they have come to trust him to do the right thing not only for himself but also for them. But, of course, not everyone does do the right thing. Some people know the right thing to do but commit the crime anyway. They pursue crime of their own volition—in what we might call "of sound mind and body"—and not because they were in any way forced into it by something internally "wrong" or by external circumstances. This is something that I have yet to discuss in this book, and points me to the fourth chapter, in which I will explore the framing of criminality that represents crime as a conscious choice. The tensions between agency and contingency in the Modern age manifest themselves in the differing way of representing criminality. Whereas I have looked closely at the emergence of three of the main social sciences in the late nineteenth and early twentieth centuries and considered them through the lens of how these theorists posited criminality, I will now turn to a different way of thinking about criminality that has everything to do with choice.

NOTES

1. *Boys Town*. Dir. Norman Taurog. Perf. Spencer Tracy and Mickey Rooney. MGM, 1938. DVD.

2. The most comprehensive history of the Chicago School is Martin Bulmer's *The Chicago School of Sociology*, published in 1984 by the University of Chicago Press. Lester Kurtz's *Evaluating Chicago Sociology*, again published in 1984 by the University of Chicago Press, provides a contextualized guide to the scope and influence of the Chicago School and includes an extensive Annotated Bibliography of works published by faculty and graduate students. Finally, Robert E. L. Faris offers a more personalized portrait of the time period considered here in *Chicago Sociology, 1920–1932*, again published by the University of Chicago, in 1967.

3. For a background in the history of American Sociology, a good place to start would be two books by Roscoe C Hinkle: *Founding Theory of American Sociology, 1881–1915* (London: Routledge and Kegan Paul, 1980) and *Developments in American Sociological Theory, 1915–1950* (Albany, NY: State University of New

York Press, 1994). Also see Craig Calhoun, ed., *Sociology in America: A History* (Chicago: University of Chicago Press, 2007). For a different perspective, Stephen Turner and Jonathan Turner published a somewhat inflammatory critique of the discipline and its historical development in *The Impossible Science: An Institutional Analysis of American Sociology* (Newbury Park, CA: Sage, 1990).

4. Kurtz, Lester, *Evaluating Chicago Sociology* (Chicago: University of Chicago Press, 1984), 61.

5. Bulmer, Martin. *The Chicago School of Sociology* (Chicago: University of Chicago Press, 1984), 94.

6. Park, Robert, R. D. McKenzie, and Ernest Burgess. *The City: Suggestions for the Study of Human Nature in the Urban Environment* (Chicago: University of Chicago Press, 1925), 1–2.

7. I use the word "force" here quite consciously, to echo the sociologists' use of the word in *The City* but also to point back to terms used by the naturalists that I discussed in the second chapter. The connections in the rhetoric reveal a similar way of thinking about issues of agency and contingency between the sociologists and the naturalists, which should not come as much of a surprise in that Herbert Spencer, the noted British social scientist, is an oft-cited influence on British naturalism.

8. Park et al., *The City: Suggestions for the Study of Human Nature in the Urban Environment*, 4.

9. Park et al., *The City: Suggestions for the Study of Human Nature in the Urban Environment*, 25.

10. Park et al., *The City: Suggestions for the Study of Human Nature in the Urban Environment*, 104–105.

11. Park et al., *The City: Suggestions for the Study of Human Nature in the Urban Environment*, 111.

12. Park writes in *The City*, "Largely on the basis of the experiment which these new [social services] agencies are making, a new social science is coming into existence. Under the impetus which the social agencies have given to social investigation and social research, sociology is ceasing to be a mere philosophy and is assuming more and more the character of an empirical, if not an exact, science." Robert Park, R. D. McKenzie, and Ernest Burgess, *The City: Suggestions for the Study of Human Nature in the Urban Environment* (Chicago: University of Chicago Press, 1925), 110.

13. Wirth, Louis. *The Ghetto* (Chicago: University of Chicago Press, 1928), 288.

14. Wirth, *The Ghetto*, 287.

15. Wirth, *The Ghetto*, 287.

16. Zorbaugh, Harvey Warren. *The Gold Coast and the Slum* (Chicago: University of Chicago Press, 1929), 82.

17. Zorbaugh, *The Gold Coast and the Slum*, 82.

18. Zorbaugh, *The Gold Coast and the Slum*, 83–84.

19. Zorbaugh, *The Gold Coast and the Slum*, 151.

20. Zorbaugh, *The Gold Coast and the Slum*, 157.

21. Faris, Robert E. L. *Chicago Sociology, 1920–1932* (Chicago: University of Chicago Press, 1967), 73.

22. Thrasher, Frederic. *The Gang* (Chicago: University of Chicago Press, 1927), 487.

23. Thrasher, *The Gang*, 488.

24. Faris, *Chicago Sociology, 1920–1932*, 74.

25. Thrasher, *The Gang*, 488.

26. Lester Kurtz notes that Thrasher's book was one of the "most important early works" on social disorganization. Although some studies took issue with Thrasher's conception of how the gangs operated as a substitute for conventional social groups, other studies have lent support to his arguments. Lester Kurtz, *Evaluating Chicago Sociology* (Chicago: University of Chicago Press, 1984), 73–74.

27. Martin Bulmer writes of these books, "The life history was an impressive demonstration of the importance of social (as well as individual) factors in delinquency, in the interplay between a person's environment and that person's own individual personality." Bulmer, *The Chicago School of Sociology*, 108. In specific reference to *The Jack-Roller*, Bulmer asserts that "factors in the home and neighborhood, in delinquent and criminal groups outside and especially inside correctional and penal institutions had an influence on Stanley's attitudes and values so powerful as to control, in almost deterministic fashion, his behavior." Bulmer, *The Chicago School of Sociology*, 108.

28. Shaw, Clifford. *The Natural History of a Delinquent Career* (Chicago: University of Chicago Press, 1931), 8.

29. Shaw, *The Natural History of a Delinquent Career*, 14.

30. Shaw, *The Natural History of a Delinquent Career*, 15.

31. Their theories about the root sources of delinquency were not universally accepted, of course. For instance, some scholars and critics believed broken homes were important in causing delinquency. Clifford Shaw and Henry McKay, in *Social Factors in Juvenile Delinquency* (Washington, DC: U.S. Printing Office, 1931), found less of a correlation than previously postulated (273–284). For more on the emphasis on social disorganization as the underlying cause of delinquency, see Faris, *Chicago Sociology, 1920–1932*, 74–75 and Kurtz, *Evaluating Chicago Sociology*, 74–76.

32. Shaw, Clifford. *The Jack-Roller* (Chicago: University of Chicago Press, 1930), 14.

33. Shaw, *The Jack-Roller*, 25.

34. Shaw, *The Jack-Roller*, 164–165.

35. Shaw, *The Jack-Roller*, 165.

36. Shaw, *The Jack-Roller*, 165.

37. Shaw, *The Jack-Roller*, 193.

38. Shaw, *The Jack-Roller*, 1.

39. Shaw, *The Jack-Roller*, 3–4.

40. Shaw, *The Jack-Roller*, 3.

41. Shaw, *The Jack-Roller*, 47.

42. Shaw, *The Jack-Roller*, 49–50.

43. Shaw, *The Jack-Roller*, 72.

44. Shaw, *The Jack-Roller*, 111.

45. Shaw, *The Jack-Roller*, 81.

46. Shaw, *The Jack-Roller*, 81.
47. Shaw, *The Jack-Roller*, 81.
48. Shaw, *The Jack-Roller*, 158.
49. Shaw, *The Jack-Roller*, 7.
50. Shaw, *The Jack-Roller*, 7.
51. Shaw, *The Jack-Roller*, 3.
52. Shaw, *The Jack-Roller*, 2.
53. Shaw, *The Jack-Roller*, 2.
54. Kurtz, *Evaluating Chicago Sociology*, 74.
55. Kurtz, *Evaluating Chicago Sociology*, 74.
56. Bulmer, *The Chicago School of Sociology*, 107.
57. Bulmer, *The Chicago School of Sociology*, 108.
58. As Bulmer writes of Stanley, these factors—inside and outside the home, in institutions and in peer groups—"had an influence on Stanley's attitudes and values so powerful as to control, in almost deterministic fashion, his behavior." Bulmer's term "almost deterministic" is worth noting. See Bulmer, *The Chicago School of Sociology*, 108.
59. Shaw, *The Jack-Roller*, 21.
60. Shaw, *The Jack-Roller*, 19.
61. Shaw, *The Jack-Roller*, 1.
62. Shaw, *The Jack-Roller*, 3.
63. Shaw, *The Jack-Roller*, 166.
64. Shaw, *The Jack-Roller*, 166.
65. Shaw, *The Natural History of a Delinquent Career*, 229.
66. Shaw, *The Natural History of a Delinquent Career*, 233.
67. Most critics would agree that Robert Warshow jumpstarted the critical interest in crime or gangster films with the publication in 1948 in *Partisan Review* of "The Gangster as Tragic Hero." Early crime film studies that helped establish the field include Carlos Clarens's *Crime Movies: From Griffith to the Godfather and Beyond* (London: Secker and Warburg, 1980), Harry Hossent's *Gangster Movies: Gangsters, Hoodlums, and Tough Guys on the Screen* (London: Octopus Books, 1974), Eugene Rosow's *Born to Lose: The Gangster Film in America* (New York: Oxford University Press, 1978), and Jack Shadoian's *Dreams and Dead Ends: The American Gangster Film.* 1977 (New York: Oxford University Press, 2003). When it comes to films that explore "social ills," see *The Hollywood Social Problem Film: Madness, Despair, and Politics from the Depression to the Fifties* by Peter Roffman and Jim Purdy (Bloomington, IN: Indiana University Press, 1981).
68. The definitive history of the Dead End Kids is *The Films of The Bowery Boys* (Secaucus, NJ: Citadel Press, 1984), by David Hayes and Brent Walker.
69. For more on the Little Rascals, otherwise known as Our Gang, see Leonard Maltin and Richard W. Bann, *The Little Rascals: The Life & Times of Our Gang* (New York: Crown Publishing/Three Rivers Press: 1977, rev. 1992).
70. There has been limited critical interest in the Dead End Kids. Of special note is Pamela Wojcik's "Vernacular Modernism as Child's Play," *New German Critique* 122 (Summer 2014): 83–95. Wojcik explores the way in which the Dead End Kids'

performance of urbanism—in *Dead End, Angels with Dirty Faces*, and other films—
exposes how "the contradictions of modernity are played out through the figure of
the child . . . by balancing a kind of social miserablism with a sense of mobility,
spatial freedom, and play." See Wojcik, "Vernacular Modernism as Child's Play,"
86. Alternatively, James A. Clapp, "Growing Up Urban: The City, the Cinema, and
American Youth," *Journal of Popular Culture* 40, no. 4 (2007): 601–629, writes
briefly on *Dead End* and *Angels with Dirty Faces*, and includes a brief mention of
Boys Town. His essay is more a straightforward historical account of films that detail
the difficult status of urban youth than an argument about how those films dramatize
a particular ideology about Modernism or a prescription for battling urban conditions.

71. *Angels with Dirty Faces*. Dir. Michael Curtiz. Perf. James Cagney, Pat
O'Brien, Humphrey Bogart. Warner Brothers, 1938. DVD.

72. While acknowledging the role of environmental determinism on Rocky,
Fran Mason has a distinctly different take on the montage early in the film and
what it shows about Rocky's path. He writes that the montage "places a moral
around Rocky's criminality by showing how he has no control over his descent
into the underworld but its main importance is in the way it shows the thrilling,
pleasurable, and glamorous lifestyle that the gangster leads, creating a conflicted
image of the gangster as both a pariah and a role model to aspire to." See Mason,
Fran. *American Gangster Cinema: From 'Scarface' to 'Pulp Fiction'* (Palgrave
Macmillan, 2002), 44–45.

73. Ruth, David. *Inventing the Public Enemy: The Gangster in American Culture,
1918–1934* (Chicago: University of Chicago Press, 1996), 145.

74. There are a number of scholars who have written well on the history of film
gangsters. Two of the best are Jonathan Munby, *Public Enemies, Public Heroes:
Screening the Gangster from* Little Caesar *to* Touch of Evil (Chicago: University
of Chicago Press, 1996) and Ruth, *Inventing the Public Enemy: The Gangster in
American Culture, 1918–1934*. See also Marilyn Yaquinto, *Pump 'Em Full of Lead:
A Look at Gangsters on Film* (New York: Twayne, 1998) and Richard Maltby: "The
Spectacle of Criminality," in *Violence and American Cinema*, ed. J. David Slocum
(New York: Routledge, 2001: 117–147).

75. To compare to earlier films and to consider film representations of violence
and immorality, see Thomas Doherty, *Pre-Code Hollywood: Sex, Immorality, and
Insurrection in American Cinema, 1930–1934* (New York: Columbia University
Press, 1999).

76. In *American Gangster Cinema: From 'Scarface' to 'Pulp Fiction* (Palgrave
Macmillan, 2002), Fran Mason rejects this reading of the film altogether, labeling
Father Connolly a "hypocrite" and "manipulative person who betrays Rocky's loy-
alty for his own ends." See Mason, *American Gangster Cinema: From 'Scarface' to
'Pulp Fiction'*, 45. I would argue, however, that Mason's own analysis is undercut
by what he interprets as the appeal of the gangster's life and his insistence that
Rocky outsmarts everyone else in the film. If that were so, however, why does
he end up on death row? He claims the ending of the film—the boys' rejection of
Rocky and willingness to follow Father Connolly—is "ambiguous," but I would
suggest that this is somewhat disingenuous in its own imposed rejection of Father

Connolly's attempts to intervene positively in the fight for the boys' economic futures and directions. Mason finds Rocky to be more compelling, charismatic, and loyal than Father Connolly and wants the characters in the film to agree. That the boys go with Father Connolly at the end is an affront to him. But viewers do not get to determine how characters respond. Is the film persuasive that Father Connolly's path is better than Rocky's? I would argue yes, in that Rocky's way entails violence and danger and ultimately an early death.

77. Other critics have noted the ways in which the film dramatizes some of the central questions raised by the Chicago School. See Richard Maltby, "Why Boys Go Wrong: Gangsters, Hoodlums, and the Natural History of Delinquent Careers," in *Mob Culture: Hidden Histories of the American Gangster Film*, ed. Lee Grieveson, Esther Sonnet, and Peter Stanfield (New Brunswick, NJ: Rutgers University Press, 2005), 41–66. Maltby "examin[es] the relationship between cinematic and sociological discourses on delinquency and criminality in the 1930s" and focuses especially on the gang history of Chicago and its influence on the films of James Cagney, with most of its focus on *The Public Enemy*. See Maltby, "Why Boys Go Wrong: Gangsters, Hoodlums, and the Natural History of Delinquent Careers," 42. Frederik Byrn Køhlert likewise articulates a connection between the film and the Chicago School but he mainly focuses his argument on the appeal of the gangster to urban youth and that films about gangsters had a particular allure for such kids. For Køhlert, the gangster represented a dangerous alternative for the American Dream—a concept I will address in great detail in the next chapter. In his reading of the film, that appeal, in addition to the studios' reaction to the Hays Production Code, leads to the construction of the film's moral framework. See Frederik Byrn Køhlert, "In the Ghetto: Sociology, the Cagney Gangster, and the 'Dead End' Kids in *Angels with Dirty Faces*," *Journal of Popular Culture* 47, no. 4 (2014): 857–876.

78. *Boys Town*. Dir. Norman Taurog. Perf. Spencer Tracy and Mickey Rooney. MGM, 1938. DVD.

79. For more on the film's disregard of changing the conditions that led to the boys' delinquency, see Kenneth B. Kidd, *Making American Boys: Boyology and the Feral Tale* (Minneapolis, MN: University of Minnesota Press, 2004).

80. For more on the roots of the actual Boys Town, see Clifford Stevens, "Father Flanagan and the Founding of Boys Town: Omaha, Nebraska (1917–1925)," *American Catholic Studies* 121, no. 1 (Spring 2010): 91–97.

81. For a history of the notion of criminality originating in something "internally" wrong, see Karen Haltunnen, "The Murderer as Mental Alien," *Murder Most Foul: The Killer and the American Gothic Imagination*. I previously discussed this book in the Introduction and in the first chapter.

82. Whereas we tend to have greater sympathy for crime narratives that present situations where the individual seems to have little choice but to commit the crime, or where the individual cannot seem to imagine other possibilities. Because of the sense of mitigated circumstances, readers/viewers tend to interpret these situations more leniently.

Chapter 4

The Criminal as Self-Made Man

Near the end of F. Scott Fitzgerald's *The Great Gatsby*, Gatsby's father says of his son, "If he'd of lived, he'd of been a great man. A man like James J. Hill. He'd of helped build up the country."[1] At this point in the novel, Gatsby is dead, a victim of the wrath of the crazed George Wilson, who shot Gatsby in the mistaken belief that he had been the driver of the car that had run Wilson's wife down and killed her. Having come East to help bury his son, Gatsby's father thinks of his son—whose given name was James Gatz—on equal terms with one of the handful of men who had helped reshape the American economy in the previous fifty years. Notwithstanding the paternal pride evident in his claim of his son's destiny for greatness, this brief but significant reference to Hill—an American railroad tycoon of the late nineteenth and early twentieth century—is an especially revealing moment, for it positions Gatsby as a self-made man and suggests his equivalency to major industrialist Robber Barons such as Hill, John D. Rockefeller, and Andrew Carnegie. Perhaps such a comparison would make sense to Mr. Gatz, as his son lived on an estate on Long Island Sound; threw lavish parties for friends, acquaintances, and apparently much of the New York social scene; and had compiled a library full of books he hadn't read and two cabinets full of shirts "piled like bricks in stacks a dozen high."[2] His possessions, in other words, signified financial success made manifest through what Thorstein Veblen defined as conspicuous consumption. Nonetheless, a comparison to a Robber Baron is rather rarefied air for a front man for a bootlegging, gambling, and loansharking syndicate—which is what Gatsby was.

I am identifying this scene in *The Great Gatsby* as a key moment because it speaks to an ethos of the early twentieth century itself, one that explicitly connected business and crime. That connection works in two ways: as comparison and as a desire for emulation. The comparison positions criminals such as

133

Gatsby as individuals making conscious decisions to pursue crime as a means of socioeconomic advancement—not because of environmental factors that led to what they imagined as limited potential options but because they saw crime as a morally, ethically, and economically viable path toward success. Jay Gatsby is one of the most well-known fictional representations of this type of figure, although a number of real-life characters, such as Al Capone, embodied a similar ethos of criminality. They made a rational choice to pursue crime as their path toward self-making. Moreover, they imagined their stories as ethically legitimate (or, the writers who told their stories did) and even as inherently "American." After all, their narratives followed along similar lines as Hill, Carnegie, Rockefeller, and others who had built the United States into the global economic power that would rule the twentieth century.

Of course, the comparison between criminals and businessmen is less complimentary toward the businessmen. While criminals like Gatsby, Capone, and the Corleone family (from *The Godfather* films) would come to treat crime as a business and to operate in that realm with both efficiency and violence, the comparison to the Robber Barons also points to how those men operated in ruthless, unethical, and even criminal ways themselves. As models for men such as Gatsby, Capone, and the Corleones to emulate, the Robber Barons demonstrated the financial reward in a business philosophy that demanded success at any cost and a mind-set that the end results always justify the means of operation—even if those means are exploitative and at times even against the law. These men embraced the principles of free market capitalism and perceived business as a competition and financial success as the equivalent of winning. They were "better" at business than their competitors because they committed themselves to choices that exploited competitive advantages regardless of the ethics (or legality) of those choices.

Fitzgerald's characterization of Gatsby fits into a long narrative tradition that, at its heart, explores the choices that an individual makes to move forward on the path to socioeconomic advancement. In contrast to the crime narratives of the previous three chapters, the traditional American Dream narrative is a story of choices—of commitment, discipline, steadfastness, and a sharp eye for opportunity. The model first proffered by Benjamin Franklin had linked financial success to moral self-improvement. However, as the self-making narrative evolved culturally in the late nineteenth century, men like James J. Hill—men who were willing to do what it meant to "win" at any cost, so long as it led to the results they sought—came to serve as a new model to emulate. Fitzgerald and others recognized this cultural shift and constructed stories that illustrated a logical endpoint for this transition: gangsters imagined as businessmen, making conscious choices to purse crime as a means of accumulating wealth, unconcerned with the ethical implications of their work because—after all, as Michael Corleone would later explain—it was "not personal. It's strictly business."[3]

By the end of the nineteenth century and the beginning of the twentieth, the concept of self-making had evolved, as cultural historian John Cawelti put it in *Apostles of the Self-Made Man*, "away from the earlier balance of political, moral, religious, and economic values [as originally laid out in Franklin's *Autobiography*] and in the direction of an overriding emphasis on the pursuit and use of wealth."[4] The pursuit and use of wealth in American culture was the focus of the economist Thorstein Veblen's influential treatise, *The Theory of the Leisure Class*, published in 1899, a book that had wide influence in the early decades of the twentieth century. Veblen had grown up in Minnesota, graduated from Carleton College, and studied philosophy at Johns Hopkins and Yale, where he earned a PhD in 1884. He was not able to locate a teaching position so returned home for a number of years before entering Cornell as a graduate student, where he worked with James Laughlin. When Laughlin accepted the position to oversee the Political Economy Department at the University of Chicago in 1892, he brought Veblen with him.[5] Beginning as a fellow there, becoming an instructor a few years later, and eventually achieving the rank of assistant professor, he left Chicago and became an associate professor at Stanford before ultimately ending up as a lecturer at the University of Missouri.[6]

As John B. Parrish details in "Rise of Economics as an Academic Discipline: The Formative Years to 1900," economics became a valued social science in the American university in the last decades of the nineteenth century (although almost all of these departments were called "Political Economy" at the time, before taking on the new name in the twentieth century).[7] The first courses in the field were offered at Harvard, Yale, Johns Hopkins, and Carleton in the 1870s, with initial PhD degrees first conferred in that decade as well. Between 1880 and 1900 American universities expanded course offerings, professorships, and the number of degrees awarded at both the undergraduate and graduate levels.[8] While most departments were heavily influenced by classicists such as Adam Smith and David Ricardo, John Stuart Mill's critique of the notion of equitable wealth distribution within capitalism and Jean Baptiste Say's examination of the production, distribution, and consumption of wealth were increasingly influential as the century progressed. As economics transitioned into a social science it became less reliant on its theoretical origins and more connected to an investigation of how economies played out in actuality. Veblen's work fits well into how the discipline evolved, for his work in its early years is more descriptive than theoretical and is based on his analysis of capitalism at work in the socioeconomic dynamics of American culture. As derived from the work of Mill and Say, Veblen and other early American economists wrote specifically how wealth operated within the nineteenth and twentieth centuries.

It was while he was working and teaching at the University of Chicago that Veblen published the two books—*The Theory of the Leisure Class* and *The Theory of Business Enterprise* (1904)—on which his reputation most heavily rests. As I mentioned in the third chapter's brief history of the Department of Sociology at the University of Chicago, the institution was the epicenter of much of the most important work in the social sciences in the fin de siècle decades, and Veblen's work was among the most notable for how he thought about economics, capitalism, and wealth.

As an economist, Veblen—like many other early social scientists—was grounded in the work of Marx and Darwin. He was struck by Marx's concepts of the stages of historical economic development that were founded on superior systems replacing inferior and inefficient ones. He also was influenced by Darwinist principles of evolution and change that came through variation and predominance. Within both of these influences Veblen located a logic of development and movement toward an inevitable endpoint, which he applied to his work. A self-identified pessimist, Veblen did not equate that evolution as progress in economic terms but instead saw in capitalism a system that encouraged particular human instincts toward predation and emulation. A founder of what came later to be known as evolutionary economics, Veblen believed that economies were organized according to principles of evolution—especially as related to efficiency—that derived from social determinants outside of individual motivations.[9] Accordingly, Veblen repeatedly asserted the importance of placing economic theory in the context of social and cultural circumstances. He argued in *The Theory of the Leisure Class* that the social values privileged within capitalism were power and status and that these were directly determined by wealth.[10] If one were to look at the American economy of the nineteenth century, in its development into an Industrial Age world economic power, one can see how the rise of the Robber Barons was almost inevitable within Veblen's schema. Their embrace of accumulating wealth as a way to gain power and to assert it was wildly successful in re-shaping the American economy and in re-shaping the nation's social and cultural landscape. They were self-made men, many of them, but they did not adhere to Franklinian ideals of self-improvement through a critical examination of their moral character. They focused on wealth and what came with it as the sign of their success. Within Veblen's conception, the Robber Barons's embrace of privileging the monetary value of the end results over the ethical values associated with the methods of arriving at those results seemed as inevitable as Darwin's notion of biological evolution.

Veblen's debt to Marx and Darwin is evident in how he thinks in clearly systematic ways that privilege historical sequences and movements. His concern in this treatise is with the accumulation and use of wealth within capitalism, an economic system in which private property and the custom of ownership are central. In capitalist systems, wealth has a fundamental "utility" because the "possession of wealth confers honour; it is an invidious distinction."[11] Because wealth operates this way in the social and cultural context, bestowing status and power on those who have it, ownership and the consumption of goods distinctly signify success. In this social context, then, "the motive that lies at the root of ownership is emulation" because the accumulation of private property and wealth is the sign of success and power and emulating others' ownership becomes the means of achieving that distinction.[12]

As capitalism develops, Veblen says, "[property serves] as evidence of the prepotence of the possessor of these good over other individuals within the community. The invidious comparison now becomes primarily a comparison of the owner with the other members of the group."[13] Property, therein, becomes a "trophy of success" and with "the growth of settled industry, the possession of wealth gains in relative importance and effectiveness as a customary basis of repute and esteem."[14] Moreover, over time, property, "as distinguished from heroic or signal achievements . . . becomes the conventional basis of esteem."[15] He goes on to assert that "in order to stand well in the eyes of the community, it is necessary to come up to a certain, somewhat indefinite standard of wealth."[16] Finally, in relation to emulation and competition within the social and cultural spheres for status and power, "it is necessary, in order to his own peace of mind, that an individual should possess as large a portion of goods as others with whom he is accustomed to class himself; and it is extremely gratifying to possess something more than others."[17]

In tracing this seeming inevitability in how property and ownership are perceived over time within capitalism, Veblen's logic again derives from Marxist and Darwinist principles of historical evolution that have to do with efficiency and effectiveness within the system itself. As capitalism moves through its stages, "the power conferred by wealth also affords a motive to accumulation. . . . When [man] enters upon the predatory stage, where self-seeking in the narrower sense becomes the dominant note . . . the propensity for achievement and the repugnance to futility remain the underlying economic motive."[18] In Veblen's articulation of the development of capitalism, notions of virtue, civic-mindedness, and the communal good all are superfluous to the primary motives of the way people live, where "self-seeking" is dominant.

Veblen's *The Theory of the Leisure Class* serves as a valuable lens through which we can read a transition in American culture in the late nineteenth century regarding ideas about business and economic success. As America moved from a primarily agrarian economy to an industrial one and as the rise of monopolies and the corporatization of American business took greater hold, the primary focus of success within much of America evolved from communal to individual. Whereas John Winthrop had once preached the centrality of generosity, forgiveness, and charity as the benchmarks of success in the American Experiment, by 1900 the exemplars of success were supremely wealthy white men who exploited and abused their employees to better maximize their personal profits. In pursuit of market efficiencies that they could exploit for personal gain, these individuals privileged the accumulation of wealth over just and ethical business practices—and doing so paid off. Their means of success established an acceptance of the unethical as logical, rational, and justifiable for others to use as their path to advance socioeconomically. By the early 1920s, the meaning of success in America was in transition from a traditional notion that linked work with virtue to an "increasingly secular understanding of 'The American Dream'" that was "entirely economic and free of moral obligation."[19]

This context of success defined in economic and not moral terms provides a useful means to consider the representation of the criminal in Fitzgerald's novel, now through the lens of Veblen's *The Theory of the Leisure Class.* The association of Gatsby to Hill reveals broad cultural implications in the connections between businessmen and gangsters and between the criminal and the self-made man during the 1920s. By that time, within the self-making narrative, criminality was not imagined as a product of circumscribed possibilities but as a directed choice of agency for personal gain and advancement. Such a representation of criminality is strikingly different than those I outlined in the previous three chapters.

The origins of the American self-making narrative were not centered on the accumulation of wealth and the resulting status that one achieved through it. In his *Autobiography*, perhaps the foundational narrative of success in America, Benjamin Franklin articulated an ideology of self-making that had its roots in Puritan notions of hard work and virtue, as well as in the early capitalism of Adam Smith. Franklin lays out how he set out to make his fortune as a young man in Philadelphia while at the same time focusing on self-improvement in terms of his habits, and he suggests that the latter leads to the former. He details his attempts to improve his character, focusing on such virtues as temperance, frugality, industry, justice, and humility. He draws a strong correlation between his socioeconomic rise and his deep commitment to virtuous behavior, claiming that "in the world a Number of rich Merchants, nobility, States and Princes . . . have need of honest Instruments for the Management of their Affairs, and such being so rare, [I] have endeavored to convince young Persons, that no Qualities were so likely to make a poor Man's Fortune as those of Probity and Integrity."[20] For Franklin, hard work and the drive toward self-improvement bring with it the means to advancement.[21] Indeed, John Cawelti argues, "Franklin believed that the habit of industry and prudence . . . would create virtuous and happy people. How better stimulate men to the practice of this habit than by showing that wealth and comfort could be achieved by this means?"[22] His *Autobiography*, then, is meant to serve as a model for others for how they too can improve their status.

Implicit in Franklin's narrative and his ideology of individual success is the importance of recognizing avenues of opportunity. This is an element that Horatio Alger also endorsed in his nineteenth-century juvenile biographies of famous men such as President James Garfield and his fictional narratives of industrious young men out to make their name and fortune. Alger was a prodigious writer, whose books were invariably best sellers. His fictional bootblacks and newsboys, in such titles as *Ragged Dick*, *Strive to Succeed*, and *Struggling Upward*, find economic success and locate a respected place for themselves in society through their own hard work, diligence, and attention to opportunity. Part of that attention to opportunity, in the thinking of both Franklin and Alger, had to do with luck—finding yourself, at a propitious moment, in a situation from which you could benefit. But it also had to do with the ability to recognize opportunity and with the ability to take advantage of it. Moreover, in alignment with Franklin's linking of virtue and economic success, Alger's characters focus on moral self-improvement and achieve their success at least in part due to their honesty and good works.

When Henry Gatz relates his vision of his son to Nick Carraway in *The Great Gatsby*, he clearly means it as a lament for what his son could have been, a dream of the dazzling accomplishments he could have pulled off, if he had only had enough time. However, Fitzgerald's use of Hill does not merely serve as a suggestion of the greatness that Gatsby might have achieved; it is part of a larger narrative conception of self-making that is very much at the heart of the novel and of American culture itself, a Machiavellian schema that suggests that the means to success do not matter so much as its ultimate realization.

James J. Hill was a well-known figure to early twentieth-century Americans, especially those with roots in the Northwest or the Midwest, such as Fitzgerald. Hill was instrumental in opening up the railroad passage between the Great Lakes and the Pacific and he served as a useful model of the self-made man, having come from modest origins but eventually prospering and rising to great social and economic heights through his hard work and intelligence. At fourteen, following his father's death, Hill began working to support his family and three years later left home and settled in St. Paul, quickly finding a place there in the shipping business. Recognizing the evolving importance of transporting goods across and through the Midwest, he was fortunate enough to be in a position to take advantage of the vast economic opportunity that rail transportation offered. He embarked on a series of fortuitous and ultimately prosperous partnerships with a group of other businessmen to invest in rail transportation across the Northern Plains. By virtue of these wise alliances, he vastly increased his range of influence and power. Thereafter, Hill grew into the foremost railroad tycoon of the Northwest, and one of the leading industrialists in the country, owning and operating the Great Northern Railway, which ultimately extended from Minnesota to the Pacific Ocean (See Figure 4.1.).

Just a few years before Fitzgerald wrote *The Great Gatsby*, Joseph G. Pyle published the biography of Hill that its subject officially recognized as definitive and authorized.[23] *The Life of James J. Hill*, in two volumes, stands as a fascinating document of hagiography, presenting Hill's story as an Algeresque narrative of socioeconomic advancement from poverty to wealth and glory.[24] Pyle repeatedly stresses that Hill's achievements came as a result of his willingness to work hard, arguing that Hill reached greatness through sheer will and determination. "These two conditioning circumstances, money

JAMES J. HILL, "THE EMPIRE BUILDER"

Figure 4.1   James J. Hill. *Source:* Library of Congress, Prints & Photographs Division [reproduction number, e.g., LC-B2-1234].

and opportunity," he writes, "are external, and neither is particularly important. The real sources of success lie within: knowledge, foresight, courage,
honesty, labour."[25] Moreover, at numerous moments Pyle follows the traditional plot of the Franklinian self-making narrative. He describes Hill's
"kindness of heart," his charity, and his generosity; he claims that Hill distinguished himself with his perspicacity, his "incalculable prescience;" and he
suggests that Hill was destined for success because of his "familiarity with
conditions and the grasp of details which displayed in relation to almost every
kind of business."[26]

However, not all of his contemporaries viewed Hill as such a positive
model of the businessman.[27] For instance, the historian Frederick Lewis Allen
in *Lords of Creation*, his 1935 account of the economic expansion between
1890 and 1930, details the notorious battle over control of Northern Pacific
stock in the spring of 1901. Along with J. Pierpont Morgan, Hill sought to
fight off the attempt of E. H. Harriman to gain a foothold in the corporate
powerbase that controlled so many of the Western railroads. In their week-
long battle over the common stock, these men caused a Wall Street panic
as they cornered the market for Northern Pacific stock. Allen writes of the
aftermath of the stock fight, "The one sure victor in the battle—a battle which
from any broad social point of view, considering the railroads as public car-
riers rather than as pawns in a game of grab, appeared almost completely
senseless—was the principle of consolidation and concentration of capital.
The losers were the speculators and investors, large and small, who had been
trapped between the contending armies."[28] Allen's contemporary, Matthew
Josephson, also writes of Hill's desire to win at all costs in his 1934 history, *The Robber Barons*. The railroad tycoon, he asserts, "had no small
scruples."[29] "With his low costs, his economical planning," Josephson says
of Hill, "he was equipped to compete as mercilessly as Rockefeller in his
large-scale oil-refining. And like Rockefeller, Hill meant to 'rule or ruin.'"[30]

Though he had passed away in 1916, Hill's impact and influence certainly
still resonated in the middle of the 1920s. The reputations of the Robber
Barons, however, were decidedly mixed. Historians had chronicled their
ruthlessness in business matters from the beginning of their reign over the
American scene. Their strict adherence to the tenets of capitalism, especially
their stockpiling of and display of wealth while other Americans were suf-
fering economic hardships, illustrated that personal success achieved through
unfettered moral scruples could have serious costs for the broader community. In this regard, being a great man, "a man like James J. Hill," was
not inherently a compliment. Indeed, Pyle himself, in his biography of Hill,
reveals the perception of a link between the Robber Barons and criminality.
He writes, rather unconvincingly, "Some few people in the muck-raking
period included Mr. Hill in their general denunciation of the rich man as a

criminal ipso fact. But the public as a whole showed juster discrimination. He alone, among the very wealthy individuals of his day, was singled out for a respect revealed by unmistakable indications."[31] Further, his language in asserting that the basis of Hill's fortune, "judged by any accepted standard, is sound and above reproach," speaks most strikingly of an anxiety that the basis of his fortune might *not* be interpreted as above reproach.[32]

Matthew Josephson argues that Robber Barons such as Hill, Rockefeller, Jay Gould, and others

> were aggressive men, as were the first feudal barons; sometimes they were lawless; in important crises, nearly all of them tended to act without those established moral principles which fixed more or less the conduct of the common people of the community. At the same time, it has been noted, many of them showed volcanic energy and qualities of courage which, under another economic clime, might have fitted them for immensely useful social constructions, and rendered them glorious rather than hateful to their people.[33]

By the end of World War I, the gilded age of the Robber Barons was essentially over. Hill, Harriman, Morgan, Carnegie, and Jay Gould were all dead. Regardless of one's feelings about this small group of men, Allen writes, one must recognize "the pervasive social influence—in the broadest sense—of the financial and industrial leaders; for they largely constituted our American upper class, and their standards and ideas tended to permeate the whole population."[34] The public reception of these men in the first third of the twentieth century was, not surprisingly, complex and even contradictory. They pushed for great changes that had profound effects on the lives of many, and they gave great sums and efforts to charitable causes, but their business methods were often deeply unprincipled and selfish. The Robber Barons brought vast changes in the economy and turned the nation into a "unified industrial society"; however, they also made sure to ensure that the control of that society was, disturbingly, "lodged in the hands of a hierarchy."[35]

The recognition of this "paradox," as Josephson puts it—that these larger-than-life public figures instigated positive change but that they failed as models of moral conduct—points to the complexity of what it means to be a great man, or even what "great" might mean. As Veblen points out, within capitalism "great" is not defined in relation to one's contributions to the community or the culture as a whole but in relation to one's wealth. In an economy where status is designated to the wealthy and achievements are defined through one's property, greatness is not moral but financial and business success becomes a justification for ethical shortcuts in one's self-making narrative. Fitzgerald recognized this in *The Great Gatsby*, though he was not the only writer to do so. In the first decades of the twentieth century, in conjunction with the movement away from self-making narratives rooted in a "balance of political, moral, religious, and economic values," a number of writers composed novels that focused on businessmen who pursued success with a disregard for accepted ethical standards or legalities.[36] These novels differed from Alger's idealized portraits of plucky, ultimately well-meaning Ragged Dicks, and instead were grounded more in the tenets of Veblen's articulation of a socioeconomic marketplace wherein property and wealth served as the ultimate arbiter of worth.

In Abraham Cahan's *The Rise of David Levinsky*, published in 1917, Levinsky is a Russian Jewish immigrant living in New York City who decides to formulate his own garment manufacturing business. In the early days of this venture, he is forced to devise a number of financial "subterfuges" to keep his business solvent, including sending unsigned checks to creditors or placing them in the wrong envelope so that the payments would arrive late, but on time for him to deposit enough money in the account to cover the check. Although he admits that these "could not exactly be called honorable," he excuses them with the claim that "business honor and business dignity are often a luxury in which only those in the front ranks of success can indulge."[37] He later adopts such business "strategies" as stealing designs and undercutting pay scales that the unions had negotiated with manufacturers. He does not try to excuse these strategies, but instead identifies them as "American business ways," presenting Herbert Spencer and Darwin as his guides to life and claiming to a competitor, "The fittest survives."[38]

As a Jew, Levinsky has to operate outside of the traditional WASP avenues of access, but he still glories in any perceived connection to American business leaders. Indeed, Levinsky glories in the negative attacks in the press that he receives for his manipulations with the union, noting that "the same organ assailed the Vanderbilts, the Goulds, the Rothschilds, and by calling me a 'fleecer of labor' it placed me in their class."[39] In this coupling of the Russian Jewish clothes manufacturer and the Robber Barons, Cahan seems almost to foreshadow Fitzgerald's later yoking together of Gatsby and James J. Hill, though Cahan does not go so far as to suggest that Levinsky is actually a criminal. Instead, he dramatizes the ways in which businessmen adopt unethical means in their pursuit of success and the rhetoric of social Darwinism they use to excuse those means. Levinsky believes in his own ability to negotiate the dangers and pitfalls of modern business, as well as modern life, and he does not hesitate to follow any means necessary in order to achieve his financial objectives.[40]

In his 1912 novel, *The Financier*, Dreiser establishes his portrayal of Frank Cowperwood on a similar rhetorical foundation as Cahan, emphasizing the pursuit of individual success regardless of the moral implications. He begins *The Financier* with an exemplary moment in which Frank observes a lobster kill a squid. Extrapolating from this scene, Frank considers the logic of power:

> The incident made a great impression on him. It answered in a rough way that riddle which had been annoying him so much in the past: "How is life organized?" Things lived on each other—that was it. Lobsters lived on squids and other things. What lived on lobsters? Men, of course! Sure, that was it. And what lived on men? he asked himself. Was it other men? . . . Sure, men lived on men. Look at the slaves. They were men. That's what all this excitement was about these days. Men killing other men—negroes.
>   He went on home quite pleased with himself at his solution.[41]

Frank's perception of a ladder of mastery—culminating in his consideration of slavery—with one being lording over another, leaves little room for such things as morality, compassion, or ethics. In this formative moment, Frank decides that the universe is cold, brutal, and efficient. Dreiser ends this opening chapter with Frank thinking further of this world and his place in it, writing that "for days and weeks Frank thought of this and of the life he was tossed into, for he was already pondering on what he should be in this world and how he should get along. From seeing his father count money, he was sure he would like banking."[42] Dreiser's portrait of Cowperwood as an adolescent serves as a harbinger of the choices he makes as an adult in *The Financier*, when he engages in a series of legally questionable acts to cover burdensome loans during a financial panic. In Dreiser's follow-up novel, 1914's *The Titan*, Frank continues his financial manipulations to secure his wealth and power. Although the connection between cold, brutal efficiency and banking lacks subtlety, the correlation between violence and finance captures the rhetorical shift in formulating the concept of self-improvement as in any way connected to virtue or ethics.[43]

Extrapolating from Cahan and Dreiser, Fitzgerald was prescient in recognizing the emerging cultural figure of the gangster as businessman, a figure rhetorically derived from the varied portrayals of businessmen as ruthless, often unethical, and always results oriented. Fitzgerald's novel implies that gangsters were now linked with business and should be understood in that context. Culturally speaking, by the time of Prohibition criminality was a legitimate path to economic success in that it was an economically logical response to market conditions: wherein the government had rendered certain goods and services illegal when the demand for those goods and services continued to run apace. Bootleggers stepped in to satisfy that demand and responded to the market. It's not hard to see how some might see those men as operating as smart businessmen in recognizing an opportunity and seeking to capitalize on it. But, of course, that perspective quietly elides the reality that those "businessmen" were not only involved in bootlegging but also prostitution, gambling, stock manipulation, and countless other crimes, and that the ultimate factor in their success was just how willing they were to turn to violence and murder to get their way. After all, the alcohol business was a nasty and rough venture and you had to be willing to do anything to protect your market share.

To understand how some members of the public came to accept gangsters for the violence they perpetrated, we need to recognize how they came to treat these criminals as businessmen who were simply making choices based on sound business principles and the logic of Veblen's conception of capitalism. In a change from the past reception of criminals as a danger to society, for some Americans, crime became a culturally viable and even legitimate path toward advancement. Following a postwar recession at the start of the 1920s, the American economy climbed to newfound economic heights, with the gross national product rising nearly 40 percent. This outstanding growth was stimulated in great part by the demand for consumer products, particularly the automobile—at the start of the decade 9 million vehicles were on the road, while by 1930 there were 27 million. This demand for consumer products offered new opportunities to those who were able to take advantage of the emerging markets for goods and services. And those markets included new ones created by the Volstead Act. The Prohibition years saw an upsurge in crime directly resulting from the need to supply a demand for alcohol and other related services that continued regardless of legality. In economic terms, gangsters recognized a market that they could capitalize on and they pursued that market with little care for virtue and little hindrance from ethics. In *The Great Gatsby*, the "services" that Gatsby and Wolfsheim provide their clients remain somewhat murky, but include bootlegging, gambling, loansharking, and selling stolen bonds. Like the real-life gangsters whose deeds these characters mirrored—men such as Lucky Luciano and Legs Diamond—they met the demand for leisure activities that included drinking alcohol and the other illegal outlets such as gambling and prostitution that often went hand in hand with the market for alcohol. Their wealth demonstrated that they were highly successful in their business.[44]

Gatsby's dream was to get rich so that he could win back Daisy Fay, the debutante with whom he fell in love while waiting to be deployed overseas in World War I. Daisy did not "wait" for him, as promised, and instead she got married to the independently wealthy Tom Buchanan while Gatsby was in Europe. Without a formal education or any business connections, Gatsby embraces crime as his best opportunity for financial success. As Tom Buchanan tells Nick Carraway, rather petulantly, but with a touch of legitimacy, "A lot of these newly rich people are just big bootleggers, you know."[45] That may be true—certainly it is for Gatsby—but, as Veblen pointed out, a level of wealth brings status with it. The spoils of the gangster life grant Gatsby entrée, if not a secure foothold, into the higher echelons of society that he desperately desires. Much of upper-class New York society flocks to his mansion for his lavish parties, including, eventually, Daisy Buchanan.

Even if he is a finely dressed and good-looking dandy, Gatsby is still a gangster who serves as little more than the handsome and elegant façade for Meyer Wolfsheim's criminal enterprises. Nonetheless, he does offer a captivating example of self-making and the pursuit of the American Dream. The young James Gatz was a dreamer with bigger plans than a life of working an unsuccessful farm in the Northern Plains. Even as a young boy he had kept a daily schedule and list of General Resolves in his ragged copy of *Hopalong Cassidy*. This list for improving himself and his station—with such items as "Bath every other day" and "Read one improving book or magazine per week"—is, of course, strikingly reminiscent of the tenets set out by Ben Franklin in his *Autobiography*.[46] As a teen, James Gatz's "heart was in a constant, turbulent riot. The most grotesque and fantastic conceits haunted him in his bed at night. A universe of ineffable gaudiness spun itself out in his brain."[47] Obsessed with making a better life for himself and puffed up by these romantic dreams of greatness and future glory, he stumbles upon the figure of Dan Cody. A self-made man who had recognized an opportunity, Cody had made his fortune in Montana copper. He was "a product of the Nevada silver fields, of the Yukon, of every rush for metal since Seventy-five."[48] When James Gatz sees Cody drop anchor in the shallows along the shore of Lake Superior, he rows out to the yacht to warn him that a strong wind might endanger the boat there. To the young man, Fitzgerald writes, "that yacht represented all the beauty and glamor in the world."[49] He tells Cody that his name is Jay Gatsby and wins Cody over with his "quick, and extravagantly ambitious" personality.[50] The older man soon becomes the mentor for the younger one, who embarks on the rest of his life with a new name and a new identity.

Fitzgerald's construction of Cody emphasizes the self-making tradition so central to the novel, harkening back to autonomous and independent frontiersmen while also hinting at the new type of successful man in industrial America. The "education" that Gatsby receives from Cody—"the pioneer debauchee who during one phase of American life brought back to the eastern seaboard the savage violence of the frontier brothel and saloon"—clearly emphasizes the possibility of the American individual to realize his dreams if he is willing to do whatever it takes, including "savage violence," to attain them.[51] As John Cawelti points, by the early twentieth century, "The old ideal of the moral pursuit of wealth had been replaced by new visions of sudden and massive enrichment."[52] Cody embodies this ethos, as Fitzgerald's characterization of him as Gatsby's first mentor hints at how the mentee comes to so readily to conflate crime with business. From Cody's example, Gatsby learns to value the ends over the means, further distancing himself from his boyhood adherence to Franklin's tenets of improvement that linked virtue and monetary gain. Thus, it should not come as a surprise that the penniless Gatsby, having returned Stateside after serving his country in the war, forms a partnership with the gangster Meyer Wolfsheim: this decision is a logical extension of what he has learned from Cody and what he has learned about how to succeed in America.

The gangsters of the 1920s, as represented in the novel by Wolfsheim and Gatsby, represent a new type of entrepreneur, willing to use "savage violence" to win in the marketplace. Wolfsheim shows off his cufflinks made of human molars and tells stories of the shooting deaths of his friends. At the same time, he poses as a businessman offering to set up "a business gonnegtion."[53] Explicitly using the rhetoric of the self-making narrative, Wolfsheim says of his protégé, "I raised him up out of nothing, right out of the gutter. I saw right away he was a fine appearing gentlemanly young man and when he told me he was an Oggsford I knew I could use him good."[54] He even goes so far as to claim, when Nick asks him if he started Gatsby in business, "Start him! I made him."[55] Wolfsheim, as many critics have noted, is at least partly modeled after Arnold Rothstein. Rothstein was a well-known criminal figure in the 1920s, a gambler, bootlegger, pawnbroker, dealer of narcotics, and more.[56] He was a mainstay in the exploding world of crime that overtook New York and all of urban America in the years following the implementation of the Volstead Act in 1919. Along with Capone and Luciano and others, Rothstein occupied a dangerous world. In New York alone, more than 1,000 gangsters were killed during the 1920s. In winning the fight over the new markets created by Prohibition, Capone, Luciano, Rothstein, and select others came to emblematize the individual success story during the Roaring Twenties and rose to prominence on the front pages of the tabloid newspapers (See Figure 4.2.).

Fitzgerald places his narrative securely within this culture, referring specifically to the Herman Rosenthal murder in 1912 by placing Wolfsheim at the scene with Rosenthal before he was killed, even though Rosenthal had in fact been sitting alone.[57] Fitzgerald also has Gatsby explicitly state that Wolfsheim fixed the 1919 World Series, which was widely reputed to be the doings of Arnold Rothstein.[58] Moreover, the allusion to stolen bonds near the end of the novel recalls the Fuller-McGee trial of the mid-1920s, in which Edward Fuller and William McGee were convicted of embezzling $4 million and Rothstein and others were implicated in the scheme to steal securities and other assets.[59] Certainly Fitzgerald was well aware of the place of gangsters in the cultural imagination as he composed the novel, as critics have pointed out connections between Gatsby himself and such real-life figures

Figure 4.2   Arnold Rothstein. *Source:* Library of Congress, Prints and Photographs Division, NYWT&S Collection [reproduction number, e.g., LC-USZ62-90145].

as Max Gerlach, George Remus, and Dapper Dan Collins. That he modeled Rothstein and Gatsby after contemporary gangsters is well established.[60] In situating that modeling within the sociocultural dynamics of the 1920s, I am highlighting that, like the protagonists in most classic rags-to-riches stories, these gangsters—real and fictional—came from humble origins yet made a great deal of money. They recognized and exploited emerging markets and operated as entrepreneurs who answered the demands of their time. Some turned to crime in order to provide for the basic necessities of food, sustenance, or shelter, while others approached it as a career, stealing from local merchants, conning dupes of their money, pickpocketing visitors to the city, controlling districts in the city, and offering "protection services" to inhabitants of a neighborhood or town. Nonetheless, regardless of their intentions, these gangsters and the crimes they committed had taken on a romanticized allure that illustrated the close parallel between a particular definition of success and the lionization of great wealth in a way that was distinctly similar to how Veblen had posited it in *The Theory of the Leisure Class.*

In 1925, with *The Great Gatsby*, Fitzgerald was at the forefront of this type of characterization as he extended the novels of Dreiser and Cahan and put into dramatic form Veblen's ideas about capitalism, emulation, and the role of wealth as status signification, regardless of how that wealth was amassed. His portrayal of Gatsby gets at the complicated nuances of a man who is celebrated for his financial success but ultimately criticized for the way he achieved it. Fitzgerald was strikingly prescient in his recognition of a new type of cultural figure. Indeed, the novel provides one of the first representations of an emerging type of hero in the 1920s—the gangster as businessman. Fitzgerald recognized a shift in the culture not so much in terms of how businessmen were sometimes portrayed as criminals, for certainly that was not something new.[61] Instead, Fitzgerald recognized the deeper implications of what it might mean if the inverse were the case: if a gangster was represented as a mere businessman. Those implications, I would suggest, were captured in Henry Gatz's comment that Jay Gatsby could have been "a great man. A man like James J. Hill."

To conceive of criminality as nothing more than business not only undercuts much of the value built into creating and running a business—the production of jobs, important goods and services, and community goodwill, for instance—but it also flattens the moral and ethical wrongdoings involved in the criminal act to little more than the regular practices that businessmen and businesswomen commit every day in the workplace. Crimes serve then, culturally, more as commonplace events than the polluting, corrupting, dangerous social actions that anthropologists, psychologists, and sociologists imagined them to be. To understand crime as a form of business regularizes and legitimizes it, no longer allowing one to perceive it as outside of the accepted norms of individual behavior. Indeed, to see gangsters as businessmen is to see them as taking a rational, logical, profit-based approach to their work that derives from sound business practices, again "regularizing" crime as a valid enterprise and taking the implications of Veblen's work to its logical conclusion that if the primary objective of our economic system is the accumulation of wealth and status, then the use of crime to accumulate property is fully justifiable as long as it leads to the desired outcome. Criminality, in this conception, is not the product of forces outside of an individual's control—biological, psychological, social, or economic—but instead a conscious and rational act of agency wherein the individual chooses a criminal path as the best means toward empowerment and success.

It is through another representation of criminality that was written in the same time period, that we can perhaps best see what this looks like in practice. Like Fitzgerald's novel, Fred D. Pasley's 1930 "tell-all" biography, entitled provocatively, *Al Capone: Biography of a Self-Made Man*, offers a self-making narrative of social mobility and the rise to economic heights through the frame of presenting Capone as a gangster who is an excellent businessman. Pasley imagines Capone's story along the lines of the rags-to-riches narrative implied in the subtitle, writing early on in the book, "Coming to Chicago in 1920 an impecunious hoodlum, in 1929 [Capone] was estimated by attachés of the internal revenue service to be worth $20,000,000" (9). Moreover, Pasley lays out his vision of Capone's rise to heights in the criminal under-world of Chicago using many of the same linguistic and rhetorical tropes as the classic self-making narrative: "Poor little rich boy—the Horatio Alger lad of prohibition—the gamin from the sidewalks of New York, who made good in a Big Shot way in Chicago—General Al the Scarface, who won the war to make the world safe for public demand" (355). Regardless of the purple prose and use of irony in this summation of Capone's career, Pasley's allusion to Alger suggests that he discerns a clear connection between the gangster and the traditional American story of upward mobility.

Much of what Pasley writes follows the model that Alger had popular-ized in the nineteenth century. Pasley relates that Capone was forced early into labor and the responsibilities of adulthood, writing that he "had quit school in the fourth grade to help his parents in the struggle for existence in the slums." Learning early the ways of being street smart, Capone "had learned to prowl the streets and alleys with the sharp wits of those who begin as mischievous gamins, pillaging vegetable carts, and end as wharf rats, looting trucks and warehouses. He soon commanded respect by reason of his fighting ability and fast thinking" (17). Not only did Capone learn to adapt to the conditions of the streets to survive, he distinguished himself, the passage implies, not only through his physical exploits but also through his intelligence. In this regard, again, Pasley's framing of the story follows Alger's model. At the same time as portraying Capone within this tradi-tion, however, Pasley also recognizes that Capone's ascent in the Chicago underworld was not without its social consequences. He writes that at the height of Capone's reign over Chicago, in 1928, "there were 367 murder, 129 of which were either unsolved or the principals not apprehended. Of those arrested, 37 were acquitted, 39 received jail sentences, 16 were sent to insane asylums, 16 committed suicide, and 11 (gangster cases) were killed. There were no executions. In other words, on the 1928 record, a murderer had a 300-to-0 chance that he would not be sentenced to death in Chicago" (p. 151). Pasley bemoans the lawlessness of Capone's control of the city but he can't seem but to admire the acumen that brought Capone to his heights, valorizing him even while asserting his viciousness (See Figure 4.3.).

That valorization most often emerges from Pasley's embrace of the rags-to-riches structure for Capone's story. First comes a childhood of poverty, struggle, and adapting to the laws of the streets. Later comes an apprentice-ship and learning how best to get ahead in a challenging marketplace. Last

Figure 4.3   Al Capone's Mugshot Photo, Miami, FL 1930. *Source:* Library of Congress, Prints and Photographs Division, NYWT&S Collection [reproduction number, e.g., LC-USZ62-90145].

comes the financial rewards that are the result of adaptability, perspicacity, and guts. Central to Pasley's version is his portrayal of Capone as a business innovator, a figure who imports new ideas of efficiency and procedure into a stagnant industry, revolutionizing it through his savvy and intelligence. He writes,

> The unknown Capone of 1920, making a lowly debut into the Chicago under-world at the behest of Johnny Torrio, was ostensibly just one of the bourgeoisie; loud of dress, free of profanity; no paunch then; stout-muscled, hard-knuckled; a vulgar person; a tough baby from Five Points, New York City; bouncer and boss of the Four Deuces; Torrio's all-round handy man.

> Unheralded his coming, and considerable time was to elapse before the unsus-pecting public and authorities were to be made aware of his presence and its epochal significance. For Capone was to revolutionize crime and corruption by putting both on an efficiency basis, and to instill into a reorganized gangland firm business methods of procedure. He had served with the A.E.F. overseas in the World War and the instilling was to be with machine guns.[62]

Pasley's allusion to Capone's use of "machine guns" as the means of tak-ing control of the bootlegging, gambling, and prostitution markets posi-tions "savage violence" as not only an efficient business strategy but also as a justifiable choice. The shift in this passage in his representation of Capone—from vulgar underling who relied on his strength to astute leader who, just five or six years later, sagely reshaped the workings of his organization for maximum efficiency—speaks to a logic of self-making that is a radical shift from that of Franklin and Alger. While these two had imagined individual success as a product of education and the pursuit of a virtuous life, Pasley consciously positions Capone—a notorious gangster who embraced violence and murder as methods of business efficiency—within that same tradition of individual self-making.

However, Pasley also makes conscious nods to the evolution of that tradition by often connecting Capone to the Robber Barons and their business practices. Capone's success in dominating the illicit liquor market leads Pasley to more than once describe him as "the John D. Rockefeller of some twenty thousand anti-Volstead filling-stations."[63] Like Rockefeller, who owned both refineries and gas stations, Capone understood the value of controlling both the manufacture and sale of the product: he commanded "the sources of supply from Canada and the Florida east coast and the operations of local wildcat breweries and distilleries."[64] In summing up his organization, Pasley asserts, with seeming admiration, "Here was a supertrust operating with the efficiency of a great corporation. It had a complete auditing system, maintained by a clerical staff of twenty-five persons. There were loose-leaf ledgers, card indexes, memorandum accounts, and day-books. No item was overlooked."[65] Pasley's analysis of the organization portrays Capone as a new type of criminal who recognized the power of strong corporate procedures as a means of maximizing profit and who had recognized the importance of modern efficiencies in manufacturing and distribution and mastered them in how he conducted business. What Pasley leaves out in these moments is that "mastering" came through violence and death. While his business "practices" were therein not quite the equivalent to what the Robber Barons had done in forging their own fortunes, they were the logical next step in the historical sequence of capitalism that Veblen had identified in *The Theory of the Leisure Class*. While Capone was a vicious thug who used violence to intimidate and destroy competitors, Pasley portrays him at the same time as an astute businessman who forged control over the available markets for the services he provided, in the process gaining further wealth and stature.

Pasley's characterization of Capone's rise and his repeated associations of Capone with the tycoon Rockefeller demonstrate how the framing of gangsters as businessmen takes narrative shape. Capone's thuggery is legitimized because he took a rational, logical, profit-based approach to his work. In adopting the "sound business practices" he had learned from Rockefeller and the other Robber Barons, Capone's criminality is rhetorically "regularized" as a valid business enterprise. Indeed, if we see these texts through the lens of Veblen's economic theory, we can recognize that the interpolation of the rhetoric of self-making into the realm of the crime narrative was an inevitable next step from the representation of the Robber Barons and their own brutal business practices as an evolution of the American Dream narrative. Once again, if the primary objective of our economic system is the accumulation of wealth and status, then the use of crime to accumulate property is fully justifiable as long as it leads to the desired outcome.

During and after Prohibition, the figure of the criminal as a self-made man had a rich cultural resonance; it offered a way to imagine criminality as something that derived from choice, agency, and rationality. These were not men acting out of circumstances they could not control. Instead, they represented a type of rugged individualism that centered their own agency in their narratives. Numerous pulp writers of the later 1920s and early 1930s implemented the trope of the gangster as businessman: Donald Henderson Clarke's *Louis Beretti* (1929), W. R. Burnett's *Little Caesar* (1929), and Benjamin Appel's *Brain Guy* (1934) are three such crime narratives that closely follow the self-making model. The Warner Brothers' gangster films of the same years often also pursued the same narrative arc. Many years later, of course, in 1969, Mario Puzo would update the figure of the criminal as businessman in *The Godfather* and make famous the phrase, "It's not personal. It's strictly business." That novel sold over 9 million copies and spent over a year on the *New York Times* best seller list. However, it reached its true apogee in relation to cultural relevance and power, I would argue, with the release of Francis Ford Coppola's *The Godfather* in 1972 and *The Godfather Part II* in 1974.

The Godfather was a substantial commercial and critical success, grossing more than any other film that year and earning three Academy Awards and a historical legacy of critical appreciation. The film focuses on the later years of Vito Corleone, the titular lead character and paterfamilias of the Corleone family, and the rise of his son Michael to the same role by the film's end. *The Godfather Part II*, which skillfully weaves together flashbacks from Vito's younger life with Michael's attempts to move the family business toward legal gambling in Nevada and Cuba, was a commercial success, though not on the level of the first film.

Together the two films capture the self-making story of Vito Andolini, a young man from Sicily who, after witnessing the murders of his father, mother, and older brother, escapes and immigrates to America. Upon arrival he becomes Vito Corleone and grows up in New York. He finds work in a grocery but loses that job because the local mob boss wants his position for his own nephew. Vito has a young family and in order to provide for them accepts the invitation of two new acquaintances to join them in crimes of larceny and selling stolen goods. In his mind, these activities serve simply as a way to make money in a system that cares little for his well-being. Eventually their crimes attract the attention of that same mob boss, who insists they pay him as the price of doing business in his neighborhood. While the others agree, Vito decides to solve the problem by killing that boss and succeeding him in the local community where he garners a powerful reputation as dangerous but also fair. Eventually he consolidates more and more power and property and grows to become head of one of the Five Families of the New York City mafia. He has made his fortune as a businessman by making his fortune as a gangster.[66]

As head of the Corleone family, Vito oversees a highly successful criminal enterprise fronted by the Genco Pura Olive Oil Company. His "business" operations include loansharking, money laundering, prostitution, illegal gambling, hijacking, extortion, and any other number of illegal activities. At the heart of his business, though, is his ability to wield political influence and legal protection—the "politicians that [he carries] in his pocket like so many nickels and dimes," as one character says to him. In economic terms, Vito recognizes a market opportunity and capitalizes on it, taking advantage of a need in the marketplace and using it to secure his value. In much the same way that Pasley represents Capone's business enterprise, the *Godfather* films present the Corleones as businessmen who seek to maximize opportunities and efficiencies to succeed in the marketplace. Vito's (and later Michael's) "friendship" with these powerful public figures in the political and legal realms protects his employees and his enterprise from prosecution, a facet of his business empire that his competitors in the mafia are jealous of.

That friction comes to a head when Virgil "The Turk" Sollozzo, backed by Corleone rival Don Tattaglia, comes to Vito with an offer to form a joint enterprise to import and distribute heroin. Sollozzo seeks financing for his operation, along with the political and legal protection that only Vito can provide. In turn, Vito would receive 30 percent of the profits, with a return in the first year that would triple his $1 million cash loan to get the operation going. To prepare for the meeting Vito meets with Sonny Corleone, his eldest child and heir apparent, and Tom Hagen, the informally adopted son who acts as consigliere, or close family counselor. Sonny advocates accepting the deal, saying simply, "There's a lot of money in that white powder."[67] Tom is more forward thinking, suggesting they should do the deal not because of the profit margin but because if they don't do it one of their competitors will and that money will enrich and embolden them to buy the political power so important to the Corleones. For Tom, the opportunity cost of rejecting the deal is too high, as it has the potential to threaten the niche market that the Corleones currently control. Ultimately, though, Vito rejects Sollozzo's offer because getting into the drug business has the potential to make his "friends" with political influence uncomfortable, thereby jeopardizing the political influence and legal protection that make him powerful. Because those connections separate him from his competitors, Vito is wise enough to treat that part of his business with utmost care.

The director Francis Ford Coppola stages this scene as a business meeting with a discussion between associates about in a potential investment in a new market, followed by a face-to-face meeting with the interested partner. The deal is solely discussed in economic terms and Coppola represents the Corleones as thoughtful businessmen weighing the pros and cons of a proposal. When they meet with Sollozzo, the demeanor of all involved is cordial and respectful. There are no threats in the dialogue, no attempts to intimidate, no implications of violence. Vito's rejection of Sollozzo's proposal is respectful, polite, and presented as a logical response to what he believes the partnership would lead to—the loss of the core of his business. More than short-term gains or long-term worries, Vito values what makes the Corleone family business special. He understands the distinct nature of his business enterprise and knows how to value it. In rejecting Sollozzo's proposal, he is essentially protecting "the brand."[68]

Significantly, Coppola frames this scene as a business discussion divorced from any ethical considerations—Vito even says at one point that "it makes no difference to me how a man makes his living." Coppola presents a face-to-face meeting between two parties considering a multimillion partnership wherein they will import a product from overseas, establish a market for that product, and seek to profit from it. Missing from the scene is any consideration of the damage that heroin causes on an individual and community level and the tremendous social costs that would result from the proposal in New York and beyond. Coppola's decision to omit this element of the discussion dramatizes how the social and ethical implications of business transactions are of little import to people who imagine crime as a business and gangsters as businessmen. For men like the Corleones and Sollozzo, the money they would gain (or potentially lose) is the only consideration worth having. What is at stake here is wealth and status, not awards nor commemorations for individual achievements in good citizenship.

The reality is that Vito Corleone is a gangster and a mobster. He claims at one point, "We're not murderers," but they are. As a young man, Vito has to make a decision about his future when the mob boss, Don Fanucci, asks for a payoff to allow Vito and his associates to continue their illegal operations in his neighborhood. While the other two agree to the payoff, he decides to simply kill Fanucci, taking over the neighborhood and then raking in the protection money that others had been paying the now-dead boss. Coppola presents this murder as an effective and extremely useful business strategy. It eliminates, in a Capone-like way, the individual threatening his profit margin while also offering a way to set up the Genco Pura Olive Oil Company, to gain influence in the neighborhood, and to reap further financial rewards.[69] Vito

Figure 4.4   Al Pacino (Left) and Marlon Brando as Michael and Vito Corleone in
The Godfather. *Source:* Coppola, Francis Ford. 1972. *The Godfather.* United States:
Paramount Pictures.

recognized an opportunity for advancement and, from that point on, his ascent
is inevitable. Does it matter that he committed murder to get there? Not to him.

Indeed, Coppola presents all of Vito's criminal acts, rather tellingly, as
logical, rational choices that he makes to secure upward mobility for his family. When film producer Jack Woltz refuses to cast Johnny Fontane—Vito's
godson—in his upcoming blockbuster, Vito advocates for Johnny by sending
Tom Hagen to meet with Woltz, instructing him to "make him an offer he
can't refuse." That offer entails threatening Woltz by having one of Vito's
henchmen kill his prize stud horse and leaving its severed head in Woltz's
bed.[70] He sees himself as the head of a family business; it's just that the family's business is a vast web of criminal enterprise.

The ultimate self-making achievement, in Vito's eyes, is for the Corleones
to have standing as legitimate businessmen and positive contributors to their
community. He wanted his third son, Michael, not to be the agent of that
ascension but to be its product, but that was not to be (See Figure 4.4.). In a
tender moment, the two of them speak of Vito's disappointment in what he
wasn't able to ultimately do to help his family achieve "legitimacy" as a successful American enterprise:

> I knew that Santino was going to have to go through all this. And Fredo . . .
> Fredo was . . . sigh. . . . But I never, I never wanted this for you. I worked my
> whole life. I don't apologize to take care of my family and I refused to be a fool
> dancing on the string held by all those bigshots. I don't apologize, that's my life,

but I thought that when it was your time that you would be the one to hold the strings. Senator Corleone. Governor Corleone.

I'm not a pezzonovante [bigshot].

Well. . . . There just wasn't enough time, Michael. Wasn't enough time.

We'll get there Pop. We'll get there.

Michael was not meant to be the Don. He was the Ivy League graduate. The war hero. He was meant to be someone who did not need the crime narrative to explain his socioeconomic status. The opening sequence of the film establishes Michael as an outsider to the rest of his family—in his clothing, in his late arrival with his fiancée Kay, in how he never enters the house. Coppola repeatedly shows Vito opening the curtains of his office to look out the window, hoping to catch Michael's entrance to the wedding. The final scene of the film stages Michael now at the center of that room, with the door closing tightly against Kay, now his wife. Although Vito had imagined that his firstborn, Sonny, would be in charge, he was too hotheaded to run the business successfully. His second son, Fredo, did not have the intelligence nor the constitution to run the business. With how Coppola stages this last scene, Michael takes his rightful place, the true heir to his father in terms of his business acumen. He embraces his part of a larger family legacy—his responsibility as head of the business and head of the family. The second film, *Godfather II*, tracks in part Michael's attempts to gain a gambling license in Nevada so that he can finally make the family business legal and legitimate.

However, Michael, like his father, is ultimately a gangster who is fully willing to use violence against those who endanger the family or the business. On the day he becomes godfather to his nephew, he has all of the other heads of the Five Families murdered and then explains his strategy with a statement that invokes the language of a boardroom squabble: "Today I settle all family business." There is no irony in this declaration for Michael. To him, planning and carrying out these assassinations is equivalent to a business decision that takes care of past debts and expands the family's financial position. While there is vengeance involved—payback for the shooting of his father, the murder of his brother, and a number of betrayals for which he wants to enact punishment—Michael couches his actions as choices he has made to protect the family and strengthen the family business. In so doing, he justifies a series of horrific murders as a strategy to eliminate competition and to secure the financial footing of the family business by boldly taking control of the market. The methods to achieve his goals do not matter him, only the results. Repeatedly Michael turns to violence or even just the threat of violence to get his way. After Sollozzo orchestrates an attempt on his father's life, starting a war between the families, Michael has the opportunity to negotiate a peace with him. Instead, he kills Sollozzo. At a later moment, he intimidates a witness set to testify against him in front of a congressional hearing by bringing the witness's brother with him to the hearing room, sending a clear message that if the witness speaks against Michael he will be endangering his brother's life. The witness quickly backtracks on his testimony.

In the conversation with Michael where Vito wishes for more time to enact his plans and laments the need to thrust Michael into the role of Don, Vito explains that he has no remorse for the things that he has done "to take care of my family." He also offers a powerful image that has driven his decisions—that he "refused to be a fool dancing on the string held by all those bigshots." Vito strove always to have agency, to be able to make the decisions that *he* wanted to make, and to do what *he* thought best for the family and the business. The cost of that insistence on agency, however, is high. The Corleone narrative is a rejection of the self-making tradition laid out by Franklin and Alger.[71] Neither Vito nor Michael is invested in the idea of moral self-improvement, nor its potential connection to financial success. They have other plans.[72] The fact that they do it through criminal acts and that the films showcase those acts (as well as the rhetorical gestures toward the traditional self-making narrative that they ultimately end up rejecting) makes clear that "savage violence" is an inherent part of any American Dream story. Vito consciously chooses violence and crime as a path toward wealth and Michael continues with that strategy. He frames these choices as business decisions that have to do with the success of the family, but he is not forced into them. He makes them freely. And there is great personal cost that comes with those choices. At the end of the first film Michael has his brother-in-law killed, and therein alienates his sister from him forever. At the end of the second film he has his brother Fredo killed. Coppola's final shot of *The Godfather II* is Michael, sitting alone, isolated from everyone he once cared about.

The portrayal of criminality in *The Godfather* films, like that in *The Great Gatsby* as well as in Pasley's biography of Al Capone, is one of self-interest couched in the trappings of logical and efficient business dealings. Murder *is* personal and not strictly business. Gatsby's attempt to reclaim the woman he loves and, in the process, break up her marriage and separate her from her young daughter is a terrible thing to do. Capone running roughshod over the city of Chicago is a problem, especially with the huge increase in violent crime that his "business principles" brought. While these images of criminality demonstrate agency in a way that is fundamentally different than the portrayals I have detailed in the previous chapters, they are deeply problematic. In the first, these individuals wreak social and personal havoc all around them. But secondly, we should interrogate the cost of agency if the end product is what we see in these stories. Gatsby is murdered. Capone dies in prison. Do we truly want to end up alone like Michael Corleone, surrounded only by sycophants, all of his family either dead by his hand or else deeply afraid of him? Is that what we want control over one's life to look like? *The Godfather* films have been widely influential in the portrayal of gangsters and criminals in American popular culture, but we might want to consider why—in the era of late capitalism—it would be better to be a gangster than a regular "citizen," as Michael was identified early on in the first film. As contemporary emblems of the ideology of socioeconomic mobility that Benjamin Franklin had once tied to virtue and self-improvement, Michael Corleone and the representations of popular criminality who followed him—Tony Montana in Oliver Stone's remake of *Scarface*, Tony Soprano, Avon Barksdale, and Stringer Bell in *The Wire*—all represent a central fact of American life that Veblen seemed to recognize intuitively: the American Dream, always more myth than reality, was always and inevitably a deeply corrupt conception.

NOTES

1. Fitzgerald, F. Scott. *The Great Gatsby*. 1925 (New York: Collier, 1992), 176.

2. Fitzgerald, *The Great Gatsby*, 97.

3. *The Godfather*. Dir. Francis Ford Coppola. Perf. Marlon Brando, Al Pacino, James Caan. Paramount, 1972. DVD.

4. Cawelti, John. *Apostles of the Self-Made Man: Changing Concepts of Success in America* (Chicago: The University of Chicago Press, 1965), 169.

5. The Department of Political Economy was re-named the Department of Economics in 1925. This was the case for most Economics Departments in the decades of the late nineteenth century and early twentieth century.

6. Veblen lost his position at the University of Chicago as well as his position at Stanford due to marital and personal difficulties. His position at Missouri was a significant step down, especially for someone with his scholarly reputation, that was a direct result of those personal behavioral issues. For more on Veblen, his biography, and his work, see early Veblen biographies by Joseph Dorfman, *Thorstein Veblen and His America* (New York: Viking Press, 1934); David Reisman, *Thorstein Veblen* (New York: Charles Scribner's Sons, 1954); and John P. Diggins, *The Bard of Savagery: Thorstein Veblen and Modern Social Theory* (New York: Seabury Press, 1978). In the early 1990s two scholars wrote noteworthy volumes on Veblen: John Wood published *The Life of Thorstein Veblen and Perspectives on his Thought* (New York: Routledge, 1993) and Rick Tilman published *Thorstein Veblen and His Critics, 1891–1963: Conservative, Liberal, and Radical Perspectives* (Princeton, NJ: Princeton University Press, 1992). Lastly, Irving Louis Horowitz edited a volume on Veblen entitled *Veblen's Century: A Collective Portrait* (New Brunswick, NJ: Transaction, 2001).

7. Parrish, John B. "Rise of Economics as an Academic Discipline: The Formative Years to 1900," *The Southern Economic Journal* 34, no. 1 (July 1967): 1–16.

8. Perhaps a further useful context to this perspective might be the rise of business schools across the United States, beginning in 1881 with the Wharton School

of Business at the University of Pennsylvania and then in 1898 at the University of California and also the University of Chicago. By the mid-1920s there were dozens of business schools across the country, including undergraduate, masters, and doctoral programs. The main degrees in these programs tended to be business administration, management, and accounting, and the focus of education in these schools was teaching sound business principles and operations. They not only encouraged notions of efficiency within those business principles, but also innovation, all while advocating for an ethics to be at the heart of the business enterprise. Of course, that ethics can be challenging within an economic system such as free market capitalism.

Regardless of the moves made by the federal government in the early 1900s toward regulating some industries, the economy of the United States in the late nineteenth and early twentieth century was very much a space of product and service innovation, of exploitation of natural resources and markets, and of deep and often cutthroat competition. The fact that business schools were forming all across the country illustrates just how much cultural emphasis there was for young men (and it was of course mostly gendered as such) to go into and succeed in the business world. It served as a democratic vehicle toward socioeconomic advancement—in that it was available for all who earned admission. The approach of thinking about business principles and practices "scientifically," often through an examination of case studies, emphasized empirical thinking that could be transferred to other situations, making the education portable to the workplace following graduation. And at the heart of that approach was how to maximize profit, for profit and economic wealth were the hallmark of business success.

As a contrast, and to recall the focus of the previous three chapters, the rise of the Social Sciences—specifically in this instance of anthropology, psychology, and sociology—was not predicated on the value of creating economic wealth. Those disciplines were meant as explorations of human behavior to better understand how people operate as social beings, as individuals living in a community. The disciplines of accounting, management, and business administration have as their ends a different purpose.

9. Veblen's approach to economics is often identified as Evolutionary Economics, a term he himself coined in "Why Is Economics Not an Evolutionary Science?", *Quarterly Journal of Economics* 12, no. 3 (July 1898): 373–397. For more, see Geoffrey M. Hodgson, *The Evolution of Institutional Economics: Agency, Structure and Darwinism in American Institutionalism* (New York: Routledge, 2004).

10. Veblen's work has also been identified as a part of the field Institutional Economics. For more, see Bernard Chavance, *Institutional Economics* (New York: Routledge, 2009).

11. Veblen, Thorstein. *The Theory of the Leisure Class*. 1899 (New York: Penguin, 1994), 26.

12. Veblen, *The Theory of the Leisure Class*, 25.

13. Veblen, *The Theory of the Leisure Class*, 28.

14. Veblen, *The Theory of the Leisure Class*, 28.

15. Veblen, *The Theory of the Leisure Class*, 29.

16. Veblen, *The Theory of the Leisure Class*, 30.

17. Veblen, *The Theory of the Leisure Class*, 31.

18. Veblen, *The Theory of the Leisure Class*, 32–33.

19. Berman, Ronald. *The Great Gatsby and Modern Times* (Urbana, IL: University of Illinois Press, 1994), 178; 172–173. Berman is one of the few critics who mention Hill in their analyses of the novel. While Berman is interested in conceptions of success in the novel, he does not try to fully explore the implications of the connection between Gatsby and Hill.

20. Franklin, Benjamin. *Autobiography* (New York: Vintage, 1988), 88.

21. In *Apostles of the Self-Made Man*, John Cawelti argues that "Franklin believed that the habit of industry and prudence . . . would create virtuous and happy people. How better stimulate men to the practice of this habit than by showing that wealth and comfort could be achieved by this means?" See Cawelti, *Apostles of the Self-Made Man: Changing Concepts of Success in America*, 15.

22. Cawelti, *Apostles of the Self-Made Man: Changing Concepts of Success in America*, 15.

23. While Pyle's biography was recognized by Hill as the "authorized" one, it lacks any sense of objectivity in its portrayal of its subject. Much better are two later biographies: Albro Martin, *James J. Hill and the Opening of the Northwest* (New York: Oxford University Press, 1976) and Michael Malone, *James J. Hill: Empire Builder of the Northwest* (Norman, OK: University of Oklahoma Press, 1996).

24. Indeed, Berman draws a straight connection between Alger and the Robber Barons in terms of the recognition of opportunity for gain, even if that gain derived from illicit means. Berman writes, for instance, that the "Alger hero necessarily has a lot of Hill and Vanderbilt in him." See Berman, *The Great Gatsby and Modern Times*, 170–171. For more on Gatsby, Hill, and self-making, see Stephen Brauer, "Jay Gatsby and the Prohibition Gangster as Businessman," *The F. Scott Fitzgerald Review* 2 (2003), 51–71 and Stephen Brauer, "What Makes Him Great? Teaching The Great Gatsby and the New Historicism," *Approaches to Teaching Fitzgerald's* The Great Gatsby, Eds. Jackson R. Bryer and Nancy P. VanArsdale (New York: MLA, 2009), 84–92.

25. Pyle, Joseph G. *The Life of James J. Hill*, Vol. I and II (Garden City, NY: Doubleday, Page and Co., 1917), Vol. II, 378–379.

26. Pyle, *The Life of James J. Hill*, Vol. I, 37; 77; 180. It is this tone of "cheerleading" that led Malone, one of Hill's later biographers, to label Pyle "obsequious" in his approach to the railroad tycoon. See Malone, *James J. Hill: Empire Builder of the Northwest*, 283.

27. Pyle acknowledges the negative ways that Hill was portrayed at times in the newspapers and by contemporary critics, but he directly seeks to subvert any notions of wrongdoing. He writes, "Some few people in the muck-raking period included Mr. Hill in their general denunciation of the rich man as a criminal *ipso facto*. But the public as a whole showed juster discrimination. He alone, among the very wealthy individuals of his day, was singled out for a respect revealed by unmistakable indications" (I, 290). His attempt to defuse any sense of Hill as anything other than exemplary is telling here, for it not bespeaks a type of anxiety about the means through which Hill

accumulated his wealth, it also shows Pyle's awareness that many of Hill's wealthy contemporaries were seen as "criminals."

28. Allen, Frederick Lewis. *Lords of Creation* (New York: Harper and Brothers, 1935), 65.

29. Josephson, Matthew. *The Robber Barons: The Great American Capitalists, 1861–1901* (New York: Harcourt, Brace and Co., 1934), 236. While Allen is admirably measured in his approach to the Robber Barons, Josephson has more of the sense of the muckraker to him. However, his work was widely respected for its accuracy and attention to detail and went through numerous printings. For a truly vociferous attack on the Robber Barons from this same era, see John McConaughy, *Who Rules America?* (New York: Longmans, Green and Co., 1934).

30. Josephson, *The Robber Barons: The Great American Capitalists, 1861–1901*, 237. Michael Malone claims that Hill "was not a man to disappoint, anger or cross" and, in contrast to Pyle's portrayal of his subject, suggests that Hill was guilty of such malfeasance as corporate sabotage, collusion, and even bribery. See Malone, *James J. Hill: Empire Builder of the Northwest*, 28; 63; 127.

31. Pyle, *The Life of James J. Hill*, Vol. I, 290.

32. Pyle, *The Life of James J. Hill*, Vol. I, 292.

33. Josephson, *The Robber Barons: The Great American Capitalists, 1861–1901*, vii.

34. Allen, *Lords of Creation*, xi.

35. Josephson, *The Robber Barons: The Great American Capitalists, 1861–1901*, vii.

36. Cawelti, *Apostles of the Self-Made Man*, 169.

37. Cahan, Abraham. *The Rise of David Levinsky*. 1917 (New York: Modern Library, 2001), 232.

38. Cahan, *The Rise of David Levinsky*, 364.

39. Cahan, *The Rise of David Levinsky*, 266.

40. Critics generally agree. For a representative example, in "Money vs. *Mitzvot*: The Figure of the Businessman in Novels by American Jewish Writers," *Yiddish* 6, no. 4 (1987): 48–55, Sylvia Huberman Scholnick argues that Levinsky replaces not only traditional Jewish values but also Judaism itself "with a different belief system, the profit motive" (52).

41. Dreiser, Theodore. *The Financier*. 1912 (New York: Plume, 1988), 8–9.

42. Dreiser, *The Financier*, 9.

43. Alex Pitofsky, "Dreiser's *The Financier* and the Horatio Alger Myth," *Twentieth Century Literature* 44, no. 3 (Fall 1998): 276–290, disagrees with my critique of Dreiser's style and didacticism, arguing that in the novel Dreiser renders a "subtle and modulated representation of the interplay of commerce and ethics." See Pitofsky, "Dreiser's *The Financier* and the Horatio Alger Myth," 276.

44. Berman even goes so far as to suggest that Wolfsheim, just as much as the drastically more naïve and sheltered Henry Gatz, was a believer "in the morality of success" because he "takes it on faith that success is a matter of character and belief." See Berman, *The Great Gatsby and Modern Times*, 168. The link between Meyer Wolfsheim and Ben Franklin is wonderfully evocative.

45. Fitzgerald, *The Great Gatsby*, 114.
46. Fitzgerald, *The Great Gatsby*, 181–182.
47. Fitzgerald, *The Great Gatsby*, 105.
48. Fitzgerald, *The Great Gatsby*, 105. Philip Castille has pointed out that Cody, who by virtue of his name seems to be something of an amalgam of Daniel Boone and Buffalo Bill Cody, symbolizes a type of frontier hero to the recent college dropout, an echo of his earlier interest in Hopalong Cassidy. (Castille, "The Smuggler as Frontier Hero," *The University of Mississippi Studies in Fiction* 10 (1992): 232.) However, Joseph Corso has convincingly articulated the close resemblance of the fictional Dan Cody to the industrialist Edward Robert Gilman. (Corso, "One Not-So Forgotten Summer Night: Sources for Fictional Symbols of American Character in *The Great Gatsby*," *Fitzgerald/Hemingway Annual* 8 (1976): 9–34.) As Cody did in the novel with Gatsby, Gilman had taken on the young Robert Kerr and provided him with what Fitzgerald calls in the novel a "singularly appropriate education" (Fitzgerald, *The Great Gatsby*, 107). Castille, Corso, and Matthew Bruccoli have done important work in determining the historical sources for Cody and other characters in the novel, and their work has enabled other critics to now focus attention on the larger socioeconomic and historical dynamics implicit in the choices Fitzgerald made. (See Matthew Bruccoli, "*The Great Gatsby* as Social History," in *F. Scott Fitzgerald's* The Great Gatsby: *A Literary Reference*, ed. Bruccoli (New York: Carroll & Graf, 2000), 16–19. This is an excellent book for sources for the novel and includes selections from many of the sources cited in this chapter.)
49. Fitzgerald, *The Great Gatsby*, 106.
50. Fitzgerald, *The Great Gatsby*, 106.
51. Fitzgerald, *The Great Gatsby*, 106.
52. Fitzgerald, *The Great Gatsby*, 110.
53. Fitzgerald, *The Great Gatsby*, 75.
54. Fitzgerald, *The Great Gatsby*, 179.
55. Fitzgerald, *The Great Gatsby*, 179. A number of recent critics have noted connections between the rhetoric of self-making and the representations of criminals in the 1920s and 1930s. Jonathan Munby, for example, argues in *Public Enemies, Public Heroes*, that the cinematic gangsters of such films as *Little Caesar*, *Public Enemy*, and *Scarface*—characters based at least in part on Al Capone—"came to express the desires of the culturally and economically ghettoized in an ethnic street vernacular . . . [that] help[ed] foster the nation's collective identification with the desires of 'new' Americans for a fairer share of the American pie." See Munby, *Public Enemies, Public Heroes*, 4. The gangster figure in these films sought a successful future, like any other working-class American pursuing his version of the American Dream of moving from the margins of society to a more secure economic status. In *Inventing the Public Enemy*, his study of the urban gangster figure in the 1920s and early 1930s, David Ruth notes that in media portrayals of the gangster, the "public enemy, energetic and confident, was successful in a competitive, highly organized business. A model of stylish consumption, he wore fine clothes, rode in a gleaming automobile, and reveled in expensive nightlife." See Ruth, *Inventing the Public Enemy*, 2. What is new in this type of representation of the criminal, and what both Munby and Ruth

recognize, is the way that crime was operating as a move from the margins toward the mainstream.

56. For the fullest portrait of Rothstein, see Leo Katcher, *The Big Bankroll: The Life and Times of Arnold Rothstein* (New York: Harper, 1959).

57. For more on this incident, see Dalton H. Gross, "The Death of Rosy Rosenthal: A Note on Fitzgerald's Use of Background in *The Great Gatsby*," *Notes and Queries* 23, no. 1 (1976): 22–23.

58. Thomas Pauly has suggested that Rothstein serves not so much as a model for Wolfsheim, but for Gatsby himself. Pauly emphasizes Rothstein's conservative appearance, his ties to upper-class gamblers, and his large Long Island estate, along with Fitzgerald's notes that he had met Rothstein, to suggest that Rothstein more closely resembled Gatsby than Wolfsheim. See Thomas Pauly, "Gatsby as Gangster," *Studies in American Fiction* 21, no. 2 (Autumn 1993): 220–231.

59. For more on the trial and its relation to the novel, see Henry Dan Piper, "The Fuller-McGee Case," in *Fitzgerald's The Great Gatsby*, ed. Piper (New York: Scribner's, 1970): 171–184. Piper draws a correlation between Gatsby and Fuller himself.

60. Matthew Bruccoli, for instance, has suggested the influence of Max Gerlach, a minor bootlegger and Fitzgerald's neighbor in the summer of 1923, on Fitzgerald's creation of Gatsby and Horst Kruse has recently offered an in-depth study of this connection that has extended and reinforced Bruccoli's supposition. See Bruccoli, "How Are You and the Family Old Sport—Gerlach and Gatsby," *Fitzgerald/Hemingway Annual* (1975): 33–36. See also Bruccoli, *Some Sort of Epic Grandeur: The Life of F. Scott Fitzgerald* (New York: Harcourt Brace, 1981), 183–184. And see Horst Kruse, "The Real Jay Gatsby: Max Von Gerlach, F. Scott Fitzgerald, and the Compositional History of *The Great Gatsby*," *The Fitzgerald Review* 1 (2002): 45–83. Pauly contrasts Rothstein with Gerlach and George Remus, a successful owner of drugstores that sold alcohol and who threw lavish Gatsby-like parties at his Long Island mansion in the early 1920s, as possible models for Gatsby, suggesting that Rothstein's machinations more closely resembled the schemes that Gatsby was involved in, including the sale of stolen bonds. See Pauly, "Gatsby as Gangster," 226–229. While Pauly suggests that Gatsby was more than just a front man for Wolfsheim, he also points out striking resemblances between Gatsby and Dapper Dan Collins, Rothstein's own front man, a connection also recognized by Philip Castille. See Pauly "Gatsby as Gangster," 235 and Castille, "Jay Gatsby: The Smuggler as Frontier Hero," 231.

61. Other than Dreiser and Cahan, writers who had previously explored the criminality of businessmen include Herman Melville in *The Confidence-Man* (1857) and Frank Norris in *The Octopus* (1901) and *The Pit* (1902). In *Manhattan Transfer*, published in 1925 along with *The Great Gatsby*, John Dos Passos does offer a representation of a gangster as businessman in the character of Congo Jake. Like Gatsby, Congo is an immensely likable and charismatic figure to other characters in the novel.

62. Pasley, Fred D. *Al Capone: Biography of a Self-Made Man* (New York: Ives Washburn, 1930), 10–11.

63. Pasley, *Al Capone: Biography of a Self-Made Man*, 9; 144. Peter Baida, in *Poor Richard's Legacy*, his recent survey of American business values from Franklin

to Donald Trump, shows that Rockefeller defended his business practices—such as rebates, bribes, and price-fixing—as evolving from "the natural laws of trade," though Baida notes that many of these practices had been made illegal by the Interstate Commerce Act of 1887. "Though its critics may have exaggerated," Baida concludes, "it would be difficult to argue that Standard Oil did nothing to deserve its reputation of ruthlessness." See Baida, *Poor Richard's Legacy: American Business Values from Benjamin Franklin to Donald Trump* (New York: William Morrow, 1990), 117. For more on readings of Rockefeller and Standard Oil from an earlier perspective, see two very different texts: Allan Nevins, *John D. Rockefeller: The Heroic Age of American Enterprise* (New York: Scribner's, 1940) and Ida M. Tarbell, *History of the Standard Oil Company* (New York: Harper and Brothers, 1904). Nevins is perhaps overly sympathetic to Rockefeller, while Tarbell represents the muckraking perspective that was so bent on damning the Robber Barons.

64. Pasley, *Al Capone: Biography of a Self-Made Man*, 9.

65. Pasley, *Al Capone: Biography of a Self-Made Man*, 70.

66. Over the last twenty-five years, there have been sparse critical resources dedicated to *The Godfather* films. Carlos Clarens, *Crime Movies: From Griffith to the Godfather and Beyond* (London: Secker and Warburg, 1980) remains a touchstone for those who place the film in a tradition of crime films. In 2003, Jack Shadoian updated his 1977 classic, *Dreams and Dead Ends: The American Gangster Film* (New York: Oxford University Press, 2003). For a collection of essays specifically on the films, see Nick Browne, ed. *Francis Ford Coppola's* The Godfather Trilogy (Cambridge: Cambridge University Press, 2012).

67. *The Godfather*. Dir. Francis Ford Coppola. Perf. Marlon Brando, Al Pacino, James Caan. Paramount, 1972. DVD.

68. Coppola represents Vito first and foremost as a listener. The opening of the film positions Vito as quietly listening to Bonasera's story of his daughter's assault. In multiple scenes he likewise stages Vito as patiently listening to others talk—in the boardroom, in his office, in his bedroom as his house erupts in pain at the news of Sonny's death. Vito is perspicacious and he is able to divine what others are thinking and revealing not only in what they say but in how they say it. He rejects Bonasera's plea for justice by murder by pointing out that his daughter is not dead. He can readily tell that Tattaglia—who he calls "a pimp"—does not have the smarts to outwit Sonny to lead him to the ambush that killed him. He also recognizes that Sonny is having an adulterous affair merely by watching his son and daughter-in-law and recognizing that Sonny's absences from the family business have to do with his sexual proclivities. And he can tell that—as he says to Tom—"I never thought you were a bad consigliere. I thought Santino was a bad Don, rest in peace."

This is most explicit in the boardroom scene where the heads of the Five Families, along with representatives from across the country, convene to call a truce to the war between the Corleone and Tattaglia families. Don Barzini serves as moderator for a discussion, mainly centered on the violence, that is having an effect on all of them.

Vito first states that he has always agreed to share his political and legal protection with the others, "except for one time. And why? Because I believe this drug business is going to destroy us in the years to come." While Tattaglia would be the logical one to respond—as Sollozzo's sponsor and the rival in the war—instead it is Barzini who answers. He says, "Times have changed. It's not like the old days, where we can do anything we want. A refusal is not like the act of a friend. If Don Corleone had all of the judges and politicians in New York, then he must share them . . . he must let us draw the water from the well. Certainly he can present a bill for such services." In this moment of abandoning his role as moderator in this business meeting, Barzini reveals his own position as the one pushing for entry into narcotics. He is not impartial. He has a vested interest and is insisting that Vito relent, even under the guise of moderator acting as peacekeeper. Eventually, the leaders agree "to control [the drugs] as a business, to keep it respectable." But Vito had already known he would have to concede that in order to keep his son Michael alive from future attacks on his life. Vito's genius was to use the meeting to ferret out who his real enemy was.

69. Film critic Manohla Dargis places the film in the long history of American gangster films and sees it as an extension of the Warner Brothers' gangster films of the early 1930s. She also recognizes the correlations between crime and twentieth-century American business: "It would be truer to say that Cagney's original Public Enemy, Robinson's Little Caesar, and Pacino's reluctant don, Michael Corleone, incarnate the logic of the Free Market, only with substantially less influence than the average captain of industry—this last being precisely the identity that Michael covets and comes close to attaining by the finish of the Godfather cycle. The irony is that in the logic of the classic gangster film, violence is not irrational but rational, because it serves the gangster's needs: blood is the price of his ambitions." See "Dark Side of the Dream," *Sight and Sound* 6, no. 8 (August 1996): 15–18.

70. Near the beginning of the film, Michael tells his fiancée Kay a story about Johnny Fontane, who was an incredibly talented and popular singer who wanted out of his contract with a big band leader. Johnny appealed for Vito's help when the band leader refused his request and Vito made the big band leader "an offer he couldn't refuse" by having his associate hang him out a window by holding him at the ankles. The band leader then signed a release for Fontane's contract.

71. In contrast to my assertion that the film insists on the inherent violence built into the American Dream narrative, as seen in the late nineteenth and twentieth centuries, Gogsu Gigi Akkan asserts that the film does not embody that violence nor dramatizes it but instead rejects the self-making mythology of the American Dream. See Gogsu Gigi Akkan, "The Godfather and the American Dream," *Journal of Media Critiques* 3, no. 9 (2017): 25–32.

72. Paul Cantor sees a different dynamic at play in the films in relation to self-making and the American Dream. He argues that the dynamic has to do with a tension between "family versus business and Europe versus America (or more broadly: the Old World versus the New)." He writes:

> Devotion to one's family often comes into conflict with commitment to one's business. The demands of his business may draw a man away from his family, just as family loyalties may get in the way of business responsibilities. The Godfather films also question whether it is possible to make a smooth transition from the Old World to the New. Their

epic scale gives a wide geographic and historical scope to the films. Coppola portrays what it is to move from Europe to America and from the nineteenth century to the twentieth, and neither journey goes well for the immigrant. Carrying over Old World habits to the New may interfere with pursuing the American dream, while adapting to the fast pace of change in America can be disorienting to the Old World immigrant. The New World way of life may undermine the immigrant's Old World customs and traditions, leaving him without a moral compass. The Godfather films present America as the land of modernization, but they also raise questions about modernity as a way of life.

See Paul Cantor, *Pop Culture and the Dark Side of the American Dream* (Lexington, KY: University of Kentucky Press, 2019), 49.

Conclusion

The Crime Narrative in Late Capitalism

The film is *New Jack City*. The date is New Year's Eve. The Cash Money Brothers (CMB), a drug syndicate operating in New York City, have gathered to celebrate the New Year and to enjoy the financial successes of their business venture. Inside the spotlight, the nightclub they own and use as their headquarters, we hear the MC welcoming us to the party while the camera pans through the crowd, eventually leading us to the inner sanctum of the nightclub and the boardroom of the CMB. Their leader, Nino Brown, dressed in a bright red suit, is giving a toast at the head of a corporate table: "This is the fruit of our hard work. The belief in the entrepreneurial spirit. The New American Dream. A toast to my family. In life until death. Happy New Year. To CMB. On and on!"[1] This scene clearly illustrates how the film treats the CMB as a business operation as much as it pictures them as drug dealers. These characters see themselves not so much as criminals but as businessmen. Nino frames this gathering as one centered on family, in which they all support each other and they all profit from the company's success. His toast invokes the idea of the American Dream, with its faith in the value of hard work and entrepreneurialism. They are celebrating the vision Nino laid out in his business plan for the syndicate, and he imagines—"On and on!"—continued gains, with no real reason to doubt the value of that vision or his faith in the validity of the American Dream.

The setting is New York City and the timeframe is the late 1980s. Ronald Reagan's economic plan at the start of his administration in 1980 has led to financial rewards for free market capitalists let loose from the restrictions of government regulations. And Nino Brown is just such a man—someone with a vision, someone not afraid of risk, someone who understands the value of integration in a business context. Nino comes to the rest of the company with a plan—to produce their product and to distribute it in the same setting, radically cutting costs and maximizing profits. He is, in the words of one of his lieutenants, "a genius." He is also the biggest drug dealer in the city and a ruthless and cold-blooded killer willing to use children as shields in a gunfight. In his 1990 monograph, *Streetwise: Race, Class, and Change in an Urban Community*, sociologist Elijah Anderson identified real-life drug dealers as "young, often a product of the street gang, and at best indifferent to the law and traditional values" and this description fits Nino extremely well. [2] In his study, Anderson noted "new role models emerg[ed]" in 1980's urban American culture, men like Nino who sought to exploit urban blight within the free market system and to profit from their communities' malaise.[3] In *New Jack City*, Nino may not be a good man, but he is certainly a man of his times.

Directed by Mario Van Peebles as his feature film debut, *New Jack City* was released in March 1991 to strong reviews and went on to become the highest-grossing independent film of the year. The film focuses on the rise and fall of the CMB, a drug-dealing enterprise in the 1980s that capitalizes on the crack epidemic to reach economic heights before crashing following an extensive police investigation and prosecution. Wesley Snipes plays Nino Brown and Allen Payne is Gee Money, the two leaders of the organization. Ice-T and Judd Nelson play the two police officers heading up the investigation and Van Peebles performs the role of the lieutenant overseeing that operation. Chris Rock appears as a junkie who reforms and works with the police to try to bring the CMB down, only to suffer a relapse that leads to his death. In its portrayal of Nino Brown as a contemporary criminal who idolizes fictional gangsters such as Vito and Michael Corleone, the film makes conscious nods to earlier representations of the gangster who fashions himself as a self-made man. At one point in the film, in an echo of what Michael Corleone says repeatedly in the *Godfather* movies, Nino tells another character that the murders he commits are always "business, never personal." Of special note is Nino's viewing of Oliver Stone's *Scarface*, starring Al Pacino, which of course is a remake of the original 1932 movie that fictionalized the rise and fall of Al Capone and which operates in this film as a type of mirror narrative for Nino. In these ways and more, the filmmakers of *New Jack City* explicitly represent Nino as part of a long tradition of criminals in American culture: a businessman trying to run a business—to be sure, one who operates in a volatile and violent marketplace—in the face of multiple market constraints from competitors and also from law enforcement. Nino's success, as is evident from the New Year's Eve scene, is portrayed as a result of his business acumen, much as Capone's was represented in *Al Capone: Biography of a Self-Made Man*. Six decades after that book's publication, the filmmakers of *New Jack City* imagined criminality within that same context of self-making and socioeconomic advancement.

However, a central element of this strategy is how the film positions Nino as a criminal within more than one type of tradition. The filmmakers also imagine Nino within the concept of criminality wherein individual agency is circumscribed by larger socioeconomic and cultural forces. Key to this is sociohistorical context of the American 1980s, especially within the African American urban community. In *Streetwise*, Anderson identifies "an employment bind" for African Americans at that time, with low-skill manufacturing jobs in decline and jobs in the emerging service economy too low in pay or too far from home. He writes that "opportunities for poorer blacks to participate in the regular economy are limited, as evidenced by recurrent by high levels of black unemployment and underemployment."[4] He continues later:

> Whereas the older generation of local men were able to work in the regular job market and earn wages that allowed them to live much like the American middle class, the changed economy has made this extremely difficult for the younger generation. Largely unskilled and with serious educational deficiencies, the youth of today are left to participate only at the lowest levels of the emerging service-oriented economy. . . . This social context of persistent poverty becomes a fertile field for the growth of the drug culture.[5]

This passage has strong rhetorical echoes of the Chicago School and its emphasis on social ecology—indeed, at one point, Anderson sounds distinctly like one of Robert Park's protégées when he notes in the African American community "an atmosphere of estrangement, segmentation, and social distance."[6] And he understands that the drug dealers offer something crucial to members of that community, arguing that they respond "to an important need for the local underclass—employment. The drug dealers promise money and the material 'good life' where for many there is little hope."[7] In Anderson's view, criminality in urban America in the late 1980s and early 1990s, spurred on by the crack epidemic, was a response to the socioeconomic limitations that young black men faced—or, at the least, the limitations that those young black men *believed* that they faced.

The sociological perspective on crime that Anderson brings to his work on race, class, and crime in the 1980s derives from an earlier understanding of criminality, as passed down by the Chicago School, and *New Jack City* does represent crime as a result—at least in part—of the socioeconomic conditions of the time. However, the film complicates its representation of crime by positioning Nino explicitly as a self-made man. Early in the film, Nino articulates what he perceives as the limitations for moving up the socioeconomic ladder in contemporary America. As he previews his business plan for the rest of the CMB, he asserts, "You gotta rob to get rich in the Reagan era." Nino ultimately sees himself less as a drug dealer and more as a businessman.

To him, the product that he is selling doesn't particularly matter because he is simply operating on the same business principles that he sees others use. His logic is that he is simply applying those principles for a new but highly popular product. He articulates his work as recognizing a niche in the public marketplace and satisfying the demand. It is Gee Money, his main partner (or "his brother," as he calls him), who first notices that demand. The CMB sell cocaine in nightclubs and Gee Money has been doing an "experimentation" by selling not cocaine powder but instead substituting crack cocaine, or "freebase" as he calls it. He explains to Nino: "At the clubs, right? Some of the fellas were getting ready to step away from the blackjack tables to the bar getting ready to buy a $50 or a $100 worth of sniff, and I set them up in the backroom with a hit of the base, and yo—15 minutes after leaving the club they be back with two and three people with them. . . . They didn't come back from the cocaine! They came back for the base!" Because the effects of crack are so strong and yet so brief, users feel compelled to return for more in order to achieve that same high again and again. Nino takes Gee Money's recognition that "base"—crack—will create an emerging market with high demand and turns that market realization into a stunning business model: Nino will produce and distribute the crack at the same site, first cutting overhead in production and then risk in distribution and thereby maximizing profit for the CMB.

In its representation of Nino Brown as a contemporary businessman in the 1980s who responds to the crack epidemic by looking for innovative ways to exploit the demand, *New Jack City* harkens back to the language and rhetoric of the Prohibition years and the way Al Capone adapted business strategies to run his own business enterprise. Nino has a brilliant strategy for success, though of course he gives little thought to the welfare of his workers, his customers, or the public itself. In this way, he operates as something of a modern-day Robber Baron or someone "in the tradition of Joe Kennedy," as one character says to him.

Nino's first great business skill is his perception of the marketplace. In the first meeting of the entire CMB operation that we see, Nino refers to the rough socioeconomic conditions in urban America in the 1980s and explains how those conditions lead to particular behavioral choices that perceptive businessmen can exploit. Holding up a vial of crack, he says to his partners, "In times like these, people want to get high. Real high and real fast. This is gonna do it. And make us rich." But recognizing a market demand and perceiving a business opportunity are only part of his business acumen. He also has the ability to adapt what others have done to meet new circumstances. He continues, "The Columbians and the Dominicans have shown us the way. And the shit is large! But, we gonna do it differently. Gone are the days of selling on the street corners. You change the product, you change the marketing strategy." Nino here demonstrates his second strength, the ability to innovate—he plans to take over an apartment complex in a depressed urban neighborhood, where he will set up a lab to produce the crack, a computer system to watch out for the workers, the product, and the money, and a space for purchasing and distribution. The CMB makes the crack in one part of the complex, users are screened for entry at another secure point in the complex, and then they buy the crack and use it all in a third secure place.

In coming up with this plan Nino recognizes the economic advantages of meeting the demand where it is and then exploiting the opportunity to maximize profit by situating his manufacturing and distribution sites in the same place. Moreover, by having his customers use the product there—a product whose effects wear off quickly—he encourages them to purchase that product over and over again without ever having to leave. He says to his team that "we're talking about combinating and consolidating," showing that while he does not have a formal education or the full language of the contemporary businessman, he does have the ability to read the market, to innovate, and to operate in a truly entrepreneurial way. He finishes with this prediction: "One place to make the product, one place to collect our money. We will own this fucking city." And he does.

At the time of its release, in 1991, *New Jack City* was often linked with a series of other films featuring predominantly black casts operating in contemporary urban settings with drugs and crime at the heart of their narratives. These films were often known as "hood films." Beginning with the release of Dennis Hopper's *Colors* in 1988, with its focus on gangs and law enforcement in contemporary Los Angeles, and Spike Lee's *Do the Right Thing* in 1989, with its story of racial tensions in Brooklyn that culminated in a police officer choking a black man to death, these hood films in the late 1980s and early 1990s dramatized contemporary racial and socioeconomic unrest in urban America. As Anderson notes in *Streetwise*, the cost of Reaganomics on the lives of people of color was significant in terms of social disorganization and that cost was often at the heart of these stories, with many of these films written and directed by African American men. Indeed, with Lee's *She's Gotta Have It* in 1986, along with the comedies *Hollywood Shuffle* and *I'm Gonna Git You Sucka* (directed by Robert Townsend and Keenan Ivory Wayans, respectively), African Americans in the late 1980s and early 1990s got the chance to direct films in numbers not seen since the heyday of blaxploitation in the 1970s. Lee's *Do the Right Thing* in 1989 received a great deal of critical acclaim—including end-of-year prizes for members of its cast and for Lee's writing and nominations in Cannes and at the Academy Awards—and commercial attention for films centered on contemporary African American narratives.

In 1991, the same year that *New Jack City* came out, African American directors released sixteen commercial films, the most in decades. These included the critically acclaimed *Straight Out of Brooklyn* (written and directed by Matty Rich) and *Boyz N the Hood* (written and directed by John Singleton).[8] Indeed, *Boyz N the Hood* and *Straight Out of Brooklyn* overshadowed *New Jack City* critically (though not commercially), with Singleton's film garnering worldwide critical attention at its Cannes premiere and scoring a pair of Academy Award nominations. The following few years would see the release of *Juice, Menace II Society, Poetic Justice, Fresh, Dangerous Minds*, and *Set It Off*, among others. Again, the setting for most of these films was urban, usually New York or Los Angeles, and heavily influenced by the burgeoning hip hop culture—especially the form known as gangsta rap—centered on the two coasts. Many of these films were not only inspired by rap but also often starred rappers who had little to no acting experience but who lent the film a certain credibility due to the actors' own backgrounds in those settings. Ice Cube, Ice-T, Tupac Shakur, and Queen Latifah all had starring roles in one of these films in the 1990s, catapulting them to greater fame than even their music had brought them.

New Jack City was originally a screenplay by Thomas Lee Wright before it was adapted by Barry Michael Cooper, based on an article he had written about the drug wars in Detroit.[9]

For the revised screenplay, in keeping with other "hood films," Cooper re-situated the story to New York. Most "hood films" center the tension of their narratives around African American teen boys seeking a stable environment in a community ravaged by the drug wars, usually culminating in them either joining or resisting a gang, with the narrative almost always ending in personal tragedy. These young men are often products of broken homes. They have jailed fathers and working mothers and the gangs offer the apparent allure of a second family and a type of institution that would support them. The narrative appeal of these stories is clear—at the heart is a choice about what these fictional young men want to be and what path they choose to pursue that life. The stories often fall neatly into moral, ethical, and aesthetic stereotypes that closely align with the hip hop narratives of the day that position rival gangs and the police as the dangers that young, black men face in contemporary urban America. Unspoken in much of these films are the socioeconomic realities and social disorganization that young, black men faced in the 1980s—poverty, unemployment and underemployment, incarceration, and a crumbling urban infrastructure that could no longer support them as they moved into adulthood. In many ways, the hood films of the 1990s were an update on the juvenile delinquency films of the 1930s. In how they represent criminality and its roots, the more contemporary films evolve naturally from those of the earlier era. In both genres, individuals were operating in an environment where they could see few if any opportunities for economic advancement other than crime. Both genres portray a type of economic determinism—or, perhaps better, a belief in economic determinism—that delimits what many of the characters can imagine as possible futures for themselves.

Nino imagines himself as an heir of Michael Corleone and Tony Montana—fictional gangsters who turned to crime as their means of self-making—but *New Jack City* also explicitly engages the framework of crime as a by-product of the lack of viable options for advancement. In his testimony at his trial near the end of the film, Nino adopts the language of contingency that resonates with the rhetoric of the juvenile delinquency in earlier decades. At one moment during his testimony, Prosecuting Attorney Hawkins asks him, quite bluntly, if he was "head of the narcotics consortium, the murderously bloody CMB": "Yes, I was a member [of the CMB]. But I was forced into this way of life. Hey look, I've been dealing drugs ever since I was twelve years old. See I didn't have the chances that you had, Miss Hawkins. I wasn't born with a silver spoon in my mouth, Miss Hawkins. I wanted to get out but they threatened to kill my mother." By speaking to the paucity of "chances" that he had, as opposed to others, Nino articulates his belief that he had limited agency when he was young. It was hard for him to imagine how he could get ahead in urban America other than through joining a gang and turning to crime. The allure of the gang was strong for Nino, and—as mentioned earlier—the thread of gang life is a common trope to hood films, as filmmakers often portrayed gangs as serving as an alternative family to the broken homes young men grow up in, as well as an alternative route to financial success. Of course, the film offers an alternative to Nino, another young man who grew up in difficult circumstances but who did not turn to crime. That man is Scotty Appleton, the police officer heading up the investigation into Nino and his drug syndicate. Scotty turns to law enforcement because he is able to see a different possibility.[10] Similarly to what Father Flanagan preached in the 1930s, Scotty made himself a productive citizen through his commitment to education, hard work, and self-improvement. He represents an alternative to Nino, a counternarrative to Nino's insistence that young men who grew up in poverty and crippling socioeconomic conditions had to turn to dealing drugs. The utility of Scotty's narrative for the film is how it allows the viewer to recognize that Nino was not actually forced into a life of crime. Instead he chose it, while other young men—like Scotty, who lost his mother at a young age—went down other paths.[11]

Nino, however, argues that he is not responsible for what he has done wrong and that instead he has simply played the cards dealt to him by the economic environment of late capitalism in America. He says in his testimony,

I'm not guilty. You're the one who's guilty. The lawmakers, the politicians, the Columbian druglords—all you who lobbied against making drugs legal. Just like you did with alcohol during the Prohibition. You're the one who's guilty. I mean, come on, let's kick the ballistics here. Ain't no uzis made in Harlem. I mean, not one of us in here owns a poppy field. This thing is bigger than Nino Brown. This is big business. This is the American way.

As someone marginalized by the socioeconomic superstructures in late twentieth-century America, Nino can only perceive two options: adapt or die. He believes that he has little agency in his world, so that he must learn to acclimate to the realities and rules of the system that controls individuals within it. Nino has an awareness of and ability to articulate the domestic and international economics and politics that have led to his success—the forces that forced him to adapt to "the game" of socioeconomic advancement: "You gotta rob to get rich in the Reagan era." He recognizes the rules of the game and he capitalizes on them. He is a criminal. At the same time, he also believes himself to be just one small piece in a much larger puzzle, a pawn in a game controlled by economic/social/cultural/political forces much more powerful than himself. How can we think that he has full agency over his actions if he is not ultimately in control? In essence, his defense is that his acts of crime are small potatoes in comparison to those committed by bigger forces: we just have not recognized that he is not the real problem.

As an exploration of criminality in late capitalism, *New Jack City* is a product of its time in how it represents crime as inevitable in how socioeconomic realities leave the marginalized with few other options for material success. In so doing, it takes up much the same thinking about young black men, economic disenfranchisement, and the allure of drugs that Elijah Anderson points out in *Streetwise*. The film also represents the material success of the drug dealers as defined through the ideological lens of self-making. While that representation is of its time, that lens is also a product of the past. In its storytelling, especially with the character foils of Nino and Scotty, the film negotiates many of the same tropes of agency and contingency that were the centerpieces of understanding criminality at the beginning of the twentieth century. Those structural and thematic elements also illustrate how those concepts continue to inform and dominate our thinking about criminality over 100 years later.[12] Culturally speaking, Americans continue to imagine criminality as behavior that is either the result of some type of force beyond the individual's control or the result of a conscious and rational choice—or, occasionally, even as both. Indeed, Nino seems to think of himself as a product of the streets, though someone who was smarter and better at crime than others. In other words, he thinks of himself as both marginalized and empowered at the same time. Moreover, he clearly articulates a geopolitical worldview that places his criminality as just one small piece in a much larger scheme, a worldview that accounts for the ways in which late capitalism is built on exploitation and power. But, again, he also sees himself as successful and powerful in that pecking order, even if he knows he is nowhere near the top of that hierarchy and knows he is beholden to forces beyond his reach and control. In this film, criminality is complicated in a number of different ways and defies easy categorization.

Other contemporary cultural productions have proffered similar representations of criminality that blur the different models set up by the social sciences over 100 years ago, including *The Sopranos*, *The Wire*, and *Breaking Bad*. In the latter, while Walter White turns to crime because of impending medical costs that will financially overwhelm his family, he continues in crime for more complicated psychological reasons that go beyond the economic limitations of his salary and health care coverage as a high school chemistry teacher. Similarly, *The Sopranos* offers a complicated psychological portrait of Tony Soprano and his navigation of the contemporary mob, allowing us entrée into an individual's unconscious desires and anxieties while also showing us an update of the model of the gangster as businessman laid out in Pasley's biography of Al Capone and in *The Godfather* films. Finally, *The Wire* offers perhaps the most complex representation of criminality, in that it offers a broad range of characters committing crimes with different motivations, purposes, and strategies. From the tug-of-war rivalry between the ruthless, streetcorner-obsessed Avon Barksdale and the enterprise-building Stringer Bell (who was taking business courses and looking for ways to diversify the company), to the psychologically volatile upcoming gang boss Marlo Stanfield, to the oddly heroic Omar Little, who robbed only from drug dealers and who doled out his own notion of justice—it would be impossible to posit that *The Wire* sets out a case for one way of thinking about criminality in terms of the models put forth 100 years ago by social scientists of the early twentieth century. Nonetheless, creator David Simon invests in dramatizing the byplay of institutions and individuals and how the complicated dynamics of individual agency and contingency continue in the era of late capitalism.

The anxieties about crime that still exist in America today are, in many ways, extensions and reflections of the questions about the roots of human behavior that were fundamental to American culture over a century ago. As I have pointed out throughout this book, the rise of the social sciences as a means of categorizing and cataloging human behavior came hand in hand with attempts to understand criminality. This is not particularly surprising, as one of the fundamental questions about human behavior is why people would do things that go against accepted norms—in this case, why do they commit crime? As I have illustrated throughout the previous four chapters, different social sciences—and different social scientists—pursued this question from different angles and from different ideological positions. However, at the heart of all their inquiries was the central question of Modernism itself: how much control and/or choice do individuals have in their lives? Each of the chapters has taken up this question in some manner. The issues of individual agency and contingency that were a primary concern at that time still shape our cultural conversations about free will and choice in the contemporary moment, and the figure of the criminal continues to function as an illuminating figure through whom we can understand who we are and what we believe about ourselves. From stories of racial profiling to the criminalizing of immigrants in the Trump administration, from the stories of motorists who cannot control their road rage to daytime dramas that feature illicit lovers planning the murder of a duped husband, from the "hood films" of the 1990s to the coddled and spoiled protagonists of the Billionaire Boys Club who never learned discipline or ethics, from the mantras of Logan Roy in *Succession* espousing that "You have to be a killer!" to the machinations of Jordan Belfort in *The Wolf of Wall Street*—these contemporary crime narratives all continue to employ the concept of the criminal type, the trope of the criminal who cannot control his impulse, the logic of environmental determinism, or the figure of the criminal as a self-made man. These are all updates on stories of the past, not re-imaginings. American culture is repeating itself and in so doing is failing, in its representation of criminality, to truly reckon with or understand human behavior that operates outside of the law. And Nino Brown is a terrific example of that.

The nuances and complexities of Nino as a character are worth noting, for his intelligence and perspicacity are signs that he is more than just a gangster from the hood, more than just a product of the streets, and more than just a ruthless killer. He is all of these and more. His formulation of the CMB and his articulation of that group as his family indicate that he is in search of a deeper connection. We need to see him not merely as a black man struggling for agency in an economy that marginalizes black men and criminalizes them, but as an individual seeking his own place and his own success in that economy and who wants to bring his loved ones with him. He is a complex man, like all of us are. We need a language to see him as he is, an imagination that allows us to understand how criminality may not be only an expression of contingency or agency, but how it might be much more complicated and nuanced than that. Although he eventually succumbs to his worst instincts and destroys his family from the inside, Nino is not a character to merely dismiss as another in the line of Tony Montana or Michael Corleone, the two filmic characters he is clearly based on. Nor is he just another black kid from the neighborhood who turned to dealing drugs and grew up to be some sort of animal. Again, he is a complex man, like all of us are. *New Jack City* illustrates how we continue to think of criminality in the ways first formulated in the early days of social science, but it also thereby demonstrates that we have not successfully moved beyond those classifications and tropes that originated a century or so ago. Instead, we are mostly stuck in them.

NOTES

1. *New Jack City*. Dir. Mario Van Peebles. Perf. Wesley Snipes, Ice-T, Allen Payne. Warner Brothers, 1991. DVD.

2. Anderson, Elijah. *Streetwise: Race, Class, and Change in an Urban Community* (Chicago: University of Chicago Press, 1990), 3.

3. Anderson, *Streetwise: Race, Class, and Change in an Urban Community*, 3.

4. Anderson, *Streetwise: Race, Class, and Change in an Urban Community*, 57.

5. Anderson, *Streetwise: Race, Class, and Change in an Urban Community*, 80–81.

6. Anderson, *Streetwise: Race, Class, and Change in an Urban Community*, 78.

7. Anderson, *Streetwise: Race, Class, and Change in an Urban Community*, 109.

8. There were a number of excellent female directors emerging at the same time, including Julie Dash, who was the first African American female director to have a full-length general theatrical release with the critically acclaimed *Daughters of the Dust*, also in 1991. "Hood films" were a genre dominated by African American male directors, with no female directors given the opportunity to direct, not even the female-centric *Set It Off* in 1996.

9. Barry Michael Cooper, "Kids Killing Kids: New Jack City Eats its Young," *The Village Voice*, December 1, 1987. Re-published on Medium by Cooper on July 11, 2013: https://medium.com/@BarryMichaelC/kids-killing-kids-new-jack-city-eats -its-young-1d63f53fd652.

10. The film's characterization of Nino and Scotty growing up under similar circumstances but then going in radically different directions as young men is analogous to the paths taken by Rocky Sullivan and Father Jerry Connolly in *Angels with Dirty Faces*.

11. In a rather awkwardly scripted scene, the audience learns that Nino was the killer of Scotty's mother. Nino claims that it was a random killing, a required initiation into the gang that he was trying to join. However, the forced machinations of the plot at that moment, the attempt to link the narratives of Nino and Scotty, ring false and as a contrivance.

12. Anderson's *Streetwise* serves as something of an example of this—a sociological treatise about race and class in 1980's urban America that foregrounds social disorganization as its main diagnosis of contemporary urban problems in much the same way that the Chicago School had 50–60 years earlier.

Bibliography

Ahnebrink, Lars. *The Beginnings of Naturalism in American Fiction*. New York: Russell & Russell, 1961.

Akkan, Gogsu Gigi. *"The Godfather* and the American Dream," *Journal of Media Critiques* 3, no. 9 (2017): 25–32.

Allen, Frederick Lewis. *Lords of Creation*. New York: Harper and Brothers, 1935.

Anderson, Elijah. *Streetwise: Race, Class, and Change in an Urban Community*. Chicago: University of Chicago Press, 1990.

Angels with Dirty Faces. Dir. Michael Curtiz. Perf. James Cagney, Pat O'Brien, Humphrey Bogart. Warner Brothers, 1938. DVD.

Appel, Benjamin. *Brain Guy*. New York: Alfred A. Knopf, 1934.

Asbury, Herbert. *The Gangs of New York*. 1927. New York: Vintage, 2008.

Avrich, Paul. *Sacco and Vanzetti: The Anarchist Background*. Princeton, NJ: Princeton University Press, 1991.

Baida, Peter. *Poor Richard's Legacy: American Business Values from Benjamin Franklin to Donald Trump*. New York: William Morrow, 1990.

Bainbridge, John. "Chester Gould," *Life* 14 (August 1944): 43.

Behrman, Gary. "We Must Learn to Understand Mental Illness," *St. Louis Post-Dispatch*, 3/8/2001: 21.

Beirne, Piers. *Inventing Criminology: Essays on the Rise of* Homo Criminalis. Albany, NY: State University of New York Press, 1993.

Berman, Marshall. *All That Is Solid Melts into Air* 1982. New York: Penguin, 1988.

Berman, Ronald. The Great Gatsby *and Modern Times*. Urbana, IL: University of Illinois Press, 1994.

Birdsell, Joseph. "Some Reflections on Fifty Years in Biological Anthropology," *Annual Review of Anthropology* 16 (1987): 1–13.

"The Bomb Plot," *New York Times*, 5/2/1919: 11.

Bowles, Scott and Martin Kasindorf. "Friends Tell of Picked-On but 'Normal' Kid," *USA Today*, 3/6/2001: 4A.

Boys Town. Dir. Norman Taurog. Perf. Spencer Tracy and Mickey Rooney. MGM, 1938. DVD.

Boyz N the Hood. Dir. John Singleton. Perf. Ice Cube, Cuba Gooding, Jr., Morris Chestnut. Columbia Pictures, 1991. DVD.

Brauer, Stephen. "Jay Gatsby and the Prohibition Gangster as Businessman," *The F. Scott Fitzgerald Review* 2 (2003): 51–71.

———. "What Makes Him Great? Teaching The Great Gatsby and the New Historicism," in *Approaches to Teaching* The Great Gatsby, ed. Jackson R. Bryer and Nancy P. VanArsdale (New York: MLA, 2009), 84–92.

Breaking Bad. Exec. Prod. Vince Gilligan, Mark Johnson, and Michelle McLaren. Prod. High Bridge Entertainment, Gran Via Productions, and Sony Pictures Television. Perf. Bryan Cranston, Aaron Paul, Anna Gunn. 2008–2013.

Broes, Arthur T. "Dick Tracy: The Early Years," *Journal of Popular Culture* 25 (Spring 1992): 110.

Brooks, Peter. *Reading for the Plot*. Cambridge, MA: Harvard University Press, 1992.

Browne, Nick, ed. *Francis Ford Coppola's* The Godfather Trilogy. Cambridge: Cambridge University Press, 2012.

Bruccoli, Matthew. "*The Great Gatsby* as Social History," in *F. Scott Fitzgerald's* The Great Gatsby: *A Literary Reference*, ed. Bruccoli. New York: Carroll & Graf, 2000.

———. "How Are You and the Family Old Sport – Gerlach and Gatsby." *Fitzgerald/Hemingway Annual* 1975: 33–36.

———. *Some Sort of Epic Grandeur: The Life of F. Scott Fitzgerald*. New York: Harcourt Brace, 1981.

Bulmer, Martin. *The Chicago School of Sociology*. Chicago: University of Chicago Press, 1984.

Burkhead, Michael Dow. *The Search for the Causes of Crime: A History of Theory in Criminology*. Jefferson, NC: McFarland & Company, 2006.

Burnett, W.R. *Little Caesar*. New York: Carroll & Graf, 1929.

Busch, Francis X. *Prisoners at the Bar*, from the Notable American Trials Series. Indianapolis, IN: The Bobbs-Merrill Company, 1952.

Cahan, Abraham. *The Rise of David Levinsky*. 1917. New York: Modern Library, 2001.

Cain, James M. *Double Indemnity*. 1943. New York: Vintage, 1989.

———. *The Postman Always Rings Twice*. 1934. New York: Vintage, 1992.

Calhoun, Craig, ed. *Sociology in America: A History*. Chicago: University of Chicago Press, 2007.

Cantor, Paul. *Pop Culture and the Dark Side of the American Dream*. Lexington, KY: University of Kentucky Press, 2019.

Capote, Truman. *In Cold Blood*. New York: New American Library, 1965.

Castille, Philip. "Jay Gatsby: The Smuggler as Frontier Hero." *The University of Mississippi Studies in Fiction* 10 (1992): 227–237.

Cawelti, John. *Apostles of the Self-Made Man: Changing Concepts of Success in America*. Chicago: The University of Chicago Press, 1965.

"Chester Gould Reminisces," Dick Tracy: *The Thirties: Tommy Guns and Hard Times*. New York: Chelsea House, 1978.

Civiello, Paul. *American Literary Naturalism and Its Twentieth-Century Transformations*. Athens, GA: University of Georgia Press, 1995.

Clapp, James A. "Growing Up Urban: The City, the Cinema, and American Youth," *Journal of Popular Culture* 40, no. 4 (2007): 601–629.

Clarens, Carlos. *Crime Movies: From Griffith to the Godfather and Beyond*. London: Secker and Warburg, 1980.

Clarke, Donald Henderson. *Louis Beretti*. New York: Grosset & Dunlap, 1929.

Coben, Stanley. *A Study in Nativism: The American Red Scare of 1919–1920*. New York: Irvington Publishers, 1964.

Coolidge, Calvin. "State of the Union Address," Calvin Coolidge Presidential Foundation, "We're All in the Same Boat Now: Coolidge on Immigration," 1/19/2016, viewed on 2/8/2020.

Cooper, Barry Michael. "Kids Killing Kids: New Jack City Eats its Young," *The Village Voice*, December 1, 1987. Re-published on Medium by Cooper on 7/11/2013: https://medium.com/@BarryMichaelC/kids-killing-kids-new-jack-city -eats-its-young-1d63f53fd652. Retrieved on 7/11/2021.

Corso, Joseph. "One Not-So Forgotten Summer Night: Sources for Fictional Symbols of American Character in *The Great Gatsby*." *Fitzgerald/Hemingway Annual* 8 (1976): 9–34.

Dargis, Manohla. "Dark Side of the Dream," *Sight and Sound* 6, no. 8 (August 1996): 15–18.

Daughters of the Dust. Dir. Julie Dash. Perf. Cora Lee Day and Alva Rogers. Kino International, 1991. DVD.

Do the Right Thing. Dir. Spike Lee. Perf. Danny Aiello, Spike Lee, John Turturro. 40 Acres and a Mule Filmworks, 1989. DVD.

Doherty, Thomas. *Pre-Code Hollywood: Sex, Immorality, and Insurrection in American Cinema, 1930–1934*. New York: Columbia University Press, 1999.

Donaldson, Scott. "Possessions in *The Great Gatsby*." *The Southern Review* 37, no. 2 (Spring 2001): 187–210.

Dos Passos, John. *Manhattan Transfer*. 1925. Boston, MA: Houghton Mifflin, 1991.

Douglas, Mary. *Purity and Danger*. 1966. London: Ark Paperbacks, 1984.

Downing, Lisa. *The Subject of Murder: Gender, Exceptionality, and the Modern Killer*. Chicago: University of Chicago Press, 2013.

Dreiser, Theodore. *An American Tragedy*. 1925. New York: Signet, 1981.

———. *The Financier*. 1912. New York: Plume, 1988.

———. *Sister Carrie*. 1900. New York: Norton Critical Edition, 1991.

———. *The Titan*. 1914. New York: First Meridian, 1984.

Dudley, John. *A Man's Game: Masculinity and the Anti-Aesthetics of American Literary Naturalism*. Tuscaloosa, AL: University of Alabama Press, 2004.

Dwyer, June. "Disease, Deformity, and Defiance: Writing the Language of Immigration Law and the Eugenics Movement on the Immigrant Body," *MELUS* 28 (Spring 2003): 105–122.

Eburne, Jonathan. *Surrealism and the Art of Crime*. Ithaca, NY: Cornell University Press, 2014.

Egan, Timothy. "Santee is Latest Blow to Myth of Suburbia's Safer Schools," *The New York Times*, 3/09/2001: A1, continued on A16.

Ellenbogen, Josh. *Reasoned and Unreasoned Images: The Photography of Bertillon, Galton, and Marey*. University Park, PA: Pennsylvania State University Press, 2012.

English, Daylanne. *Unnatural Selections: Eugenics in American Modernism and the Harlem Renaissance*. Chapel Hill, NC: University of North Carolina Press, 2004.

Faris, Robert E. L. *Chicago Sociology, 1920–1932*. Chicago: University of Chicago Press, 1967.

Fass, Paula S. "Making and Remaking an Event: The Leopold and Loeb Case in American Culture," *The Journal of American History* 80, no. 3 (December 1993): 919–951.

Finn, Jonathan. *Capturing the Criminal Image: From Mug Shot to Surveillance Society*. Minneapolis, MN: University of Minnesota Press, 2009.

Fitzgerald, F. Scott. *The Great Gatsby*. 1925. New York: Collier, 1992.

Fleissner, Jennifer. *Women, Compulsion, Modernity: The Moment of American Naturalism*. Chicago: University of Chicago Press, 2004.

Foucault, Michel. *Discipline and Punish*. 1975. Translated by Alan Sheridan. New York: Vintage, 1979.

Fraenkel, Osmond. *The Sacco-Vanzetti Case*. 1931. New York: Russell & Russell, 1969.

Franklin, Benjamin. *Autobiography*. New York: Vintage, 1988.

Freud, Sigmund. *Beyond the Pleasure Principle*. 1920. Translated and edited by James Strachey. New York: W.W. Norton & Company, 1989.

———. "Dostoevsky and Parricide," in *Die Urgestalt der Brьder Karamasoff*, ed. W.L. Komarowitsch (Munich: Piper Verlag, 1928), Translation in *Standard Edition*, XXI: 177–194.

———. *The Ego and the Id*. 1923. Translated and edited by James Strachey. New York: W.W. Norton & Company, 1989.

Galewitz, Herb. Ed., *The Celebrated Cases of Dick Tracy, 1931–1951*. Secaucus, NJ: Wellfleet Press, 1990.

Goddard, H.H. *The Criminal Imbecile: An Analysis of Three Remarkable Murder Cases*. New York: Macmillan, 1915.

———. *Feeble-Mindedness: Its Causes and Consequences*. New York: Macmillan, 1914.

———. *The Kallikak Family: A Study in the Heredity of Feeble-Mindedness*. New York: Macmillan, 1912.

———. *School Training of Defective Children*. Yonkers-on-Hudson, NY: World Book Co., 1914.

The Godfather. Dir. Francis Ford Coppola. Perf. Marlon Brando, Al Pacino, James Caan. Paramount, 1972. DVD.

The Godfather II. Dir. Francis Ford Coppola. Perf. Al Pacino, Diane Keaton, Robert Duvall. Paramount, 1974. DVD.

Goldliner, Dave. "Teen Suspect Silent in Court," *New York Daily News*, 3/8/2001: 5.

Gopnik, Adam. "The Genius of George Herriman," *The New York Review of Books*, 12/18/1986: 20.

Gould, Chester. *The Complete Dick Tracy, Volume 8: 1942–44*. San Diego, CA: IDW Publishing, 2009.

Gray, Judd. *Doomed Ship*. New York: Horace Liveright, 1928.

Green, Kristen and Bruce Lieberman. "Bullying, Ridicule of Williams Were Routine, Friends Say," *San Diego Union-Tribune*, 3/10/2001: A1.

Gross, Dalton. "The Death of Rosy Rosenthal: A Note on Fitzgerald's Use of Background in *The Great Gatsby*." *Notes and Queries* 23, no. 1 (1976): 22–23.

Hale, Jr., Nathan G. *Freud and the Americans: The Beginnings of Psychoanalysis in the United States, 1876–1917*. New York: Oxford University Press, 1971.

Halttunen, Karen. *Murder Most Foul: The Killer and the American Gothic Imagination*. Cambridge, MA: Harvard University Press, 1998.

Hayes, David and Brent Walker. *The Films of The Bowery Boys*. Secaucus, NJ: Citadel Press, 1984.

Healy, William. *Mental Conflicts and Misconduct*. Boston, MA: Little Brown & Co., 1917.

Healy, William, Augusta F. Bronner, and Anna Mae Bowers. The *Structure and Meaning of Psychoanalysis as Related to Personality and Behavior*. New York: Alfred A. Knopf, 1930.

Hinkle, Roscoe C. *Developments in American Sociological Theory, 1915–1950*. Albany, NY: State University of New York Press, 1994.

———. *Founding Theory of American Sociology, 1881–1915*. London: Routledge and Kegan Paul, 1980.

Hoag, Ernest Bryant and Edward Williams, *Crime, Abnormal Minds and the Law*. Indianapolis, IN: The Bobbs-Merrill Company, 1923.

Hodgson, Geoffrey M. *The Evolution of Institutional Economics: Agency, Structure and Darwinism in American Institutionalism*. New York: Routledge, 2004.

Hoebel, E. Adamson. *The Law of Primitive Man*. Cambridge, MA: Athenaeum, 1954.

Hooton, Earnest. *The American Criminal: An Anthropological Study, Vol. 1: The Native White Criminal of Native Parentage*. Cambridge: Harvard University Press, 1939.

———. *Crime and the Man*. Cambridge: Harvard University Press, 1939.

Horn, David G. *The Criminal Body: Lombroso and the Anatomy of Deviance*. New York: Routledge, 2003.

Horowitz, Irving Louis, ed. *Veblen's Century: A Collective Portrait*. New Brunswick, NJ: Transaction, 2001.

Hossent, Harry. *Gangster Movies: Gangsters, Hoodlums, and Tough Guys on the Screen*. London: Octopus Books, 1974.

House Committee on Rules, *Attorney-General A. Mitchell Palmer on Charges Made Against Department of Justice by Louis F. Post and Others* (Hearings, 66 Congress, 2 Session), 1920, 27.

Howard, June. *Form and History in American Literary Naturalism*. Chapel Hill, NC: University of North Carolina Press, 1985.

Ingebretsen, Edward. *At Stake: Monsters and the Rhetoric of Fear in Public Culture.* Chicago: University of Chicago Press, 2001.

Josephson, Matthew. *The Robber Barons: The Great American Capitalists, 1861–1901.* New York: Harcourt, Brace and Co., 1934.

Katcher, Leo. *The Big Bankroll: The Life and Times of Arnold Rothstein.* New York: Harper, 1959.

Kidd, Kenneth B. *Making American Boys: Boyology and the Feral Tale.* Minneapolis, MN: University of Minnesota Press, 2004.

Kobler, John, ed. *The Trial of Ruth Snyder and John Gray.* Garden City, NY: Doubleday, Doran & Co., 1938.

Køhlert, Frederick Byrn. "In the Ghetto: Sociology, the Cagney Gangster, and the 'Dead End' Kids in *Angels with Dirty Faces*," *Journal of Popular Culture* 47, no. 4 (2014): 857–876.

Krugman, Wilton Marion. "Review of *The American Criminal*." *American Anthropologist* 41, no. 3 (July-September 1939): 504–509.

Kruse, Horst. "The Real Jay Gatsby: Max von Gerlach, F. Scott Fitzgerald, and the Compositional History of *The Great Gatsby*." *The Fitzgerald Review* 1 (2002): 45–83.

Kurtz, Lester. *Evaluating Chicago Sociology.* Chicago: University of Chicago Press, 1984.

Lansing, Robert. "Spread of Bolshevism in the United States," July 26, 1919. The Papers of Robert Lansing, Library of Congress.

Laughlin, W. S. "Earnest Albert Hooton 1887–1954," *American Antiquity* 20, no. 2 (October 1954): 158–159.

Lehan, Richard. *Theodore Dreiser: His World and His Novels.* Carbondale, IL: Southern Illinois University Press, 1969.

Leopold, Nathan. *Life Plus 99 Years.* New York: Doubleday, 1958.

Levay, Matthew. *Violent Minds: Modernism and the Criminal.* Cambridge: Cambridge University Press, 2019.

Lombroso, Cesare. *Crime: Its Causes and Remedies.* 1911. Translated by Henry Horton. Montclair, NJ: Patterson Smith, 1968.

Lombroso-Ferrero, Gina. *Lombroso's Criminal Man.* Glen Ridge, NJ: Patterson Smith, 1972.

Loos, Anita. *Gentlemen Prefer Blondes.* 1925. New York: Liveright, 1998.

Malinowski, Bronislaw. *Crime and Custom in Savage Society.* 1926. Totowa, NJ: Littlefield, Adams & Co., 1982.

Malone, Michael. *James J. Hill: Empire Builder of the Northwest.* Norman, OK: University of Oklahoma Press, 1996.

Maltby, Richard. "The Spectacle of Criminality," in *Violence and American Cinema*, ed. J. David Slocum. New York: Routledge, 2001, 117–147.

———. "Why Boys Go Wrong: Gangsters, Hoodlums, and the Natural History of Delinquent Careers" in *Mob Culture: Hidden Histories of the American Gangster Film*, ed. Lee Grieveson, Esther Sonnet, and Peter Stanfield. New Brunswick, NJ: Rutgers University Press, 2005, 41–66.

Maltin, Leonard and Richard W. Bann, *The Little Rascals: The Life & Times of Our Gang.* New York: Crown Publishing/Three Rivers Press, 1977, rev. 1992.

Martin, Albro. *James J. Hill and the Opening of the Northwest*. New York: Oxford University Press, 1976.

Mason, Fran. *American Gangster Cinema: From 'Scarface' to 'Pulp Fiction'*. Palgrave Macmillan, 2002.

McConaughy, John. *Who Rules America?* New York: Longmans, Green and Co., 1934.

McCormick, Thomas C. "Review of *The American Criminal*." *American Sociological Review* 5, no. 2 (April 1940): 252–254.

McKernan, Maureen. *The Amazing Crime and Trial of Leopold and Loeb*. Chicago: The Plymouth Court Press, 1924.

Meloy, J. R. *A Psychoanalytic View of the Psychopath*. San Diego, CA: San Diego Psychoanalytic Society and Institute, 2008.

Merton, Robert K. and M. F. Ashley-Montagu, "Crime and the Anthropologist," *American Anthropologist* 42, no. 3, Part 1 (July-September 1940): 384–408.

Michaels, Walter Benn. *The Gold Standard and the Logic of Naturalism*. Berkeley, CA: University of California Press, 1988.

Mitchell, David. *1919: Red Mirage*. New York: Macmillan, 1970.

Mitchell, Lee Clark. *Determined Fictions*. Columbia University Press, 1989.

Munby, Jonathan. *Public Enemies, Public Heroes: Screening the Gangster from* Little Caesar *to* Touch of Evil. Chicago: University of Chicago Press, 1999.

———. *Under a Bad Sign: Criminal Self-Representation in African American Popular Culture*. Chicago: University of Chicago Press, 2011.

Murray, Robert. *Red Scare: A Study in National Hysteria*. Minneapolis, MN: University of Minnesota Press, 1955.

Nevins, Allan. *John D. Rockefeller: The Heroic Age of American Enterprise*. New York: Scribner's, 1940.

New Jack City. Dir. Mario Van Peebles. Perf. Wesley Snipes, Ice-T, Allen Payne. Warner Brothers, 1991. DVD.

Nies, Betsy L. *Eugenic Fantasies: Racial Ideology in the Literature and Popular Culture of the 1920's*. New York: Routledge, 2002.

Norris, Frank. *McTeague*. 1899. New York: Signet, 1981.

Park, Robert, R. D. McKenzie, and Ernest Burgess. *The City: Suggestions for the Study of Human Nature in the Urban Environment*. Chicago: University of Chicago Press, 1925.

Parrish, John B. "Rise of Economics as an Academic Discipline: The Formative Years to 1900." *The Southern Economic Journal* 34, no. 1 (July 1967): 1–16.

Pasley, Fred D. *Al Capone: Biography of a Self-Made Man*. New York: Ives Washburn, 1930.

Pauly, Thomas H. "Gatsby as Gangster." *Studies in American Fiction* 21, no. 2 (Autumn 1993): 225–236.

The Petrified Forest. Dir. Archie Mayo. Perf. Leslie Howard, Bette Davis, Humphrey Bogart. Warner Brothers, 1936. DVD.

Piper, Henry Dan. "The Fuller-McGee Case." in *Fitzgerald's* The Great Gatsby, ed. Piper. New York: Scribner's, 1970, 171–184.

Pitofsky, Alex. "Dreiser's *The Financier* and the Horatio Alger Myth," *Twentieth Century Literature* 44, no. 3 (Fall 1998): 276–290.

Pizer, Donald. *Realism and Naturalism in Nineteenth Century America.* Carbondale, IL: Southern Illinois University Press, 1967.

Posnock, Ross. "'A New World, Material Without Being Real': Fitzgerald's Critique of Capitalism in *The Great Gatsby,*" in *Critical Essays on F. Scott Fitzgerald's* The Great Gatsby, ed. Scott Donaldson. Boston, MA: G.K. Hall, 1984, 201–213.

Post, Louis F. *The Deportations Delirium of Nineteen-Twenty.* Chicago: Charles H. Kerr, 1920.

Potter, Claire. *War on Crime: Bandits, G-Men, and the Politics of Mass Culture.* New Brunswick, NJ: Rutgers University Press, 1998.

Preston, Jr., William. *Aliens and Dissenters: Federal Suppression of Radicals, 1903–1933* Chicago: University of Illinois Press, 1994.

Purdum, Todd. "Shooting at School Leaves 2 Dead and 13 Hurt," *The New York Times,* 3/6/2001: A1.

Pyle, Joseph G. *The Life of James J. Hill,* Vol. I and II. Garden City, NY: Doubleday, Page and Co., 1917.

Radford, John P. "Sterilization versus Segregation: Control of the 'Feebleminded,' 1900–1939," *Social Science and Medicine* 33, no. 4 (1991): 449–459.

Rafter, Nicole Hahn. *Creating Born Criminals.* Champaign, IL: University of Illinois Press, 1997.

Ramsden, Edmund. "Social Demography and Eugenics in the Interwar United States." *Population and Development Review* 29, no. 4 (2003): 547–598.

Reisman, David. *Thorstein Veblen.* New York: Charles Scribner's Sons, 1954.

Reuter, E.B. "Review of *Crime and the Man.*" *The American Journal of Sociology* 45, no. 1 (July 1939): 123–126.

Roberts, Garyn. *Dick Tracy and American Culture: Morality and Mythology, Text and Context.* Jefferson, NC: McFarland: 1993.

Roffman, Peter and Jim Purdy. *The Hollywood Social Problem Film: Madness, Despair, and Politics from the Depression to the Fifties.* Bloomington, IN: Indiana University Press, 1981.

Rosow, Eugene. *Born to Lose: The Gangster Film in America.* New York: Oxford University Press, 1978.

Ross, Frank Alexander. "Review of *The American Criminal.*" *The American Journal of Sociology* 45, no. 3 (November 1939): 477–480.

Russell, Francis. *Sacco and Vanzetti: The Case Resolved.* New York: Harper & Row, 1986.

———. *Tragedy at Dedham.* New York: McGraw-Hill, 1971.

Ruth, David. *Inventing the Public Enemy: The Gangster in American Culture, 1918–1934.* Chicago: University of Chicago Press, 1996.

Savitz, Leonard. "Introduction," in *Lombroso's Criminal Man.* Glen Ridge, NJ: Patterson Smith, 1972.

"Says We Face Revolution," *The New York Times,* 10/17/1919.

Schlapp, Max G. and Edward H. Smith, *The New Criminology.* New York: Boni and Liveright, 1928.

Scarface. Dir. Howard Hawks. Perf. Paul Muni, Ann Dvorak, George Raft. United Artists, 1932. DVD.

Schmid, David. *Natural Born Celebrities: Serial Killers in American Culture.* Chicago: University of Chicago Press, 2005.

Scholnick, Sylvia Huberman. "Money vs. *Mitzvot*: The Figure of the Businessman in Novels by American Jewish Writers," *Yiddish* 6, no. 4 (1987): 48–55.

Sekula, Allan. "The Body and the Archive," *October* 39 (Winter 1986): 3–64.

Seltzer, Mark. *Bodies and Machines.* New York: Routledge, 2014.

Shadoian, Jack. *Dreams and Dead Ends: The American Gangster Film.* 1977. New York: Oxford University Press, 2003.

Shaw, Clifford. *Brothers in Crime.* Chicago: University of Chicago Press, 1941.

———. *The Jack-Roller.* Chicago: University of Chicago Press, 1930.

———. *The Natural History of a Delinquent Career.* Chicago: University of Chicago Press, 1931.

Shaw, Clifford and Henry McKay. *Social Factors in Juvenile Delinquency.* Washington, DC: U.S. Printing Office, 1931.

Sheehan, Paul. *Modernism and the Aesthetics of Violence.* Cambridge: Cambridge University Press, 2013.

Smith, Shawn Michelle. *American Archives.* Princeton, NJ: Princeton University Press, 1999.

Snyder, Ruth. *Ruth Snyder's Own True Story.* New York: King Features Syndicate, 1927.

"Soldiers and Sailors Break Up Meetings," *New York Times*, 5/2/1919: 3.

The Sopranos. Exec. Prod. David Chase, Brad Grey, Robin Green, Mitchell Burgess, Ilense S. Landress, Terence Winter, Matthew Weiner. Prod. HBO, Chase Films, and Brad Grey Television. Perf. James Gandolfini, Edie Falco, Lorraine Bracco. 1999–2007.

Stallybrass, Peter and Allon White's *The Politics and Poetics of Transgression.* Ithaca, NY: Cornell University Press, 1986.

Steele, Diana and Dave Goldliner. "All Were Targets at HS," *New York Daily News*, 3/7/2001: 23.

Steinbeck, John. *The Grapes of Wrath.* New York: Viking Press, 1939.

Stevens, Clifford. "Father Flanagan and the Founding of Boys Town: Omaha, Nebraska (1917–1925)," *American Catholic Studies* 121, no. 1 (Spring 2010): 91–97.

Stone, Irving. *Clarence Darrow For the Defense.* Garden City, NY: Country Life Press, 1941.

Straight Out of Brooklyn. Dir. Matty Rich. Perf. Larry Gilliard, Jr., and George T. Odom. The Samuel Goldwyn Company, 1991. DVD.

Sutherland, Edwin. *Principles of Criminology.* Chicago: University of Chicago Press, 1924.

Tarbell, Ida M. *History of the Standard Oil Company.* New York: Harper and Brothers, 1904.

Thompson, Courtney E. *An Organ of Murder: Crime, Violence, and Phrenology in Nineteenth-Century America.* New Brunswick, NJ: Rutgers University Press, 2021.

Thornton, Kelly. "Why Gunman Did It Is Big Unanswered Question," *San Diego Union-Tribune*, 3/8/2001: A-14.

Thrasher, Frederic. *The Gang.* Chicago: University of Chicago Press, 1927.

Tilman, Rick. *Thorstein Veblen and His Critics, 1891–1963: Conservative, Liberal, and Radical Perspectives*. Princeton, NJ: Princeton University Press, 1992.

"Tucker Carlson Tonight," 1/14/2019. (https://www.youtube.com/watch?v=8KeIE6KuYus.) Viewed on 1/17/2019.

Turner, Stephen and Jonathan Turner. *The Impossible Science: An Institutional Analysis of American Sociology* (Newbury Park, CA: Sage, 1990).

Veblen, Thorstein. *The Theory of the Leisure Class*. 1899. New York: Penguin, 1994.

———. "Why Is Economics Not an Evolutionary Science?" *Quarterly Journal of Economics* 12, no. 3 (July 1898): 373–397.

Walcutt, Charles Child. *American Literary Naturalism: A Divided Stream*. Minneapolis, MN: University of Minnesota Press, 1956.

Warshow, Robert. "The Gangster as Tragic Hero," *Partisan Review* 15, no. 2 (February 1948).

Weinberger, Daniel. "A Brain Too Young for Good Judgment," *New York Times*, 3/10/2001: A13.

Wells, Ira. *Fighting Words: Polemics and Social Change in Literary Naturalism*. Tuscaloosa, AL: University of Alabama Press, 2013.

White, William A. *Crimes and Criminals*. New York: Farrar & Rinehart, 1933.

Wiegman, Robyn. *American Anatomies: Theorizing Race and Gender*. Durham, NC: Duke University Press, 1995.

The Wire. Exec. Prod. David Simon, Robert F. Colesberry, Nina Kostroff Noble. Prod. Blown Deadline Productions and HBO Entertainment. Perf. Dominic West, Wendell Pierce, Michael K. Williams. 2002–2008.

Wirth, Louis. *The Ghetto*. Chicago: University of Chicago Press, 1928.

Wojcik, Pamela. "Vernacular Modernism as Child's Play," *New German Critique* 122 (Summer 2014): 83–95.

Wood, John. *The Life of Thorstein Veblen and Perspectives on his Thought*. New York: Routledge, 1993.

Woodson, C. G. "Review of *The American Criminal*." *The Journal of Negro History* 24, no. 3 (July 1939): 359–360.

Wright, Richard. *Native Son*. 1940. New York: Harper Perennial, 1993.

Yaquinto, Marilyn. *Pump 'Em Full of Lead: A Look at Gangsters on Film*. New York: Twayne, 1998.

Zenderland, Leila. *Measuring Minds: Henry Herbert Goddard and the Origins of American Intelligence Testing*. Cambridge: Cambridge University Press, 1998.

Zorbaugh, Harvey Warren. *The Gold Coast and the Slum*. Chicago: University of Chicago Press, 1929.

Index

abuse and traumas, 2, 10
Academy Award, 173, 174
accumulation of wealth, 17, 137, 138
Addams, Jane, 99
African Americans, 171; female
  directors, 179n8; films written
  and directed by, 173–74, 179n8;
  self-representation of criminality,
  15; social disorganization, 174;
  socioeconomic limitations, 171,
  174
agency, 8, 123–26, 171, 176–78
Akkan, Gogsu Gigi, 166n71
*Al Capone: Biography of a Self-Made
  Man* (Pasley), 149–52, 170
alcohol, 63
Alger, Horatio, 110, 139, 143, 150, 152,
  158
Allen, Frederick Lewis, 141, 142
All That Is Solid Melts into Air
  (Berman), 7
American Anthropologist, 40
The American Criminal (Hooton), 36
American Dream, 17, 50n9, 131n77,
  134, 138, 146, 153, 158, 159,
  163n55, 166nn71–72, 169
American Experiment, 138
The American Journal of Sociology, 41,
  99

An American Tragedy (Dreiser), 71
Anderson, Elijah, 170, 171, 173, 176,
  179n12
Anderson, Nels, 100
Angels with Dirty Faces, 17, 101,
  116–20, 124
anthropology: criminal, 32–33;
  discipline of, 32; physical, 36
Apostles of the Self-Made Man
  (Cawelti), 135, 161n21
appearance, 24, 25, 27, 29–31, 38, 40,
  42. *See also* physical traits/features/
  characteristics
Appel, Benjamin, 153
archive, 27–28
Asbury, Herbert, 33–35
Ashley-Montagu, M. F., 40
asylums, 62
*At Stake: Monsters and the Rhetoric of
  Fear in Public Culture* (Ingebretsen),
  15
Autobiography (Franklin), 138–39, 146
autonomy, 8

Baida, Peter, 164–65n63
Behrman, Gary, 12
Belfort, Jordan, 178
Berman, Marshall, 7–8
Berman, Ronald, 161nn19, 24, 162n44

Bertillon, Alphonse, 27–29, 31, 33, 51n21
Beyond the Pleasure Principle (Freud),
    73, 78, 93n66
Billionaire Boys Club, 178
biological determinism, 27–49, 63, 69.
    See also criminal type
biological theorists, 82–83
biotype, 32
Bodies and Machines (Seltzer), 92n39
bodies of criminals, 25–26
Bogart, Humphrey, 115, 116
Boies, Henry, 26, 32, 52n35
Booth, Ernest, 111
Bowles, Scott, 19n27
Bowman, Karl, 83, 84, 86–87
Bowman-Hulbert Report, 83, 86–87,
    94n79
Boys Town, 17, 97–99, 101, 120–26
Boyz N the Hood, 174
Brain Guy (Appel), 153
Breaking Bad, 177
Brill, A. A., 68
Brooks, Peter, 5–6
Bruccoli, Matthew, 163n48, 164n60
Buchanan, Tom, 33
bullying, 8, 9
Bulmer, Martin, 100, 112, 128n27,
    129n58
Burgess, Ernest, 99–101, 106–8, 112, 124
Burnett, W. R., 153
business methods, 142
business schools, 159–60n8
business strategies, 172

Cagney, Jimmy, 115, 116
Cahan, Abraham, 143
Cain, James, 16, 72–80, 88
The Call, 44
Cantor, Paul, 166–67n72
capitalism, 17, 135–36; economic
    environment, 175; exploitation and
    power, 177; free market, 169; late,
    169–79
Capone, Al, 49n1, 134, 149–52, 154,
    158, 170

Capote, Truman, 2–3
Capturing the Criminal Image (Finn),
    15
Carnegie, Andrew, 133, 134, 142
Castille, Philip, 163n48, 164n60
causality, 27
cause and effect, 6, 7, 10, 14, 67–68,
    111–12
Caverly, John R., 88
Cawelti, John, 135, 139, 146, 161n21
celebrity culture, 14
Cerro, Henry, 48
Chicago School of Sociology, 16–17,
    98–125, 171
Chicago Tribune Company Syndicate,
    21
The City (Park, Burgess, and
    McKenzie), 100–102, 127nn7, 12
Civiello, Paul, 92n44
Clarke, Donald Henderson, 153
Clutter, Herb, 1–2
Clutter family murders, 1–3, 10
Colors, 173
Columbine High School, 9
commercialism, 15
composite photographic portraits, 29–31
compulsion. *See* repetition compulsion
confession, 61
consumerism, 14–15
contingency, 8, 126, 175–78
Cooper, Barry Michael, 174
Coppola, Francis Ford, 17, 153, 155–58,
    165–66n68
Corso, Joseph, 163n48
crack epidemic, 171
Crime and Custom in Savage Society
    (Malinowski), 4
Crime and the Man (Hooton), 36, 37, 41
Crime: Its Causes and Remedies
    (Lombroso), 26, 31
crime narratives: cultural work of, 5,
    6, 10, 14–15; ethnic socioeconomic
    mobility, 14–15; Halttunen on, 5, 6;
    impulses, 80–89; motivation, 10–11;
    as a reflection of culture, 5

crimes: anxiety about, 24; cause and effect, 10; context and, 4; as dangerous and threatening, 4; destabilizing effect/impact, 3, 4
Crimes and Criminals (White), 67, 83
Crime School, 116
The Criminal (Drahms), 32
The Criminal (Ellis), 33
The Criminal Imbecile (Goddard), 62–63
criminality: culture values of, 5; liminal space as, 5; media stories, 13; notions of, 5; representations of, 15; social sciences and, 6–8; study of, 6–7
Criminal Man (Lombroso), 26
criminals: bodies of, 25–26; as cultural figure, 5; as an illuminating figure, 178; as physiological other, 24; as powerful figure, 4
criminal type, 15–16; Bertillon's system of, 27–29, 31, 33; composite photographic portraits, 29–31; concept of, 24, 25, 36; Grotesques and, 24; physical traits/features, 16, 24–49; radicals, 33, 43–49; real-life events and, 43–49; technologies and, 25; theory of, 24
criminologists, 15–16
criminology, 7
Criminology (McDonald), 32
Cunanan, Andrew, 15
Curtiz, Michael, 116–17

Dangerous Minds, 174
Dargis, Manohla, 166n69
Darrow, Clarence, 81–83, 88, 95n90
Darwin, Charles, 136, 143
Dash, Julie, 179n8
Dead End, 116
Dead End Kids, 116
death drive, 16, 73. *See also* sex drive
Degeneracy (Talbot), 32
Dell, Floyd, 68
Determined Fictions (Mitchell), 92n43

determinism, 8, 63; biological, 27–49, 63, 69; environmental, 97–126; psychological, 62–89
Detroit Daily Mirror, 21
Dewey, John, 99
Dick Tracy (comic strip by Gould), 16, 21–24, 36
The Diseases of Society (Lydston), 33
disorganized environments, 101
Dolbeare, Harry, 48
Doomed Ship (Gray), 59, 61–62, 72, 77
Dorr, Wilson, 48
Dos Passos, John, 69, 70
Do the Right Thing, 173
Double Indemnity (Cain), 77–79
Douglas, Mary, 4–5
Drahms, August, 26, 32
Dreiser, Theodore, 70–72, 143–44, 149, 162n43
drug dealers, 170, 171; material success of, 176
drug wars, 174

Eastman, Max, 68
economics, 135–36
Egan, Timothy, 11–12
The Ego and the Id (Freud), 73
Ellis, Havelock, 33, 66
emotional shocks, 83
empiricism, 5, 112
entrepreneurialism, 169
environment/environmental determinism, 16, 97–126, 178; Hooton on, 42; social codes, 104. *See also* juvenile delinquency
essentialism, 27
ethnicity and race. *See* race and ethnicity
eugenics, 28–29, 31, 33, 90n14
Evaluating Chicago Sociology (Kurtz), 126n2

Faris, Robert E. L., 105, 126n2
Fass, Paula S., 95n100
Faulkner, John, 48

feeble-mindedness, 62–63
female directors, 179n8
The Financier (Dreiser), 143–44
fingerprinting, 28–29
Finn, Jonathan, 15
Fitzgerald, F. Scott, 33, 133–34,
    138–40, 142–44, 146–49, 163n48,
    164nn58, 60
Flanagan, Edward J., 97
*Form and History in American Literary
    Naturalism* (Howard), 92n39
Frankfurter, Felix, 47
Franklin, Benjamin, 110, 134, 135,
    138–39, 146, 147, 152, 158, 159
Franks, Bobby, 80, 81, 85
Frantello, Albert, 48
free market capitalists, 169
free will, 8
Fresh, 174
Freud, Sigmund, 16, 17, 66–68, 73, 75,
    77–80, 84, 88, 91n27–28

Galton, Francis, 27–32, 45, 52n27, 89n8
The Gang (Thrasher), 100, 105–6
The Gangs of New York (Asbury),
    33–35
gangsta rap, 174
gangster films, 115–16, 166n69; Warner
    Brothers', 153, 166n69
gangsters: Asbury's depiction of, 33–35;
    as businessman, 177; representations
    of, 170
Garfield, James, 139
Gentlemen Prefer Blondes (Loos),
    92–93n46
geopolitical worldview, 176–77
The Ghetto (Wirth), 100, 102–3
glandular system, 82–83
Glueck, Bernard, 83, 94n79, 95n90
Goddard, H. H., 62–63
The Godfather (Puzo), 153
The Godfather films, 153–59, 170, 177
The Gold Coast and Slum (Zorbaugh),
    100, 103–5
Goldliner, Dave, 10, 19n27

*The Gold Standard and the Logic of
    Naturalism* (Michaels), 92n39
Gordon, Randy, 9
Gothic narratives, 14, 18n11
Gould, Chester, 21–24, 27, 30, 31, 48,
    49–50n1, 50nn7–9
Gould, Jay, 142
The Grapes of Wrath (Steinbeck),
    69
Gray, Judd, 16, 59–65, 67, 68, 72,
    77–78, 88–89
The Great Gatsby (Fitzgerald), 33, 133–
    34, 139, 140, 142, 145–49
Great Northern Railway, 140
Green, Kristen, 11, 12
Grotesques, 23, 24, 27, 30, 36
Guthaus, Courtney, 10

Hall, G. Stanley, 89–90n9
Halttunen, Karen, 5, 6
Hamill, Ralph, 83, 94n79, 95n90
Hanson, Ole, 43
Harding, Warren, 33
Hardwick, Thomas, 43
Harris, Eric, 9
Hawks, Howard, 115
Hays Production Code, 115, 120
Healy, William, 65–66, 83, 84, 86,
    91n26, 94n79, 95n90
Helmholtz, Hermann von, 66
Henderson, C. R., 26, 32
Herbart, Johann Friedrich, 66
Heredity and Human Progress
    (McKim), 32–33
Hickock, Dick, 1–3, 10
Hill, James J., 134, 140–42
hip hop culture, 174
Hoag, Ernest Bryant, 94n72
The Hobo (Anderson), 100
Hoebel, E. Adamson, 3–4
Hollywood Shuffle, 173
Holmes, Oliver W., Jr., 43
hood films, 173–75, 178, 179n8
Hooton, Earnest, 36–43, 48, 53nn43, 49,
    54nn66, 71

Hopper, Dennis, 173
Hulbert, Harold, 83, 84, 86–87

Ice Cube, 174
Ice-T, 170, 174
imbeciles, 62–63
I'm Gonna Git You Sucka, 173
immigrants/immigration, 32, 33, 44–49;
    Immigration Act of 1924 and, 33;
    white supremacy and, 33
Immigration Act of 1924, 33
impulses, 12–13, 16, 61, 64–67, 69,
    75–77, 79–89, 110, 125
In Cold Blood (Capote), 2–3, 79
The Indians of Pecos Pueblo (Hooton), 36
individualism, 153
individual responsibility. *See*
    responsibility
Ingebretsen, Edward, 15
intellectually disabled, 62
interiority, 25, 26, 37
interventions, 16–17, 114–15, 123, 125,
    126; *Angels with Dirty Faces*, 17,
    116–20, 124; *Boys Town*, 17, 97–99,
    101, 120–25, 126
An Introduction to the Study of
    the Dependent, Defective, and
    Delinquent Classes (Henderson), 32
Inventing the Public Enemy (Ruth), 14, 116
IQ exams, 63

The Jack-Roller (Shaw), 106–11
James, William, 89n9
Jelliffe, Smith Ely, 68
Joint Report (White, Healy, Glueck, and
    Hamill), 86, 94n79, 95n90
Josephson, Matthew, 141, 142, 162n29
Juice, 174
juvenile delinquency, 16–17, 97–126;
    films, 116–24, 174–75; social
    disorganization and, 101. *See also*
    interventions

The Kallikak Family (Goddard), 62,
    90n12

Kasindorf, Martin, 19n27
Katzmann, Frederick G., 48
Klebold, Dylan, 9
Køhlert, Frederik Byrn, 131n77
Krafft-Ebing, Richard, 66
Kurtz, Lester, 112, 126n2, 128n26

Ladd, George Trumbull, 89–90n9
Lansing, Robert, 44
Laughlin, James, 135
laws, 3; as effective social restraint, 4;
    Hoebel on, 3–4; Malinowski on, 4;
    as prescribed behaviors, 3; social
    norms and, 3, 5
Lee, Spike, 173
Lehan, Richard, 91–92n34
Leibniz, Gottfried Wilhelm, 66
Leopold, Nathan, 80–88
Liberty Magazine, 77
Lieberman, Bruce, 11, 12
The Life of James J. Hill (Pyle), 140–42
Life Plus 99 Years (Leopold), 85
Little Caesar (Burnett), 153
Little Caesar (film), 115
Little Rascals. *See* Our Gang
Loeb, Richard, 80–88
Lombroso, Cesare, 26, 27, 31–32, 34,
    37, 42, 45, 46, 48, 51n22, 52n33
Loos, Anita, 92–93n46
Lords of Creation (Allen), 141
Louis Beretti (Clarke), 153
Luhan, Mabel Dodge, 68
Lydston, G. F., 33

"made not born" construct, 98
madness, 61–62
Malinowski, Bronislaw, 4
Manhattan Transfer (Dos Passos), 69
Marx, K., 136
Mason, Fran, 130n72, 130–31n76
McCormick, Thomas C., 41
McCoy, Horace, 70
McDonald, Arthur, 26, 32
McKenzie, Roderick, 100
McKernan, Maureen, 94–95n79

McKim, W. D., 32–33
McTeague (Norris), 69
Mead, George, 99
Menace II Society, 174
Mental Conflicts and Misconduct
    (Healy), 84
Merton, Robert K., 40
Michaels, Walter Benn, 92n39
Mill, John Stuart, 135
Mitchell, Lee Clark, 92n43
Modernism, defined, 8
modernization, 7–8
montage, 116–17, 130n72
moral monsters, 15
Morgan, J. P., 43, 141, 142
mugshot, 15, 27, 29, 34
Munby, Jonathan, 14–15, 163–64n55
murder, 5; Gothic narrative of, 14; as
    transgressive act, 10
Murder Most Foul (Halttunen), 5, 14
music, 19n27

narratives: Brooks on, 5–6; cultural
    work, 5; function, 10
Natural Born Celebrities (Schmid),
    14
*The Natural History of a Delinquent
    Career* (Shaw), 106–7, 114–15
naturalism, 92n39
Nelson, Judd, 170
New Americanists, 92nn39, 43, 44
New Jack City, 17, 169–79
New York Daily News, 10
New York Post Office, 43
Nietzsche, Friedrich, 66
Nordic Old American Criminals,
    38–39
Norris, Frank, 69, 70

O'Brien, Pat, 116
O'Neil, Daniel, 48
*An Organ of Murder: Crime, Murder,
    and Phrenology in Nineteenth-
    Century America* (Thompson), 26
Our Gang, 116

Pacino, Al, 170
Palmer, A. Mitchell, 43–49
Panken, Jacob, 55n79
Park, Robert, 99–102, 104, 108, 112,
    120, 124, 125, 171
Parrish, John B., 135
Parsons, Philip, 33
Pasley, Fred, 17, 149–52, 154, 158, 177
Pauly, Thomas H., 164nn58, 60
Payne, Allen, 170
Peirce, Charles Saunders, 89n9
people of color, 173
Pfingst, Paul, 10
phrenology, 26, 51n17
physical anthropology, 36
physical traits/features/characteristics,
    16, 24–49
Pizer, Donald, 91–92n34
Poetic Justice, 174
*The Politics and Poetics of
    Transgression* (Stallybrass and
    White), 43
pollution, 4–5
Poor Richard's Legacy (Baida), 164–
    65n63
popular culture, 15
The Postman Always Rings Twice
    (Cain), 16, 72–77
Potter, Claire Bond, 15
Predominantly Nordic Old American
    Criminals, 38, 39
Principles of Criminology (Sutherland),
    82
Principles of Psychology (James), 89n9
Prisoners and Paupers (Boies), 32,
    52n35
Prohibition, 21, 33–35, 49n1, 144, 145,
    147, 153, 172
psychoanalysis, 65–89
psychological therapy, 89
psychology/psychological determinism,
    62–89; American, 62; Scottish
    commonsense, 62
Public Enemies, Public Heroes
    (Munby), 14

Pure Nordic Old American Criminals, 38, 39
Purity and Danger (Douglas), 4
Pyle, Joseph G., 140–42

Queen Latifah, 174

race and ethnicity, 25, 31–32; physical differences, 37–42; psychological differences, 37–38; real-life events and, 43–49
racial profiling, 178
racial psychology, 37–38
radicals, 33, 43–49, 55nn78–79
Rafter, Nicole Hahn, 26, 32, 51n13, 52n35
Reading for the Plot (Brooks), 5–6
Reagan, Ronald, 169
Reaganomics, 173
Red Scare of 1919–1920, 33
repetition compulsion, 73, 75, 77–79, 88
repression, 73, 79, 80, 88
responsibility, 7, 11, 13, 29, 43, 61, 64, 65, 69, 72, 77, 90n11, 126
Responsibility for Crime (Parsons), 33
Reuter, E. B., 39–40
Ricardo, David, 135
Rich, Matty, 174
The Rise of David Levinsky (Cahan), 143
"Rise of Economics as an Academic Discipline: The Formative Years to 1900" (Parrish), 135
The Rising Tide of Color Against White World-Supremacy (Stoddard), 33
The Robber Barons (Josephson), 141
Robinson, Edgar G., 115
Rock, Chris, 170
Rockefeller, John D., 43, 133, 134, 141, 142, 152, 164n63
"Rogues Gallery," 27
rooming-house world, 104
Rooney, Mickey, 97, 123
Ross, Frank Alexander, 41
Ruiz, Peter, 9

Ruth, David, 14–15, 163–64n55
Ruth Snyder's Own True Story (Snyder), 59

Sacco, Nicola, 47–49
Salsedo, Andrea, 49
San Diego Union-Tribune, 10, 11
Santana High School, in Santee, CA. *See* Santee shooting spree
Santee shooting spree, 8–14; media coverage, 10–14; narratives, 11–14; psychological reasoning, 11–13
Say, Jean Baptiste, 135
Scarface, 35–36, 115, 170
Schlapp, Max, 94n73
Schmid, David, 14
Schopenhauer, Arthur, 66
Scottish commonsense psychology, 62
Sekula, Allan, 25, 27, 32, 52n27
self-making narratives, 17, 110, 133–59
Seltzer, Mark, 92n39
Serenade (Cain), 93n55
serial killer, 14
service economy, 171
Set It Off, 174
sex drive, 16, 64, 66, 68, 75, 91n28. *See also* death drive; impulses
Shakur, Tupac, 174
Shaw, Clifford, 101, 106–15, 120, 123–26
She's Gotta Have It, 173
Simon, David, 177
Singleton, John, 174
Sister Carrie (Dreiser), 70–71
slum, 104–5
Small, Albion, 99
Smith, Adam, 135
Smith, Edward, 94n73
Smith, Perry, 1–3, 10
Smith, Shawn Michelle, 25, 27, 29
Smith, Susan, 15
Snipes, Wesley, 170
Snyder, Albert, 59, 65, 88
Snyder, Ruth, 16, 59–61, 63–65, 72, 77, 88–89

social Darwinism, 143
social ecology, 16, 100–101, 124, 171
social norms, 3, 5
social sciences, 177–79; in academic and popular cultures, 8; as disciplines, 6–7; emergence of, 8; modernization and, 7–8
socioeconomic conditions, 171–72
socioeconomic limitations, 171
socioeconomic mobility, 14–15, 17
sociology, 101
The Sopranos, 177
Stealing Through Life (Booth), 111
Steele, Diana, 19n27
Steinbeck, John, 69, 70
St. Louis Post-Dispatch, 12
Stoddard, Lothrop, 33
Stone, Oliver, 170
Straight Out of Brooklyn, 174
Streetwise (Anderson), 170, 171, 173, 176, 179n12
Succession, 178
Sutherland, Edwin, 82
symbols, 66

Thayer, Webster, 48, 49
The Theory of the Leisure Class (Veblen), 17, 135–38, 148, 152
Thompson, Courtney E., 26
Thornton, Kelly, 10
Thrasher, Frederick, 100, 101, 105–6, 111, 128n26
Time, 37
The Titan (Dreiser), 144
Townsend, Robert, 173
Tracy, Spencer, 97
trials, 16; Leopold and Loeb, 80–88
Trump administration, 178

unconscious, 66–67, 80; Dreiser's representations of, 70–72
Under a Bad Sign (Munby), 15
Union of Russian workers, 44

University of Chicago, 99–100
Up from the Ape (Hooton), 36

Van Peebles, Mario, 17, 170
Vanzetti, Bartolomeo, 47–49
Veblen, Thorstein, 17, 99, 133, 135–38, 142–43, 145–46, 148, 149, 152, 153, 159, 159n6, 160n9
Vineland Training School for Feeble-Minded Girls and Boys, 62
Volstead Act, 145

War on Crime (Potter), 15
Warshow, Robert, 129n67
Wayans, Keenan Ivory, 173
Weinberger, Daniel, 12–13
Wellman, William, 115
Wells, Floyd, 1
West, Nathanael, 70
White, William A., 67–69, 83–84, 91n31, 94n79, 95n90
white supremacy, 33
"Why Gunman Did It Is Big Unanswered Question" (Thornton), 10
Williams, Charles, 8–14. *See also* Santee shooting spree
Williams, Edward, 94n72
Wilson, William B., 43
Winthrop, John, 138
The Wire, 177
Wirth, Louis, 100–103, 106
The Wolf of Wall Street (Belfort), 178
World War I, 45, 142
Wright, Richard, 70
Wright, Thomas Lee, 174

xenophobia, 33, 45–47

You Can't Win (Black), 111

Zorbaugh, Harvey Warren, 100, 101, 103–6, 108, 111
Zuckor, Bryan, 9

About the Author

Stephen Brauer is associate professor of English at St. John Fisher College in Rochester, NY.

www.ingramcontent.com/pod-product-compliance
Lightning Source LLC
Chambersburg PA
CBHW050649280326
41932CB00015B/2841